Purpleleaf Plums

To receive a free list of our other fine titles, just complete and return this card. We also publish books in music under our Amadeus Press imprint. Check your areas of interest:

- ☐ Gardening/Ornamental Hort.
- ☐ Forestry/Agriculture
- ☐ Botany
- ☐ Economic Horticulture
- ☐ Natural Resources Mgmt.
- ☐ Music

Name (please print)

Address

City   State   Zip

We'd also welcome your comments on this book.

Timber Press

Dioscorides Press

Purpleleaf Plums

Arthur Lee Jacobson

TIMBER PRESS
Portland, Oregon

ISBN 0-88192-255-2
Printed in Hong Kong
TIMBER PRESS, INC.
9999 S.W. Wilshire, Suite 124
Portland, Oregon 97225

Library of Congress Cataloging-in-Publication Data

Jacobson, Arthur Lee.
    Purpleleaf plums / Arthur Lee Jacobson.
        p.   cm.
    Includes bibliographical references and index.
    ISBN 0-88192-255-2
    1. Purpleleaf plums.   I. Title.
SB413.P57J33 1992
635.9'773372--dc20   92-6672
                                                      CIP

Contents

Color plates precede page 77

5

Acknowledgments

Cooperative sharing is the only way to produce a book like this one. Page after page in this volume reveals how I have borrowed from others. My gratitude extends to both the deceased authors whose quotes enliven these pages, and to my contemporaries, especially the following who contributed letters or verbal communications on the subject of purpleleaf plums: Ronald G. Brightman, Edmonds, WA; L. E. Cooke Company, Visalia, CA; Lowell Cordas, San Martin, CA; John E. Elsley, Wayside Gardens, Hodges, SC; Mary Forrest, Dublin, Ireland; M. E. Gardner, Stribling's Nurseries, Merced, CA; Robert Hartman, Puyallup, WA; Henry Field's Nursery Company, Shenandoah, IA; Richard Hildreth, San Martin, CA; Robert Kourik, Santa Rosa, CA; Roy Lancaster, Chandlers Ford, England; Michael Lee, Seattle, WA; Elwyn M. Meader, Rochester, NH; Alan Mitchell, Farnham, England; Brian O. Mulligan, Seattle, WA; Esiquio Narro, Seattle, WA; E. Charles Nelson, Dublin, Ireland; Harold P. Olmo, Davis, CA; Graham Pattison, Woking, England; Samuel J. Rich, Portland, OR; Warren G. Roberts, Davis, CA; Joyce Sherlock, Stark Bro's Nurseries, Louisiana, MO; Brian R. Smith, South Dakota Experiment Station, Brookings; Floyd Swink, Morton Arboretum, Lisle, IL; Robert L. Ticknor, Aurora, OR; Paul Thomson, Bonsall, CA; John M. Tures, Huntley, IL; Ken Vogel, Minnesota Landscape Arboretum, Chanhassen; Keith Warren, J. Frank Schmidt & Son Company, Boring, OR; John Watson, New York Experiment Station at Geneva; Brad Watts, Valley Nursery, Poulsbo, WA; Jack A. Wick, California Association of Nurserymen; Peter F. Yeo, Cambridge, England; Floyd Zaiger, Modesto, CA.

Another great debt is to the authors and publishers who granted permission to quote copyrighted material.

Thanks to all.

Part I

Identification, Cultivation, and Classification

1 Introduction

Purpleleaved plum trees stand out as dark blots in planted landscapes during the summer, after brightening our scenery with their vivid light bloom in spring. The first of these odd trees originated more than 100 years ago. Its named offspring and varieties, hybrids included, now number in the dozens. Grown in temperate countries globally, these trees are referred to as flowering, ornamental, or purpleleaf plums.

The lack of understanding about the origins and attributes of the many different kinds of purpleleaf plums is amazing—some people think they are Japanese flowering cherries. Among widely cultivated, familiar ornamental trees (weeping willows, for example), few groups match purpleleaf plums for incomplete documentation. Why, with the trees so common, is the collective knowledge of them so meager? Maybe the unwieldy, large number of different clones accounts chiefly for the poor documentation concerning them, despite their prominence in our environment.

Explanation

Most specialized works begin with a review of the existing literature on the subject, but no previous attempt has singled out and described the various kinds of purpleleaf plums. Of the many books, articles, catalogs, and references I examined, the largest number of different cultivars (cultivated varieties) mentioned in any one source was only 20 (Cochran 1962), followed by 16 (Dirr 1990), and 14 (Krüssman 1978). The present volume, which includes 50 cultivars, is the first comprehensive treatment of ornamental plums.

Seattle, my home, has thousands of flowering plums—possibly more per capita than any city. Writing a comprehensive guidebook to the city's trees, I was forced to take a close look at these "dark trees." Many and confused are the purpleleaved cultivars of the cherry plum. Books and nurseries alike present contradictory descriptions and origins of the various kinds. The most prominent names are 'Pissardii', 'Thundercloud', 'Blireiana', 'Newport', 'Vesuvius', and so forth. Despite the perplexing disagreement in sources, I tried to distinguish at least the common varieties and to cite locally planted examples of each. I sought to learn what anyone serious about ornamental trees should know—how to describe the salient differences between well-known landscape cultivars. In retrospect, it was fortunate that I live on the western coast of North America, because at least 20 cultivars originated in this region. My simple study snowballed and become something unto its own, far over and beyond the original scope of the Seattle tree guidebook, which included 19 different cultivars. I was firmly enamored of plums.

The result of my labor is contained in the present volume, which provides a detailed, complete account of ornamental plum trees. It is understandably biased towards North America, because I live here and most of the cultivars originated here. The flowering dates given, of course, are for the Northern Hemisphere; in the Southern Hemisphere, the trees bloom in August or September instead of in February or March.

Scope

Purpleleaf plum cultivars range from bushes to trees over 40 feet (12 m) tall, the latter perfectly capable of serving as shade trees for average-sized houses. Although a few are grown for fruit, most cultivars are appreciated almost exclusively for their dark foliage or bright flowers. As a group, the clan contributes the most prominent purplish cast to our landscapes, challenged in this respect only in a few areas by dark-leaved maples, beeches, and crab-apples. There are dozens of normally green trees whose cultivars sport purple leaves:

ACACIA (*Acacia Baileyana* 'Purpurea')

ALMOND (*Prunus dulcis* 'Colbrunni')

BEECH, European (*Fagus sylvatica* f. *purpurea*—about a dozen cultivars, including 'Ansorgei', 'Brocklesby', 'Dawyck Purple', 'Purple Fountain', 'Purpurea Pendula', 'Purpurea Tricolor', 'Red Obelisk', 'Riversii', 'Rohanii', 'Spaethiana', 'Swat Magret')

BIRCH, Gray (*Betula populifolia* 'Purpurea')

BIRCH, Silver or White (*Betula pendula* 'Purple Rain', 'Purple Splendor', 'Purpurea', 'Scarlet Glory')

CATALPA, Hybrid (*Catalpa* × *erubescens* 'Purpurea')

CHERRY, Bird (*Prunus Padus* 'Berg', 'Colorata', 'Purple Queen', 'Purpurea', 'Wandell')

CHERRY, Choke (*Prunus virginiana* 'Canada Red', 'Mini Schubert', 'Schubert', 'Schubert Copper')

CHERRY, Sato-zakura group (some *Prunus serrulata* hybrids such as 'Royal Burgundy')

CHESTNUT, European (*Castanea sativa* 'Purpurea')

CRAB-APPLE (*Malus* spp. and hybrids—numerous cultivars, two of the darkest being 'Purple Wave' and 'Royalty')

DOGWOOD, Flowering (*Cornus florida* 'Purple Glory', 'Redleaf')

DRACÆNA (*Cordyline australis* 'Atropurpurea', 'Purple Tower')

ELDER, Black (*Sambucus nigra* f. *porphyrophylla*)

ELM (*Ulmus* 'Purpurea')

FILBERT, Giant (*Corylus maxima* 'Fortin', 'Purpurea', 'Rote Zeller')

HAZEL (*Corylus Avellana* 'Fusco-rubra', 'Purple Avelon', 'Red Aveline')

HOP-BUSH or Ake-Ake (*Dodonæa viscosa* 'Purpurea')

HORNBEAM, European (*Carpinus Betulus* 'Purpurea')

LOCUST, Black (*Robinia Pseudoacacia* 'Purpurea')

LOCUST, Honey (*Gleditsia triacanthos* 'Ruby Lace')

MAPLE, Coliseum (*Acer cappadocicum* 'Rubrum')

MAPLE, English (*Acer campestre* 'Schwerini')

MAPLE, Horned (*Acer diabolicum* f. *purpurascens*)

MAPLE, Japanese (*Acer palmatum*—many cultivars)

MAPLE, Norway (*Acer platanoides* 'Crimson King', 'Crimson Sentry', 'Deborah', 'Faassen's Black', 'Goldworth Purple', 'Purple Heart', 'Reitenbachii', 'Royal Crimson', 'Royal Redleaf', 'Schwedleri')

MAPLE, Sycamore (*Acer Pseudoplatanus* 'Atropurpureum' or 'Spaethii')

OAK, Durmast (*Quercus petræa* 'Purpurea', 'Rubicunda')

OAK, English (*Quercus robur* f. *purpurascens*—several clones)

ORCHID-TREE (*Bauhinia variegata* 'Purpurea')

OSMANTHUS (*Osmanthus heterophyllus* 'Purpureus')

PEACH (*Prunus Persica* 'Bloodleaf', 'Foliis Rubris', 'Hiawatha', 'Kingston Redleaf', 'Rancho Redleaf', 'Royal Redleaf', 'Rutgers Redleaf')

PITTOSPORUM (*Pittosporum tenuifolium* 'Purpureum')

PSEUDOPANAX (*Pseudopanax Lessonii* × *Pseudopanax discolor* 'Purpurea', 'Sabre')

REDBUD (*Cercis canadensis* 'Forest Pansy')

SMOKE TREE, European (*Cotinus Coggygria* 'Foliis Purpureis', 'Nordine Red', 'Notcutt's Variety', 'Royal Purple', 'Velvet Cloak')

SPINDLETREE, European (*Euonymus europæus* 'Atropurpurea')

WALNUT, Black (*Juglans nigra* 'Deming Purple', 'Purpurea')

Note that no wild tree population is purple; every cultivated purpleleaf tree originated as a sport of a greenleaved tree. The above list is the most complete tabulation of purpleleaf trees and large shrubs to be found. Purplish variants of crab-apple trees alone number in the dozens. It has proved impossible to verify all the listed names due to the introduction of the same cultivar by various nurseries under names of their own devising, a common horticultural problem. So some of the names are surely synonyms or otherwise incorrect.

With many varieties, the foliage is dark in spring, then gradually becomes murky green. Thus, the very propriety of calling these trees "purple" is open to question. Many writers correctly note that the foliage can be colored bronzy, brown, reddish, maroon, or garnet, and so forth. For simplicity's sake, and in deference to custom, this volume adopts the imperfect but adequate word "purple."

It is no mere coincidence that the plums, crab-apples, beech, and some maples have the most purpleleaved cultivars, and that there are no purpleleaf pines. The genetics of pigmentation and of plant reproduction from seed, as well as the degree of human influence, together determine why some plants frequently "sport" color variations, while other plants almost never do. Chapter 8 elaborates upon this information. Appendix 3 is an account of purpleleaf *Prunus* other than plums.

With this book, readers will become aware of the surprising variety of plums and will learn which are best for special landscape roles. They will know much more about those cultivars common to their region and may be tempted to acquire other appealing cultivars. Also, readers will appreciate better (and perhaps be amazed at) how haphazard record-keeping of ornamental tree cultivars truly is. When we examine closely the history of ornamental trees, we find (as in the history of most human understanding) so few pieces of the puzzle that we must use a great deal of guesswork to complete the picture. Then we sit back to behold the work, knowing uneasily how feebly its foundations in verity are rooted. Such is life!

2 Origin and History

Asia Minor, broadly conceived, is where both the Garden of Eden and the first purpleleaf plum originated. A wild ancestral species of plum prominent there as well as in southeast Europe, *Prunus divaricata* Ledb., is a thorny, bushy little tree with small yellow fruit. An ancient cultivated race of it, probably of hybrid origin, is the cherry plum or myrobalan, *Prunus cerasifera* Ehrh. (Plate 1). John Gerard described the cherry plum in his 17th century *Herball or General Historie of Plants* (1633, 1498):

> The Mirobalan Plum tree groweth to the height of a great tree, charged with many great armes or boughes, which divide themselves into small twiggy branches, by means whereof it yeeldeth a goodly and pleasant shadow: the trunke or body is covered with a finer and thinner barke than any other Plum trees: the leaves do somewhat resemble those of the Cherry tree, they are very tender, indented about the edges: the floures be white: the fruit is round, hanging upon long foot-stalks pleasant to behold, greene in the beginning, red when it is almost ripe, and being full ripe it glistereth like purple mixed with blacke: the flesh or meate is full of juice pleasant in taste: the stone is small, of a mean bigness: the tree bringeth forth plenty of fruit every other yeare.

The cherry plum does not grow wild except when it escapes from cultivation. The tree is larger than the tree of *Prunus divaricata*, and less spiny with little sharp twigs; its fruit is larger and can be red as well as yellow; and its leaves are larger and wider. In other words, the cherry plum is a tame or lush version of *Prunus divaricata*. Some botanists treat *P. cerasifera* and *P. divaricata* as synonymous ("lump" as they say), reasoning that these two names constitute one species with wild and cultivated manifestations. This opinion may be the more logical one, but in any case the resolution of the issue is outside the scope of this book.

While the greenleaf cherry plum was grown in England in the 1600s, Western cultivation of purpleleaf plums began in 1880 when a purpleleaved *Prunus cerasifera* was exported from the Persian shah's garden near Tabriz (formerly Tauris), just over 340 miles (almost 550 km) northwest of Teheran (Tehran). Monsieur Pissard, the shah's French head gardener, is credited with this historic introduction, for it was through his action that the first purpleleaf plum (named 'Pissardii') became known to civilization. All but two other cultivars owe their existence, directly or indirectly, to 'Pissardii' (or 'Atropurpurea' as some call the clone).[1]

Pissard's purple introduction was widely cultivated in Europe and North America within a few years. Variants of it arose readily because the original 'Pissardii' clone was grown by grafting, cuttings, and sometimes by seed. The leaves of the seedlings varied in color from green to weakly bronze to as dark or even darker than the leaves of 'Pissardii' itself. Moreover, while 'Pissardii' had white flowers, some of its seedlings had pink ones. Pissard's plum was like Pandora's box. Successive introductions of purpleleaf plum variants from Persia might have additionally "muddied the picture."

As 'Pissardii' stock was dispersed, more and more opportunities arose for it to hybridize with other plants. Pollen was transferred both accidentally and intentionally between other kinds of plums (as well as related *Prunus* species) and 'Pissardii'. Now, over a hundred years later, named cultivars, excluding known synonyms, total at least 50 (Table 1), and there is every reason to believe this number will continue to grow. It is not that we do not have enough cultivars already—we have more than enough. It is the thrill of novelty and the love of acquisition that drives nurseries to propagate new aberrations as they appear.

TABLE 1. Chronologic listing of named cultivars according to their date of origin.

Hybrids[1]	Year of Origin[2]	Year Christened & Circulated	Name of Clone	Place of Origin
		1880	'Pissardii'	Persia
×		1893	'Purpleleaf Kelsey'	California, U.S.
×	1891	1895	'Coleus'	North Carolina, U.S.
×	1891	1895?	'Garnet'	North Carolina, U.S.
×	1899?	1903	'Purpurea'	France
	1894	1905?	'Moseri'	France
×	1895	1905	'Blireiana'	France
	1900?	1906	'Hessei'	Germany
×		1907	'Vesuvius'	California, U.S.
	1900?	1908	'Purpusii'	Germany
		1910?	'Nigra'	U.S.
	1905?	1910	'Woodii'	England
	1905	1910	'Othello'	California, U.S.
×	1906	1910	'Cistena'	South Dakota, U.S.
×	1906	1911	'Stanapa'	South Dakota, U.S.
×	1906	1911?	'Purple C'	South Dakota, U.S.
	1883?	1912	'Pallet'	Persia or France
×	1913	1917	'Minn. No. 1'	Minnesota, U.S.
×	1913	1917	'Minn. No. 2'	Minnesota, U.S.
		1919	'Thundercloud'	California, U.S.
×	1913	1920	'Newport'	Minnesota, U.S.
		1920?	'Roebuck Castle'	Ireland
		1920?	'R. W. Hodgins'	Australia
×		1920?	'Gaujardii'	Italy?
		1920?	'Paul's Pink'	United Kingdom
		1925?	'Diversifolia'	United Kingdom
	1922	1931	'Purple Flame'	California, U.S.
×	1932	1936	'Hollywood'	California, U.S.
		1940?	'Hazeldene Variety'	United Kingdom
×	1939	1941	'Allred'	Arkansas, U.S.
×		1948	'Purple Pigmy'	Washington, U.S.
×		1950?	'Rosea'	Netherlands
×		1950?	'Festeri'	Australia
×	1947	1954	'Trailblazer'	Oregon, U.S.
×		1955?	'Wrightii'	New Zealand
×		1956?	'Spencer Hollywood'	Oregon, U.S.
		1956	'Krauter's Vesuvius'	California, U.S.
		1962	'Purple Pony'	California, U.S.
×	1962	1962	'Gerth'	California, U.S.
×		1967	'Elsie'	California, U.S.
×		1974	'Clark Hill Redleaf'	Georgia, U.S.
×	1962	1976	'Cocheco'	New Hampshire, U.S.
		1977	'Oaks'	California, U.S.
×	1970?	1977?	'Atherton'	California, U.S.
		1980?	'Knaus'	California, U.S.
×	1975	1981	'Mt. St. Helens'	Oregon, U.S.
×	1975	1982	'Big Cis'	Oregon, U.S.
×		1983	'Citation'	California, U.S.
		1988?	'Shalom'	California, U.S.
		1990	'Mirage'	United Kingdom

[1] × = hybrid; cultivars not marked as hybrids are thought to be purebred cherry plum seedlings
[2] Year of origin = year seedling germinated

Over the decades purpleleaf plums have consistently remained very popular, as proven by their continual presence in the nursery trade, the fanfare attending new introductions, and most notably, the great number of them in the landscape. They are grown in all temperate parts of the earth. Not only are they planted intentionally, they now grow wild: various locations, such as Berkeley, California, have large, fully naturalized populations of cherry plums, showing a variety of leaf and fruit colors.

In response to this prominent popularity, which borders on pervasiveness in some areas, many people have developed a strong, vocal antipathy towards these "mudleaf marvels." By way of illustrating this attitude, I can do no better than to quote passages from two contemporaries whose views of trees are broad, and whose readership is vast—Hugh Johnson and Alan Mitchell. Johnson wrote in *The International Book of Trees* (1973, 54, 202):

> Where suburbs have gone over—as so often in England—to Nowhere trees like the dreary purple-leafed plum they need bringing back to the dominance of something real.... The purple version of the cherry plum is all too well known: the grossly over-planted purple-leaved cliché of suburban streets. The culprit for this tree was M. Pissard, the French gardener of the Shah of Persia 100 years ago—whence its name of *P. cerasifera* 'Pissardii'. There are other, slightly different cultivars, but all of them are trees of dreary hue.

Alan Mitchell, world-famous tree measurer, is even less tolerant:

> Pissard's Plum 'Atropurpurea' is a form selected in Persia by Monsieur Pissard and sent in 1880, soon to proliferate throughout suburbia. When bullfinches allow, it is well covered in flowers, with dark red leaves opening among them before they finish. But for the rest of the year it is a twiggy mess, worst in summer when bearing muddy brown "purple" foliage (Mitchell 1982, 190).

> Pissard's plum 'Pissardii' was found by Monsieur Pissard in Iran in 1880 and now pervades suburbia like privet. The very early starry white flowers from pink buds are pretty until the yellowish-brown leaves unfold among them, and spoil their effect. The leaves go on to make their gloomy, mud-purple splashes which disfigure every street and park for the rest of the summer (Mitchell 1985, 78).

> The common variety is Pissard's purple plum, 'Pissardii' found in Iran in 1880. Its fuzzy crown is a shapeless mass of twigs and its foliage, a brownish-red or muddy purple, casts gloom over huge areas of suburbs from south Ontario to Illinois and New York. It is pleasantly scarce southwards, in the Mississippi Valley and the midwest, but there are bad infestations in Houston and Amarillo, Texas, in Tulsa, Oklahoma,

Wichita, Kansas and Ames, Iowa, also near Omaha, Nebraska (Mitchell 1987, 78).

Other writers, too, have spilled negative ink in similar vein. Following are two more assaults, written particularly about 'Pissardii':

> It forms a crowded, dense tree about 20 feet high. The delightful white, or less bold pinkish-white, blossoms appear in March or early April as the red young leaves start to open. Unfortunately, the flowering is often sparse due to the evil work of bullfinches or to an in sufficiently open position, and the leaves turn later to a dark, heavy colour. The sudden blob of sullen maroon in the garden is anything but attractive in summer (Haworth-Booth 1973, 44).

> [W]ith its crude copper-red foliage and stiff, erect habit, [it is] one of the most hideous shrubs known to horticulture: it is, I am sorry to add, also one of the most popular. There is a variety even uglier than *pissardii,* called *nigra* (Hyams 1965, 45).

This U.S. writer's view is less vicious:

> I am not overly fond of any of the purple-leaved flowering plums, an irrational personal bias, perhaps. In a garden of a certain scale, they can be used judiciously, in combination with, say, a glaucous juniper or golden yellow 'Frisia' locust, or with the myriad pale jade flowers of *Clematis ligusticifolia.* But in a tiny front yard, the bulky mass of matte leaves, the color of dried blood, overwhelm the scene—a foliar Black Hole. Wasn't I tickled to find such a beast lurking just over the property line from my new garden (Sedenko 1991, 44).

I fully agree that indiscriminate, thoughtless overplanting of these dark trees is a boring blight. Still, simply dismissing the trees as visual poison and condemning the group wholesale cannot be tolerated. The world is big enough to allow for diverse plantings dictated by different tastes. Most people think purpleleaf trees (plums or otherwise) are an asset, a pleasing contrast to the normal green tones that dominate treedom. Purple foliage disgusts some people, as yellow flowers bother others. The worst sin in some eyes is to plant purpleleaf plums next to screaming yellow shrubs or trees. Yet some gardeners revel joyfully in glaring contrasts. What is "dramatically bold" to some eyes is "coarsely vulgar" to others. What some cherish as "cheerfully bright" is to others "sickly looking." "Admirable symmetry" in a row of Lombardy poplars is "boring monotony" to others. My preference is for trees of light hue: because life is dark enough to begin with, brightening it rather than darkening it proves most satisfying to me. My advice to those who like the deep color of purpleleaf plums is to plant fewer, and emphasize those with good crops of fruit.

To balance the criticism of purpleleaf plums, I sought accolades, but finding more than lukewarm praise proved difficult. Certainly I found no warmth as fervent as the vindictiveness expressed by some authors. The best I could find is as follows:

> The Purple Plum (*P. Pissardi*) is a remarkable and handsome small-growing tree in which the leaves are of a vinous purple colour, which it retains the whole season through, while it is of vigorous growth and well suited for town planting. Even in the most crowded and smoky parts of London the Purple-leaved Plum grows freely, and is valued alike for its beautiful leafage and the colour of the bark, which is at all times shining dark red, indeed frequently a deep blood-red. It is a much-branched tree with ascending twigs, the leaves, which are never dull, varying in intensity of colouring with the season, while the pure white flowers open early in March. The Purple-leaved Plum is included in the list of trees that, from experiments conducted, is recommended by the Metropolitan Public Gardens Association for planting in London (Webster 1920, 105–106).

William H. Frederick, Jr., praises 'Thundercloud' in his book titled *100 Great Garden Plants* (1975, 70):

> There is no finer plant than 'Thundercloud' Plum for attractive, lively, plum-red foliage which remains so over a long time period. Whereas the ubiquitous "Japanese Red Maples" turn dull, bronzy shades (and some become dirty green) by midsummer, this plant puts on a fine show all season. A small, compact tree, the new foliage is bronzy-pink and the new stem growth is pinkish, making a rich but subtle contrast with the duller maroon of older foliage.
>
> One of the unfortunate prejudices common in American horticulture is the dictum that plants with colored foliage are in poor taste. In my opinion, such plants have often been used unwisely and it does take greater thought to use them effectively; this does not mean, however, that they are not extremely valuable garden plants when properly sited!
>
> During the six months of the year when it sports its showy foliage, 'Thundercloud' Plum is a highly valuable "designer's" plant. The solid mass of colored foliage makes this an excellent foil and enricher for a wide variety of color combinations, a real "anchor" plant for almost any situation!

3 Flowers

Prunus is a large, highly varied genus of 200–400 species. Besides plum trees, other members of *Prunus* are cherries, almonds, apricots, nectarines, peaches, and cherry-laurels—quite a dissimilar collection. On all these trees and shrubs the individual flowers are identical in structure and approximately so in size. Because of the great variation in tree form, leaf, and fruit, some plant-classification specialists prefer to limit the name *Prunus* to plums exclusively. Cherries are then placed in a genus called *Cerasus*, almonds in genus *Amygdalus*, and so forth.

Regardless of the system chosen to sort the various *Prunus* species, almost any one is beautiful in full bloom. Some, in fact, yield second place to no blooming trees. Many are deliciously scented. Bees love the flowers. This chapter treats solely the flowering of plum trees, especially the purpleleaf kinds. Yet purpleleaf cultivars aside, almost no plum varieties are grown specifically for ornament. The few exceptions are rare:

P. cerasifera 'Angustifolia'

P. cerasifera 'Gracilis'

P. cerasifera 'Lindsayae'

P. cerasifera 'Louis Asselin' or 'Elegans'

P. cerasifera 'Pendula'

P. domestica 'Plantierensis'

P. 'Elvins'

P. mexicana 'Bright Star'

P. × *nigrella* 'Muckle' (*P. nigra* × *P. tenella*)

P. nigra 'Princess Kay'

P. spinosa 'Plena'

P. spinosa 'Variegata'

That plum trees are not grown much for ornamental purposes does not, however, mean that plum flowers are not pretty unless the leaves are purple. It merely suggests that the chief desideratum on greenleaved trees is the fruit. An examination of the whole range of wild plum and cherry species of North America and Europe shows that the ornamental value of flowers is comparable between plums and cherries. Yet the extensive breeding of Japanese flowering cherries has simply made cherries as a group seem prettier in bloom than plums.[2]

A second consideration affecting the beauty of plum flowers is that selected varieties and hybrids bred for fruit production are not necessarily as graceful or as profuse with flowers as are wild seedlings. Indeed, some are frankly ugly in bloom. Moreover, a tree pruned to produce fruit is not as handsome as one pruned to be an object of visual admiration.

In all cases the flowers appear before and/or with the unfolding leaves in spring, which in Seattle begins as early as mid-February and finishes in May. The peak bloom period is March, and to a lesser degree, early April. The flowers are either white or pink. Few are markedly fragrant. Only several cultivars have doubled flowers (that is, flowers with more than the normal five petals). The exact time of blossoming is affected by temperature—whether spring is warm and early or cool and late. In fact, the time of full bloom in one year can be an entire month later in the next year. A typical tree will be quite full and pretty for at least a week-and-a-half or two, and can be seen with some open flowers for a month. This is a leisurely pace contrasted to continental climates where the explosion of spring is relatively concentrated and brief, resulting in a fast burst of glorious awakening.

In parts of England, two problems bother cherry plum blossoms, which usually appear a month before those of other plum blossoms. One is late frosts, nipping the flowers just before or as they appear; the second problem is birds, mostly bullfinches and sparrows, which eat the buds and flowers.

Severe winter cold can kill twigs on some plum cultivars, thereby wrecking the spring floral show. Seattle's occasional great freezes, for example, are of such magnitude they damage many plants, both native and otherwise, even some that are usually hardy here. Such damage is a bother to remedy, but not deadly to the tree. One must cut off the dead twigs, then do summer pruning to remove overly vigorous sucker growth, lest the tree assume an ungainly habit.

Forcing plum twigs to bloom early indoors is a well-known practice. In my tests, 'Purple Pony', 'Newport', 'Trailblazer', and 'Vesuvius' proved inferior. As a general guide, select stout twigs with many flower buds; when the buds swell, mash one end of each twig and insert it in warm or hot water. Waiting ten days to two weeks may be necessary before the flowers open, so be sure to change the water when it turns murky. The leaf and flower colors are paler on forced twigs than on twigs left on the tree. Subtle fragrances too weak to be noticed on the tree, however, are appreciated from a vase of forced flowers.

Before turning exclusively to the purpleleaf clones, it is necessary to give a moment's consideration to greenleaf plums. The cherry plum (*Prunus cerasifera*) is an early cloud, dense as can be, of immaculate white flowers. Next to flower is the Japanese plum, *P. salicina* (*P. triflora* in old books). Compared to the cherry plum, the Japanese trees are less dense; yet I have seen them only as fruiting cultivars, not as wild trees. The last to bloom are the European (*P. domestica*) and American plums (*P. americana, P. nigra,* and several others). This flowering sequence is the same in continental climates, but occurs in a shorter period of time.

For floral ornament in Seattle's maritime climate, the best is cherry plum, second best is Japanese plum, and third best is European plum. The cultivars from eastern North America do poorly in Seattle's climate. They prefer cold winters and hot, yet moist, summers. Seattle has mild, wet winters and springs, and warm, dry summers, with an occasional shocking winter freeze or summer spell of ovenlike aridity that catches everything unguarded, thereby inflicting maximum damage. As a result, the beauty of East Coast cultivars is marred and Pacific Northwest gardeners grow few of them. When in full bloom, they are pleasant to behold. Yet since they bloom late in the Pacific Northwest, and, during the rest of the season exhibit behavior that can best be described as whining, they are scarcely worth planting.

Cherry plum blossoming is rated best for three reasons. First, it is so *early* that it gains luster or advantage by lack of competition, thus winning first place partly by default. Although some *Prunus* species bloom as early as cherry plums, none are as commonly cultivated, so the plum is the star attraction. Second, the entire tree is *bounteous* with its flowers; there is an immense satisfaction in such a lavish display, which seems the more lively in contrast to the dead-looking dark twigs. Third, the *scale* of cherry plum twigs, which are slender, even dainty, compared to the coarser branches and spurs on other plums, is impressive. Moreover, the cherry plum is often seen as a big tree in comparison to other plums, and therefore has a greater visual punch.

The following list groups purpleleaf plum cultivars by the relative merits of their flowers. It is an overview by gross categorization, and not every cultivar is included, because too little information exists about some kinds. Young trees fresh from the nursery often have fewer flowers that are smaller than the flowers on their mature counterparts. Keep this in mind if you examine the flowers on such a tree and find they seem unusually weak compared to what they are described as being.

Early: 'Atherton', 'Blireiana', 'Hollywood', 'Knaus', 'Moseri', 'Oaks', 'Purple Pigmy', 'Vesuvius'. Flowers open, or begin opening, in February, and in some years, in late January.

Early midseason: 'Allred', 'Gerth', 'Pissardii'.

Late midseason: 'Dwarf Purple Pony', 'Krauter's Vesuvius', 'Nigra', 'Spencer Hollywood', 'Thundercloud', 'Trailblazer', 'Woodii'.

Late: 'Big Cis', 'Cistena', 'Mt. St. Helens', 'Newport'. Flowering extends into early May and is quickly joined by the unfolding leaves. These cultivars have the influence of North American plums in their genes.

Sparse: 'Atherton', 'Purple Pony', 'Vesuvius'. These three are not worth growing for flowers.

Weak display: 'Newport'. Vigorous (i.e., young or carefully pruned) specimens look pleasing, but are not as showy as most cultivars.

Fragrant: 'Blireiana', 'Hollywood', 'Moseri', 'Newport', 'Spencer Hollywood'. 'Newport' is rich in nectar giving a subtle fragrance, but its flowers, although abundant, are dull. Some 'Pissardii' trees are mildly fragrant in evenings.

Double: 'Blireiana' (ca. 20–24 petals), 'Moseri' (ca. 13–17 petals), and a mystery tree of extreme rarity (ca. 20 petals).

Semi-double: 'Atherton', 'Cistena', 'Gerth', 'Hollywood' (of Seattle, not Berkeley), 'Newport', 'Spencer Hollywood', 'Trailblazer'. The flowers of these cultivars do not always have extra petals, but if you look at enough flowers you will find some with more than five petals.

Smallest: 'Atherton', 'Newport', 'Purple Pigmy'. Small flowers do not necessarily mean inferior ornamental value, but of these three cultivars only 'Purple Pigmy' is superb as a flowering plant in my eyes.

Largest: 'Hollywood' (of Seattle, not Berkeley). Since these flowers are large, fragrant, and early, they make an excellent indoor forcing stock.

Purpleleaf plum cultivars can also be categorized by petal color. Pink flowers often fade with age to pale pink. Moreover, from year to year the coloration can vary in intensity. Sometimes what appears as a pink-blooming tree from a distance is a white-petaled tree, with red sepals, flowerstalks, anthers, and unfolding leaves that provide an overall pink cast.

Petals white or with a hint of pink Total 32	Petals clearly pink Total 18
'Allred'	'Blireiana'
'Atherton' (blush)	'Citation'
'Big Cis'	'Clark Hill Redleaf'?
'Cistena'	'Festeri'
'Cocheco'	'Gaujardii'?
'Coleus'	'Hazeldene Variety'
'Diversifolia'	'Krauter's Vesuvius'
'Elsie' (blush)	'Moseri'
'Garnet'	'Nigra'
'Gerth' (blush)	'Paul's Pink'
'Hessei'	'Purple Pony'
'Hollywood'	'Purpurea'
'Knaus' (blush)	'Rosea'
'Minn. No. 1'	'R. W. Hodgins'
'Minn. No. 2'	'Spencer Hollywood'
'Mirage'?	'Thundercloud'
'Mt. St. Helens'	'Woodii'
'Newport'	'Wrightii'
'Oaks'?	
'Othello'	
'Pallet'	
'Pissardii' (blush)	
'Purple C'	
'Purple Flame' (blush)	
'Purpleleaf Kelsey'	
'Purple Pigmy' (blush)	
'Purpusii'	
'Roebuck'	
'Shalom'?	
'Stanapa'	
'Trailblazer'	
'Vesuvius'	

No one cultivar is so rich and regal, so superior, that it leaves its purple cousins far behind. It is enough that several kinds with inferior blossoms were singled out. Even if one tree does have flowers of popular appeal, it may also have wretched foliage or form. An example is 'Blireiana'; it bears gorgeous deep pink puffs of fragrance on an ugly, congested tree.

4 Foliage

Judged solely as flowering trees, ornamental plums are either overshadowed or at least equaled by cherries, but judged anywhere, anytime, as dark-leaved flowering trees, plums rout the competition. From about May through October—over half the year in my climate—they display leaves of color. Purpleleaf plums are both markedly common and diverse. Partly this is due to timing. After all, Pissard's plum has been grown since 1880. Excepting the first purpleleaf peach tree (a *Prunus Persica* selection named 'Bloodleaf' in the 1860s), all comparable trees (i.e., rose family members with showy blooms and dark foliage) originated after Pissard's freak was introduced to cultivation. No other purpleleaved flowering trees have come close to producing such an impact in the landscape. Unlike peach trees, plum trees are easily grown and relatively long-lived; they hold their purplish color better than crab-apples generally.

Leaf Color

The purple gene is the common thread linking trees in this book. It is a strong trait, holding true in many crosses and generations. Some leaves are darker, others scarcely more than bronze-tinted green. Several factors affect the depth of coloration (whether green or purple) exhibited by leaves:

1. Sunlight darkens the color; shade lightens it.
2. Good soil conditions, including sufficient summer moisture, keep the leaves darker, while dry, sterile sites result in duller, weaker-colored leaves.
3. Young, vigorously growing trees (or shoots) have darker leaves than old, weak specimens.
4. Emerging spring leaves are lighter, with more red and less purple. They darken usually, but some cultivars fade, changing from red to bronze or dark green.

For maximum darkness, choose a young specimen, plant it in good soil where it receives full sun, prune it to encourage strong shoots, then admire it in May. The same clone could be viewed much later in its life, after a dry summer, and its foliage would be paler.

Fall color is not just a joke with these trees. While many varieties drop their leaves in November with practically the same color they had in July, other varieties show an attractive change, albeit relatively subtle compared to the spectacular blaze of some maples. Two examples are 'Newport' (early) and 'Allred' (late). 'Purpurea' is good, too, but I have not seen it.

On most cultivars the leaf *undersides* are more purplish than are the topsides. This condition is exemplified also in the familiar wineleaf maple or, as the British say, wineleaf sycamore (*Acer Pseudoplatanus* 'Atropurpureum'). I do not know why this condition is prevalent. Maybe the chlorophyll concentrates on the upper leaf surface because that is where the most sunlight is received? Possibly the dark pigments deteriorate somewhat when exposed to sunlight?

The following list ranks cultivars from one extreme to another according to overall depth of leaf color:

Darkest: 'Krauter's Vesuvius', 'Nigra', 'Purple Pony', 'Thundercloud', 'Vesuvius', 'Woodii'. Only 'Vesuvius' is a hybrid. With those trees that set fruit, the skin color can match the leaf color almost exactly, making the crop inconspicuous.

Dark: 'Newport', 'Pissardii'. In late summer a strong hint of green can be noticed on the upper side of the leaf. (Many clones are called 'Pissardii' and some are as consistently dark as the clones listed above. However, the original 'Pissardii' and certainly most of the trees grown under that name are lighter in color than the trees I list as "Darkest.")

Light: 'Atherton', 'Blireiana', 'Cistena', 'Citation', 'Gerth', 'Hollywood' (of Berkeley), 'Moseri', 'Spencer Hollywood', 'Trailblazer'. All are hybrids. Young leaves are dark, but older ones are bronzy or even green on upper surfaces, thereby presenting a mottled appearance.

Lightest: 'Allred', 'Hollywood' (of Seattle). Both are hybrids. Leaves are a mere bronzy-green in summer:

Leaf Size, Shape, and Texture

Leaf color alone does not suffice as a measure of the visual merits of the various cultivars. Leaf size, shape, and texture, as well as the arrangement on the twigs, also affect our appreciation. Though 'Purple Pony' has foliage of extreme darkness, its paucity of bloom and ugly branching pattern condemn it altogether except that it offers a great feature: natural dwarfness. It is also fruitless. Where, therefore, a clean, dark little tree is desired, 'Purple Pony' is a possibility.

Leaf sizes are largest and smallest on hybrid cultivars. 'Hollywood' (of Seattle), by an easy margin, has the largest leaves; of the better known clones, 'Cistena' has the smallest leaves. Other very small leaves are on the extremely rare 'Atherton' and 'Purple Pigmy' cultivars.

Leaf shape is comfortably consistent in the *Prunus cerasifera* cultivars, but the hybrids show much variation. By this I do not suggest that any *P. cerasifera* leaf can be exchanged for another, because some differences exist, but these differences are minor compared to the extreme variation exhibited by hybrids. For example, on the hybrid 'Citation', the leaves are quite similar to those of a peach tree (that is, long and slender); on 'Blireiana', the apricot influence is obvious because the leaves are rounded.

Luster or the amount of light reflected is highest in 'Vesuvius' and in two clones whose leaves are very similar to each other: 'Gerth' and 'Spencer Hollywood'. The dullest leaves are those of 'Blireiana' and its close allies 'Atherton' and 'Moseri'. Some people prefer a matte texture ("finish"), others like a glossy surface. Since most leaves in deciduous temperate trees are dull or average in this respect, the "reflective few" do have an edge as far as novelty is considered. A dark, shiny plum tree set against staid, dull green elms and lindens provides a double contrast.

Leaf and Foliage Effect

My impressions of the leaves and foliage effect of the cultivars that I have seen and recognized are listed below. I have seen several other cultivars, but have not recognized them. Nonetheless, at least half the cultivars I have not seen are still extant and could be acquired by anyone willing to take the necessary pains (see Chapter 10 for availability of cultivars).

'**Allred**': Large leaves of pleasing arrangement. Pronounced seasonal delineation, changing from red in spring, through bronze in summer, to light red again in October—November.

'**Atherton**': Small, less than 2.25 inches (57 mm); clumsily arrayed and poorly colored. Dull because of hairs.

'**Blireiana**': A muddy blob from afar; up close, an ugly mess. Motley colors: a mix of red young leaves, greenish old leaves, and bronzy ones in between. Graceless, congested crown shape and branch arrangement. Even duller when mature in late summer.

'**Cistena**': Small, pleasing proportion, deep color, and attractively glossy. Almost devoid of hairs. Rarely seen in perfect health in a maritime climate.

'**Citation**': Too new and small to judge, but remarkable for slender peachlike leaves of weak purplish color. Usually has several prominent glands at the base of the leaf.

'Gerth': Shiny dark greenish top, deep purplish underside; like 'Spencer' except with sharper teeth, hairier leafstalks, and often with convex leaves on the long shoots.

'Hollywood': Greenish above, purplish beneath; large; widest near middle.

'Krauter's Vesuivus': Intensely dark, dense, and uniform. The leaves, if not the habit of the trees, are practically indistinguishable from 'Nigra', 'Thundercloud', and 'Woodii'.

'Moseri': Like 'Blireiana' but with slightly larger and less hairy leaves on a less offensively cluttered branching system.

'Newport': Small, bluntish (unlike most cultivars), well-arranged, richly colored leaves turn a pleasing, striking red in early autumn. Among my favorites.

'Nigra': Intensely dark, dense, and uniform. May be the darkest effect of all because of the compact density of the crown of branches.

'Pissardii': Varies, but usually a nondescript dark color; not as striking (i.e., uniformly or consistently dark) as its superior seedlings.

'Purple Pigmy': Only the type (that is, original) specimen seen, and its weakest attribute is foliage—poorly colored—but this is partly because of too much shading. The leaves are very small.

'Purple Pony': Intensely dark and uniform. Narrower and less hairy than the leaves of most similarly dark cherry plum cultivars.

'Spencer Hollywood': Uncomfortably similar to 'Gerth'. Lustrous green top, dull deep purple underside.

'Thundercloud': Intensely dark and uniform; possibly a bit less dark than 'Krauter's Vesuvius' (which see), 'Nigra', 'Purple Pony', and 'Woodii'.

'Trailblazer': Like 'Spencer Hollywood' in color and shape, but thinner, larger, slightly less glossy.

'Vesuvius': One of the most distinctive, with long, very dark, shiny leaves. Very finely toothed.

'Woodii': Intensely dark and uniform.

5 Fruit

The fruiting characteristics of the 50 cultivars treated in this book are as follows:

'**Allred':** A generous yielder. Slightly larger than average cherry plum fruit, about 1.25 inches (32 mm). Dark red skin and flesh. Grown primarily for its fruit. Ripens mid- to late July in Seattle.

'**Atherton':** Very sparingly fruitful, or fruitless. Fruit will probably be lightly fuzzy like that of 'Blireiana' and 'Moseri'.

'**Big Cis':** Fruit presumably like that of its parent, 'Cistena'.

'**Blireiana':** Sparsely produced, lightly fuzzy-skinned fruit of deep purple skin and flesh. Soft, juicy, and flavored like slightly bitter red wine or very strong grape juice. Clingstone, with a slightly hairy surface. The hairy stone is also less sharp than the stone of pure *Prunus cerasifera* stock. Late July or early August in Seattle.

'**Cistena':** Sparsely produced, very small, dark purple, inconspicuous. Not valued.

'**Citation':** A new hybrid rootstock with unknown fruiting habits. Since one parent is a peach and the other a plum, any fruit produced will likely be intermediate.

'**Clark Hill Redleaf':** Fruit small, round, "red [-skinned] with yellow to yellow-red flesh. Quality is insipid and rated only fair" (Okie 1989, 59).

'**Cocheco':** Orange-red skin, yellow-fleshed, about 1.25 inches (32 mm) in diameter; nearly freestone. High quality; but the tree needs cross-pollination to bear. Ripens mid-August in northeastern United States.

'**Coleus':** Roundish; deep red skin and flesh; stone small, flat, clinging. Low quality.

'**Diversifolia':** No information. Probably the fruit is like that of ordinary cherry plum trees.

'**Elsie':** A hybrid similar to 'Gerth' except the tree is self-sterile, and the plums are slightly larger; oval, shiny red-maroon, to 2 inches (50.5 mm) in diameter. Selected in California because its fruit is good for eating.

'**Festeri':** An Australian selection. No information.

'**Garnet':** An early ripening plum that is "roundish oval; large . . . dark garnet red . . . flesh yellowish . . . good" (Heiges, 1897, 45).

'**Gaujardii':** No information.

'Gerth': Not a copious producer. Round or nearly so, deep purple skin and flesh, 1.25–1.75 inches (32–44.5 mm); good quality. Ripens late July or early August in Seattle; early to mid-July in parts of California.

'Hazeldene Variety': An English selection. No information.

'Hessei': No information, but since this is a weak, shrubby plant, it may have little energy to spare for fruit production.

'Hollywood': Large, 1.25–2.5 inches (32–63 mm); roundish, red inside and out; good quality. Large stones containing seeds of low viability or infertile. Earliest to ripen—late June to early or mid-July in Seattle.

'Knaus': Self-sterile, very early period of blooming; if pollinated, makes oval, 1.25 inches (32 mm) wide, freestone, dark purple plums, well worth eating. Ripens early.

'Krauter's Vesuivus': Not abundant. Intensely dark and uniform, like the leaves. Flesh also deep red-purple in color.

'Minn. No. 1' and 'Minn. No. 2': No information.

'Mirage': A new introduction whose fruiting characteristics are not known.

'Moseri': Like 'Blireiana', but slightly larger, 1.5 inches (38 mm) long and almost or as wide, without being round, and less sparingly produced. Reddish with a sheen of fine fuzz on the skin. Clingstone, the stone slightly larger than that of 'Blireiana'. Flesh red. Ripens late July and early August.

'Mt. St. Helens': Fruit presumably like that of its parent, 'Cistena'.

'Newport': Scantily borne, small, 0.75–1 inch (19–25 mm), dull, deep red or purplish skin with light red flesh; neither ornamental nor good to eat.

'Nigra': Sparse. Intensely dark and uniform, hiding well in the foliage.

'Oaks': Requires pollination for adequate yields. The plums are 1.25 inch (32 mm), round, freestone, shiny red-brown, excellent flavor. Good fruit to eat. Ripens early in the season.

'Othello': An inch (25 mm) wide; deep crimson skin, much paler flesh of amber color. Good to eat. Very early.

'Pallet': No information.

'Paul's Pink': May be an English 'Nigra' or 'Woodii' lookalike, presumably with similar fruit: scant, very dark, of average cherry plum size.

'Pissardii': Varies; usually purple skinned and yellow fleshed; some trees called by this name have purple skin and flesh, others have reddish skin. Sometimes a very heavy producer.

'Purple C': Fruit presumably similar to that of its sibling 'Cistena'.

'**Purple Flame**': Yield unknown but probably bounteous. Cherry plum–sized, red inside and out, good to eat.

'**Purpleleaf Kelsey**': Dark purple skin, flesh reddish purple. Fruit larger and later ripening than that of 'Pissardii'.

'**Purple Pigmy**': Tiny and cherrylike, to 0.69 inch (17 mm) long, red, good, pretty. Small stones only 0.44 inch (11 mm) long. Ripens early July in Seattle.

'**Purple Pony**': Nearly, if not totally, fruitless. Any fruit produced will doubtless be very dark purple inside and out, and probably 1–1.25 inches (25–32 mm).

'**Purpurea**': Offspring of *Prunus spinosa*. No information.

'**Purpusii**': Probably scantily produced, nondescript cherry plum fruit. No information.

'**Roebuck Castle**': Rare old Irish cultivar. No information.

'**Rosea**': A hybrid of *Prunus spinosa*, and so its fruit, if any, may vary more than a little from the commonplace cherry plum stock. No information.

'**R. W. Hodgins**': An Australian tree, probably ordinary cherry plum fruit. No information.

'**Shalom**': Selected in California because its fruit is good for eating. "Small to medium, roundish, deep red fruits; flesh juicy, sweet, desert quality excellent; resembles Santa Rosa" (Facciola, 1990, 178).

'**Spencer Hollywood**': Abundant, breaking branches with the heavy weight; large, egg-shaped; red skinned, purplish red flesh; freestone; delicious. Ripens late July or August in Seattle.

'**Stanapa**': Presumably similar to that of its kindred 'Cistena' and 'Purple C'. No information.

'**Thundercloud**': Not abundant except in occasional years. Intensely dark and uniform, like the leaves. Flesh also deep red-purple in color.

'**Trailblazer**': Abundant, large, 1.5–2 inches (38–60 mm) long, egg-shaped, deep red skin and light red or amber flesh; delicious. Ripens very late July, primarily during August in Seattle.

'**Vesuvius**': Needs cross-pollination. Small; deep rich purplish-red skin, yellowish flesh; not especially desirable.

'**Woodii**': No information, but probably like that of 'Nigra'.

'**Wrightii**': No information. If this New Zealand clone's ascribed parentage is correct (that is, a cross of a purpleleaf plum with a peach-almond hybrid), its fruit will be fuzzy, with a large stone.

Fruit Appearance

In all cultivars, skin colors range from deep orange-red to darkest purple, but flesh color can be yellow to deep red-purple. The skin is hairy in hybrids involving the Japanese apricot (*Prunus Mume*): 'Atherton'(?), 'Blireiana', and 'Moseri'. 'Citation' and 'Wrightii' also must bear hairy fruit, if they bear any at all. Shape is round or oval, as with ordinary plums, and size ranges from the small cherrylike fruit of 'Purple Pigmy' to the 2.5 inch (63 mm) fruit reported for 'Hollywood'.

General Edibility of Fruit

In no cultivar is the fruit foul-tasting or poisonous. An unripe 'Blireiana' plum is astringent, chewy, and bitter. By unripe I mean almost or quite full sized yet still rather firm and crunchy instead of soft and juicy. Picked when fully ripe the fruit is usually plain at worst and a delight at best, but nutritious in any case. The cherry plum and some of its hybrids are worth eating even when far from fully ripe, because they have an agreeable texture, tartness, and composition. People who would not touch an unripe apple, then, can enjoy underripe purpleleaf plums.

The 10 best kinds for edible fruit are 'Allred','Cocheco','Gerth', 'Hollywood', 'Othello', some 'Pissardii' seedlings going under that name, 'Purple Flame', 'Purpleleaf Kelsey', 'Spencer Hollywood', and 'Trailblazer'. Seven of these are hybrids. Other cultivars of note include the lesser-known Californians—'Elsie', 'Knaus', 'Oaks', and 'Shalom'.

Fruit-Ripening Season

Ripening dates vary widely in written accounts. For example, 'Allred' is described as ready in early June by David Ulmer, and in early August by Henry Field's nursery. In my experience, 'Hollywood' is earliest, ripening in late June through mid-July; 'Purple Pigmy' in early July; 'Allred' in mid- to late July; 'Spencer Hollywood' and nonhybrid cherry plums generally ripen in late July; 'Gerth', 'Blireiana', and 'Moseri' in late July and early August; 'Trailblazer' is latest, in August and early September. A few cherry plums hang fresh and edible as late as mid-October.

Messiness of Fruit

Substantial crops dropped to the ground bother many people. This situation can occur when a person buys a cultivar thinking it is solely an ornamental, then watches in chagrined disbelief as a copious load of plums is borne.

Besides being unsightly, fallen fruit can be a nuisance, if not a hazard, on sidewalks, attracting wasps, fouling shoes, and making the ground slippery. Another consideration is whether the stones sprout. Weedy seedlings can be numerous in some cases. Every spring I see *Prunus cerasifera* seedlings come up in various colors: green, bronze, or purple. No hybrids reseed in a similar fashion, as far as I am aware; it would be amazing to find a hybrid that readily reproduced by seeds, although such things do exist in the plant kingdom.

Nutrition of Fruit

Plums generally are adequate, not rich, sources of vitamins, with a small number of calories. Their delicious flavor and wholesome effects are more easily felt than documented in dietary studies. That is, the fruit tastes better on the tongue and passes better through the body than its nutritional statistics look on paper. No reason exists to expect plums from purpleleaved trees to be more or less nutritious than average plums.

Ornamental Value of Fruit

'Spencer Hollywood', 'Trailblazer', 'Allred', 'Cocheco', and some trees called 'Pissardii' have bright red fruits displayed against bronze or purple foliage, affording a lovely sight for several weeks.

Prospects for Breeding Superior Eating-Plums

The best-tasting plums are from greenleaved trees. Nonetheless, some purpleleaf trees are worth growing, despite their imperfect fruit, because of their compensating ornamental value. Breeders can further improve the quality of all plums. The purpleleaf varieties doubtless echo their greenleaf kindred in having various responses to commercial production, shipping, and handling.

Role of Pollination

Give thanks to the bees! Plum crop productivity, like most fruit yields, increases to the degree that pollen from different varieties is available for fertilizing flowers. Some varieties need no pollen but their own to bring forth fruit; others cannot set any fruit unless another tree's pollen is used. 'Cocheco', 'Elsie', and 'Knaus' are self-infertile; maybe 'Vesuvius' is also. 'Oaks' benefits greatly by cross-pollination. 'Purple Pony' seems to be completely unable to set fruit. 'Newport' can set fruit and then abort it all before maturity, but this may be due to inadequate cross-pollination. 'Atherton' may be sterile.

6 Tree shape

Size

The ultimate or mature size of trees and shrubs is usually neglected by people who plant them. Or, if not ignored, the matter of size is given too little consideration. People will not cram their own feet into shoes too small, but again and again they plant trees in impossibly tight quarters, then prune them back or pull them out. Though careful pruning improves trees, most size-control pruning disfigures and maims natural branch architecture. The solution? Plant only right-sized trees for any given location. This goal sounds easy, but is rarely achieved.

Many prospective buyers ask nursery dealers: "How big will it grow?" The variables affecting tree size are legion: genetics, means of propagation, condition of tree at time of planting, depth at which it is planted, soil pH, soil texture, soil humus content, soil drainage, soil compaction, sunlight level, shelter, wind, moisture regime, influence of fertilizers, pesticides, pruning, temperature, air pollution, response to snowload, pest and disease resistance, salt-tolerance—much of which will vary from region to region.

Despite this forbiddingly long list of factors, it is possible to classify the purpleleaf plum cultivars by size, as genetic allowances are only modified so much by environmental conditions.

40 foot (12 m) trees: 'Allred', 'Hollywood', 'Pissardii'.

30 foot (9 m) trees: 'Clark Hill Redleaf', 'Coleus', 'Diversifolia', 'Elsie', 'Festeri', 'Garnet', 'Gerth', 'Hazeldene Variety', 'Krauter's Vesuvius', 'Othello', 'Pallet', 'Paul's Pink', 'Purpleleaf Kelsey', 'Purpurea', 'Purpusii', 'Roebuck Castle', 'R. W. Hodgins', 'Thundercloud', 'Woodii', 'Wrightii'.

20 foot (6 m) trees: 'Atherton', 'Cocheco', 'Knaus', 'Moseri', 'Mt. St. Helens', 'Newport', 'Nigra', 'Oaks', 'Purple Flame', 'Rosea', 'Trailblazer', 'Vesuvius'.

15 foot (4.5 m) trees or shrubs: 'Big Cis', 'Blireiana', 'Cistena', 'Citation', 'Gaujardii', 'Hessei', 'Minn. No. 1', 'Minn. No. 2', 'Mirage', 'Purple C', 'Purple Pigmy', 'Purple Pony', 'Shalom', 'Spencer Hollywood', 'Stanapa'.

The height of a tree is influenced greatly by crowding, with open-grown specimens being stouter, usually broader, and proportionately shorter. When categorizing the trees above, I considered overall size, not only height. The largest tree I have seen is a 'Pissardii' fully 47.5 feet (14.5 m) tall and 57.5 feet (17.5 m) wide! Numerous 'Pissardii' specimens are over 40 feet (12.2 m) tall, although many are much smaller, despite being every bit as old. This discrepancy is easily explained by the different clones called 'Pissardii' as well as by the variety of growing conditions experienced by the trees.

Scale in the Landscape

Purpleleaf plums are usually planted in home lawns or along roads. Many are in parks, too, but most are used in residential landscapes. In general, I suggest choosing the smallest cultivar, whether the tree is valued primarily for its flowers, dark foliage, or fruit. The pleasure will be just as much, but the work less. Choose a large-growing tree variety only if you have much room and want a shade tree to block the sunshine or some unsightly view.

Branching Habit

Trees are fascinating to behold when they are naked in winter: their elemental anatomy is revealed in skeletal fashion, devoid of obscuring foliage, though not as dead as bones. Bare trees are not heartwarming like flashy flower displays or cheerfully radiant fall coloration, but in a subtle way and for months on end, they assume importance—like quietly floating clouds, or trees far on a horizon, or the murmur of moving water.

Some trees are depressingly ugly because of congested, irregular, twiggy growth habits. Others sweep arching branches into the sky like a static dance, revealing a twig silhouette of graceful symmetry against the air. Most, to be sure, are merely ho-hum. One of the reasons I became so interested in purpleleaf plums was my bewilderment that people could endure the wretched appearance of 'Blireiana'—a hideous tree except when it is in bloom; I had much rather plant the poor-blooming 'Newport' because of its superb branching pattern and relatively fine foliage effect.

For purposes of rendering useful guidance, I should love to be able to describe or illustrate all the different cultivars in their mature, unpruned state, in winter. Alas, all I can do is convey my limited impressions.

The cherry plum group, that is, **'Pissardii'** and 19 or so other nonhybrid seedlings, tend towards an upright habit, which is normally too dense unless carefully thinned. They almost always come from nurseries with several closely spaced, strongly vertical branches, and are quite set in their ways. I believe that what most of us buy at nurseries is crippled, that most nursery stock is made to look appealing, to be compact, but the close-forking sections grow too densely and some forks often break away later. Remedial pruning can alleviate the poor structure of nursery trees, but it is a rare practice, demanding an understanding eye and patience. In fact, most pruning does more harm than good (see Chapter 9). Thus, by either neglect or mistake, most cherry plums end up looking like crude vases. The branching pattern of such trees has no ability to inspire people until decades have passed and a sort of noble, aged ambiance adds its influence to the otherwise plain branch architecture.

'**Purple Pony**' must be cursed with the worst branching habit of all the nonhybrids. I have studied how to prune purpleleaf plums for maximum beauty, but this wayward dwarf makes me despair. It is hopeless, like 'Blireiana' and some other hybrid cultivars. I think it will always look ugly regardless of how it is pruned. Perhaps, at best, it will look merely inoffensive.

'**Blireiana**' I have already condemned as hideous. It is so bad it wins a perverse credit: King of Ugly Trees. Its associated hybrids 'Atherton' and 'Moseri' are not anywhere near as bad—indeed, 'Moseri' can be almost winsome. 'Blireiana', however, because its flowers have an explosive power in their bright pink fragrance, cannot be scrapped altogether. Nevertheless, plant it in the background, not as a centerpiece or where eyes will focus on it. No amount or style of pruning can make it presentable. What an embarrassment—the prettiest flowers on the most repulsive tree, as a caustic friend remarked, "fifty-dollar flowers on a ten-cent bush." I hope that 'Blireiana' is exceptionally wretched in my climate—that elsewhere it is better behaved. For example, Alan Mitchell said (pers. com. 1991) "You are very hard on poor 'Blireiana', and seeing it in California I see your point. With us it is a better shaped, less gouty, cut-back plant."

'**Newport**' has the most consistently pleasing branch structure. Probably its sport 'Mt. St. Helens' is just as good. The influence of North American native plums on the background of this hybrid is probably the key. A horizontal tendency manifests itself, in refreshing contrast to the usually vertical cherry plum growth.

'**Spencer Hollywood**' is so fruitful that it often breaks limbs under the weight of its crop, thereby distinguishing itself from the rest of the purpleleaf plums. It is also a natural dwarf. Anyone who plants this cultivar will do so for the flowers and generous pounds of fruit, not for its wintertime appearance.

'**Trailblazer**' is usually not as fruitful as 'Spencer' and does not break up. It also grows larger, particularly wider. It is not a dense tree like 'Spencer'. With thoughtful pruning, it is as handsome as any plum tree.

'**Vesuvius**' has a unique pattern: a radiating head of elongated, gently undulating limbs of unequal length, making a rather flamboyant silhouette compared to the less spiky outlines of most cultivars. When pruning 'Vesuvius', people have a tendency to shorten the long branches, of course, thereby making the tree conform to the blob ideal exemplified by the norm.

Such branch shortening is akin to training rose-bushes into lollipop tree-form, and other silly practices.

'**Cistena**' and other shrubby cultivars are not expected to be handsome in winter, although their tree kindred are expected to look interesting. At least that is my impression. Most deciduous shrubs do better if they are occasionally chopped back to the soil line. Such pruning is best done in late winter or earliest spring, right before the roots send forth their surge of energy for new growth. Shearing is certainly to be shunned.

Longevity

Longevity, like ultimate size, is no simple matter. The oldest of the purpleleaved trees are just over 100 years, dating from the early 1880s. We do not expect them to live for centuries like some oaks, pines and redwoods. As with humans, tree age is affected by numerous environmental factors. Dry-area specimens are likely to live longer than those in wet sites. Seedling-grown specimens or those on their own roots may live longer than grafted specimens. The degree to which a given cultivar grows in the climate and soils it favors has great bearing on its performance and lifespan. Unpruned as well as carefully pruned trees usually outlive specimens mutilated by malpruning. On the other hand, some pollarded trees seem almost immortal in their ability to rejuvenate. Most purpleleaf plum trees should be considered short-lived trees, or at best trees of moderate longevity—150 years at most, perhaps. Some 'Blireiana' plums are wretchedly old-looking and weak in 25 years.

7 Hardiness

What varieties succeed where? Another way of defining hardiness is "climatic adaptability." North Dakota is too cold for most purpleleaf plums—they will not survive, let alone thrive there—and south Florida is not cold enough. Purpleleaf plum trees need a dormant season and chilly temperatures, but if they shiver too much they are hurt or killed. Any given region has a set of plants hardy there. These plants can reasonably be expected to perform well year after year. We can stretch our definition of hardy to include "half-hardy" plants. Half-hardy means more or less surviving under protest, or making some headway but then dying back in a trying year.

Plant hardiness-zone maps based upon yearly average minimum temperatures have become increasingly familiar. In the United States the most widely used standard originated at the Arnold Arboretum. The United States Department of Agriculture (USDA) version is similar but has been used less often. It is better, however, than the Arnold Arboretum version and is deservedly gaining headway.

Zone	Arnold Arboretum Hardiness Zones	USDA Hardiness Zones
2	-50° to -35° F (-45.5° to -37.3° C)	-50° to -40° F (-45.5° to 40.0° C)
3	-35° to -20° F (-37.2° to -28.9° C)	-40° to -30° F (-40.0° to -34.5° C)
4	-20° to -10° F (-28.8° to -23.4° C)	-30° to -20° F (-34.4° to -28.9° C)
5	-10° to -5° F (-23.3° to -20.6° C)	-20° to -10° F (-28.8° to 23.4° C)
6	-5° to +5° F (-20.5° to -15.0° C)	-10° to 0° F (-23.3° to -17.8° C)

Some nursery catalogs supply hardiness zone numbers, but do not specify which system they follow. Some sources contradict one another. The following chart shows the relative hardiness of selected cultivars. Of course, the plums will grow in most of the warmer hardiness zones (7, 8, 9, 10), too, but will fail when the warmth of winter becomes too much.

2, 3   'Big Cis', 'Cistena'
3, 4   'Mt. St. Helens', 'Newport'
4, 5   'Allred', 'Hollywood', 'Othello', 'Pissardii', 'Trailblazer'
5   'Krauter's Vesuvius', 'Nigra', 'Thundercloud', 'Vesuvius', 'Woodii'
5, 6   'Blireiana', 'Moseri'

For cold tolerance, bushy 'Cistena' is the hardiest known purpleleaf plum cultivar, while 'Newport' is the hardiest known purpleleaf plum tree.

Perhaps 'Big Cis' is the hardiest tree, but is so new that documentation to support this possibility is lacking. 'Purple Pigmy' should be tested in severe winter conditions, as well.

Although severe cold freezes flowerbuds and even kills the ends of twigs, cold is only one factor. A cultivar can fail to thrive in the right temperature if, for example, the soil is too dry or the winds too great. Some varieties may not endure ice or snow loads, though they can endure cold.

Establishment

An important but sometimes overlooked consideration in judging tree hardiness is establishment. Suppose a person is willing to try any means to grow a purpleleaf plum in a cold, harsh region. If that individual buys a containerized specimen from a California nursery, he or she may be unintentionally asking for trouble. Why? Because the little tree will be accustomed to a rich diet: warm temperatures, heavy fertilization, pest and disease control, and ample water. It will be a lush plant. The first winter in its new home it may suffer terribly because the shock will be so withering, and it will have had no time to adjust, to get its roots firmly anchored or its growth regulated by the dictates of the new climate. The same cultivar, if purchased from a far-north grower, might be a more prudent investment. In fact, buying plants of any kind from nurseries with climates similar to the climate in which the plants will be grown is a sound practice. Once the tree becomes several years old and is established, it can endure more cold than a typical one-year-old tree from anywhere.

Some trees are hardy enough to be worthwhile for large commercial growers; many more trees are hardy for homeowners who will take extra pains to help the tree get established. Mass-production nurseries need reliable, no-risk stock if they are to operate efficiently. If a certain tree, while young, is not sure to survive, a nursery may not carry it—even if the variety is known to take hold after a couple years of coddling. This is not to blame nurseries, but to encourage enthusiastic testing by anyone who wants to try growing a cultivar that is not a certain success.

Depending upon the area and its climate, different tactics can be employed to increase a tree's likelihood of performing well. Something as simple as a mulch can make the critical difference.

Even when a tree has proven itself adapted to a given climate, occasional marked departures from the norm can hurt it. Seattle generally has mild, wet winters and warm, dry summers. Every purpleleaf plum can grow here, although some do better than others. When we get arctic visitations, the flowerbuds and young twigs—and sometimes older twigs—are killed on many trees. Snow breaks limbs, especially those of 'Moseri', for whatever reason.

Warm Climates

Cold aside, we turn now to the other end of the spectrum. If a climate is relatively mild in winter and/or hot in summer, growing the following may be advisable: 'Allred', 'Blireiana', 'Elsie', 'Gerth', 'Knaus', 'Krauter's Vesuvius', 'Moseri', 'Newport', 'Oaks', and 'Shalom'. No purpleleaf plums succeed in truly tropical regions—the lack of chill and dormancy foils them. However, in warm-temperate zones some cultivars do perform better than others. 'Krauter's Vesuvius' accepts summer heat and dryness admirably, so is the best (of the familiar kinds, at least) for the southwestern United States. I have not traveled in subtropical climates, so cannot report on which purpleleaf plums appear to do best in such balmy conditions. Doubtless one kind or another would prove to be the preferred choice if a comparative test was made.

8 Breeding and Genetics

Our discussion of plum breeding and genetics begins with the tree that gave birth to the first purpleleaf plum. The greenleaf cherry plum or myrobalan, *Prunus cerasifera*, is a tetraploid species from southeast Europe and southwest Asia. A tetraploid is a sort of super species, with more chromosomes than normal species. In this case it suggests the possibility that the cherry plum species originated as a cross thousands of years ago between two simpler species. *Prunus divaricata* represents a logical origin. But nobody knows for sure and few people care.

Somehow a purpleleaf seedling of *Prunus cerasifera* came about. The exact cause is still unknown. It might have been a branch sport appearing on a greenleaf tree. Reddish-pigmented members of the rose family (Rosaceæ) are comparatively common, so the purpleleaved plum was by no means miraculous in degree. It is always fascinating and can be vital to know the origins of odd trees, but our cataloging of aberrations is far more thorough than our accounting of their origins. By one means or another, *P. cerasifera* has produced the following sorts of deviants from its "typical" state of green leaves, white flowers, and yellow fruit: orange or red fruit; variegated leaves ('Louis Asselin' or 'Elegans'); narrow leaves ('Angustifolia'); bunched leaves ('Gracilis'); pink flowers ('Lindsayae'); weeping habit ('Pendula'); purple leaves.

A percentage of cherry plum genes allows for purplish pigmentation. In fact, the trait is dominant. At least 13 *Prunus* species have been directly or indirectly involved in hybridizing with 'Pissardii' or its offspring to produce additional purpleleaf plum varieties:

Scientific Name(s)	English Name(s)	Native Land
P. americana Marsh.	American plum	North America
P. angustifolia Marsh.	Chickasaw plum	South-Central U.S.
P. Besseyi Bailey	Western sand-cherry	Great Plains of North America
P. dulcis (Mill.) D. A. Webb (= *P. Amygdalus* Batsch)	Almond	North Africa to Syria
P. hortulana Bailey	Miner or Hortulan plum	Eastern U.S.
P. microcarpa C. A. Meyer	Bush cherry	Southwest/south-central Asia
P. Mume (Sieb.) S. & Z.	Japanese apricot	China, Korea, Taiwan
P. nigra Ait.	Canada plum	Northeastern North America
P. Persica (L.) Batsch	Peach	China
P. pumila L.	Sand cherry	Northeastern North America
P. salicina Lindl. (= *P. triflora* Roxb.)	Japanese plum	China

Scientific Name(s)	English Name(s)	Native Land
P. Simonii Carr.	Apricot plum	North China
P. spinosa L.	European sloe (plum); blackthorn	Eurasia

We can probably add a 14th species with assurance: the common apricot (*Prunus Armeniaca* L.). California's great plant breeder, Luther Burbank, made numerous crosses between apricots and plums. The resulting hybrids he named "plumcots." Although my research has revealed no named and released purpleleaf plumcots, Burbank reported some (Burbank et al. 1914–1915, 5: 300, 302):

> By crossing some of the plumcots with the *Prunus pissardii* plum, some purple leaved plumcots have been secured. This characteristic of dark foliage is readily transmitted in the plumcot cross as it is in the plum crosses. It is expected that by this cross one or more varieties of plumcots will be secured that are valuable both for fruit and foliage.
>
> The purple-leaved plum trees have proved of great value for decorating lawns, and the plumcot trees are considered of even more value by some, because of the unique combination, and the brilliant color of the foliage.

Most of Burbank's plumcots were obtained by crossing the apricot with Japanese plums. Any crosses he made betwen the apricot and cherry plum would be referable to the binomial *Prunus* × *dasycarpa* given by Friedrich Ehrhart in 1791, for this name covers hybrids cultivated in the Old World. The cross is called the purple or black apricot. The name "pluot" is also used to describe plum/apricot hybrids.

The Mexican plum (*Prunus mexicana* Wats.) is also a likely (15th) candidate as a parent in some purpleleaf plum crosses. Native to the south-central United States and northeast Mexico, it is also called big-tree plum, as it often grows very large. Perhaps it or an allied North American native species crossed with purpleleaf plums to produce 'Allred' or 'Gerth'—two cultivars with the flowerstalks covered in short fine hairs, unlike all other cultivars excepting 'Purple Pigmy' (of Old World origin) and a rare kind I have seen but cannot name yet.

Although they can, purpleleaf plums have rarely crossed with the common, garden, or European plum (*P. domestica* L.), probably because the cherry plum is nearly or completely finished blooming when the European plum begins. Of course, some botanists think that *P. domestica* arose as a hybrid between *P. cerasifera* and *P. spinosa*. It would seem that practically any plum species might be able to hybridize with the cherry plum, as long as some of the flowers are open at the same time. However, cherries (also *Prunus* species) have not yet hybridized with purpleleaf plums. The two sand cherry plants in the above list are bushes that grow on sandy soil and are unlike familiar cherries. The very name "cherry plum" causes some confusion: the species is a plum in all respects, but its fruit was thought cherry-like—thus the name.

The possibilities in plum breeding are endless. It is curious how most (30+) of the 50 clones of purpleleaf plums treated in this book came about by chance; only 13 are known to have been bred intentionally.

Luther Burbank surpassed all other individuals or groups in originating purpleleaf plum trees, although they were a minor part of his entire life work. Disregarding the apparently long lost purpleleaf plumcots and 'Oval Crimson' plum (which see in Chapter 12), he contributed five kinds. First was a hybrid of the Japanese plum 'Kelsey' with the original purpleleaf plum 'Pissardii'. Burbank called this hybrid simply 'Purpleleaf Kelsey' and offered it in his 1893 catalog. It was the first intentional purpleleaf plum hybrid, possibly dating from 1888, and the first selection other than 'Pissardii' to be commercially available. It is now extinct or grown under another name.

In 1905 'Othello' was sold, obviously named after Shakespeare's black Moor of Venice. A dark-leaved 'Pissardii' seedling, it was valuable as a fruit-producer.

In 1907 Burbank's very unusual hybrid 'Vesuvius' débuted, named after the Italian volcano whose A.D. 79 eruption destroyed the Roman cities of Pompeii and Herculaneum and also claimed as a victim the elder Pliny despite his confident utterence, "Fortune favors the brave!"

The epitomé of Burbank's darkleaf plums proved to be his 1919 'Thundercloud'. It is the most widely sold purpleleaf plum in the United States—or at least a tree bearing this name, is the most widely sold.

Last came 'Purple Flame' in about 1922. Whether Burbank or Stark Brothers Nurseries gave it the name is unknown, but it was not commercially available until 1931. The prolific plant-breeder died in 1926.

Other than Luther Burbank's five introductions, only eight purpleleaf plum cultivars are known to have resulted from intentional work:

Cultivar	Hybridizer	Year
'Citation'	Floyd Zaiger in California	ca. 1975
'Purple Pony'	Walter Krause in California	ca. 1962
'Newport'	University of Minnesota	1913
'Minn. No. 1'	University of Minnesota	1913
'Minn. No. 2'	University of Minnesota	1913
'Cistena'	Niels Hansen in South Dakota	1906
'Purple C'	Niels Hansen in South Dakota	1906
'Stanapa'	Niels Hansen in South Dakota	1906

The remaining 37 cultivars arose as chance seedlings or sports. A sport can be a branch or bud mutation on an otherwise normal tree. The variation can then be propagated vegetatively to retain its peculiar characteristics. Many very familiar trees arose this way, perhaps most notably the Lombardy poplar (*Populus nigra* 'Italica'). Normal black poplars are not narrowly upright, but once one of them sported in Italy, it was seized upon as a desirable novelty and subsequently has been planted around the earth.

No purpleleaf plum cultivars have been reported to have witches'-brooms. Should any sport these dense, twiggy masses, the world would be presented with an opportunity to propagate yet another purpleleaf plum, of bushy dwarfhood. However vast and rich our civilization, we do not need a miniature purpleleaf plum.

Numerous Offspring

Since the cherry plum is a variable species and readily cross-pollinates with many other species of *Prunus*, and since the "purple gene" is so strong, it is not surprising that there are dozens of purpleleaf plums. The following list divides cultivars into cherry plum seedlings and hybrids. As the question marks imply, absolute certainty is not always possible.

P. cerasifera Seedlings (20)

'Diversifolia'	'Oaks'?	'Purpusii'
'Hazeldene Variety'	'Othello'	'R. W. Hodgins'
'Hessei'	'Pallet'	'Shalom'?
'Knaus'?	'Paul's Pink'	'Thundercloud'
'Krauter's Vesuvius'	'Pissardii'	'Roebuck Castle'
'Mirage'	'Purple Flame'	'Woodii'
'Nigra'	'Purple Pony'	

P. cerasifera Hybrids (30)

'Allred'	'Festeri'	'Purple C'
'Atherton'	'Garnet'	'Purpleleaf Kelsey'
'Big Cis'	'Gaujardii'	'Purple Pigmy'
'Blireiana'	'Gerth'	'Purpurea'
'Cistena'	'Hollywood'	'Rosea'
'Citation'	'Minn. No. 1'	'Spencer Hollywood'
'Clark Hill Redleaf'?	'Minn. No. 2'	'Stanapa'
'Cocheco'	'Moseri'	'Trailblazer'
'Coleus'	'Mt. St. Helens'	'Vesuvius'
'Elsie'?	'Newport'	'Wrightii'

Hybrids

Some people wonder what difference it makes whether a tree is or is not a hybrid. Briefly, hybrids are normally much more variable than seedlings of purebred species. In flower, fruit, stone, leaf, tree size, and shape, hybrids demonstrate the genetic influence of both parents, so they look different and act differently. It is like giving a painter twice as many colors to use. Seven of the ten cultivars listed in Chapter 5 as best for producing edible fruit are hybrids. All the cultivars with doubled flowers and those with markedly fragrant flowers are hybrids.

Hybrids are by no means necessarily better trees than purebred seedlings. Nor are intentional hybrids guaranteed to be better than random wild seedlings that originated from crosses. There is hybrid vigor, wherein an energy level greater than that of either parent is achieved, and there are hybrid runts. 'Blireiana' is a case of a weak, little hybrid. Plant breeding is fascinating, but it leads to a proliferation of offspring, only a fraction of which are really superior and worth growing widely. Although Luther Burbank produced dozens of valuable plum varieties, he sent thousands to their deaths by burning them as inferior rejects. In his own words:

> It is better. . . . to run the risk of losing a perfected product, through the destruction of the elements which went into it, than to issue forth to the world a lot of second bests which have in them the power of self perpetuation and multiplication, and which, if we do not destroy them now, will clutter the earth with inferiority or with mediocrity (Burbank et al. 1914–915, 1: 205–206).

How do hybrids work? The following graphic illustration is imaginary but true to life: If plum purpleleaf is a *P. cerasifera* seedling, say 'Nigra' though it could just as well be any other, and we pollinate it with plum greenleaf, a Japanese plum (*P. salicina*), by dusting the Japanese species' pollen all over the purpleleaf tree's flowers, the genes of the Japanese species will mingle with the genes of the purpleleaf species. From this "marriage" the purpleleaf species' flowers give rise to fruit, whose seeds contain a new combination of genetic material. Thus, the seedlings will exhibit intermediate characteristics: most will be bronzy rather than either rich purple or plain green. However, the offspring of these first-generation hybrid seedlings will be a fascinating grab bag of variations: some trees will be purple, some bronze, others green.

So much crossing has gone on with plums in general, that in truth probably most named plum varieties are hybrids, whether we call them so or not. The same is certainly true with purpleleaf plums. Some cultivars listed above as cherry plum seedlings could well be second-generation hybrids. It is possible for a hybrid to look very much like one of its parents, exhibiting little or no obvious influence from the other—or example, 'Purple Pony' possibly. If a tree is an obvious hybrid, we should recognize this fact. Alas, most purpleleaf plum varieties are wrongly called cultivars (i.e., clones) of *P. cerasifera*. On the trees listed above as hybrids, we should write their names as 'Hollywood' plum or *Prunus'* 'Hollywood', not *Prunus cerasifera* 'Hollywood'. Many authors continue the traditional method of loose accuracy in naming, because either they do not know better or (worse) they simply do not care. To everyday gardeners, whether a plant "variety" is a hybrid or not is almost inconsequential, but professionals, at least, ought to practice accuracy.

The 30 purpleleaf *Prunus* hybrids can be divided into five groups based upon known or suspected parentage:

Group 1. *Prunus cerasifera* × *P. salicina* **(primarily, not exclusively):**
'Allred', 'Cocheco', 'Coleus', 'Elsie', 'Festeri'?, 'Garnet', 'Gerth', 'Hollywood', 'Purpleleaf Kelsey', 'Spencer', 'Trailblazer', 'Vesuvius'.

Group 2. *Prunus cerasifera* × **North American natives:**
'Big Cis', 'Cistena', 'Clark Hill Redleaf', 'Minn. No. 1', 'Minn. No. 2', 'Mt. St. Helens', 'Newport', 'Purple A', 'Stanapa'.

Group 3. *Prunus cerasifera* × **Peach, Almond, or Apricot:**
'Atherton', 'Blireiana', 'Citation', 'Gaujardii'?, 'Moseri', 'Wrightii'.

Group 4. *Prunus cerasifera*(?) × *P. microcarpa*:
'Purple Pigmy'.

Group 5. *Prunus cerasifera* × *P. spinosa*:
'Purpurea', 'Rosea'.

Pedigree charts (Tables 2–5), showing the ascribed parentage of four North American purpleleaf plum hybrids, graphically illustrate how involved tracing genetics can be.

TABLE 2. Parentage of 'Hollywood'.

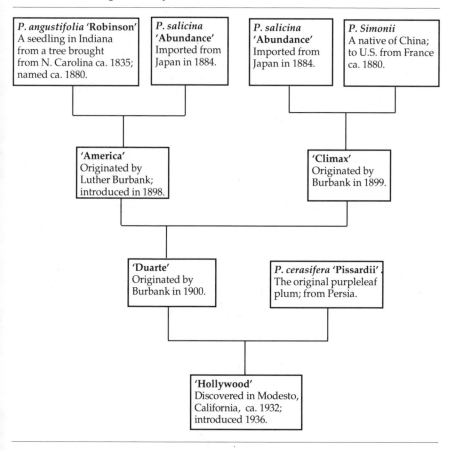

TABLE 3. Parentage of 'Minn. No. 1' and 'Minn. No. 2'.

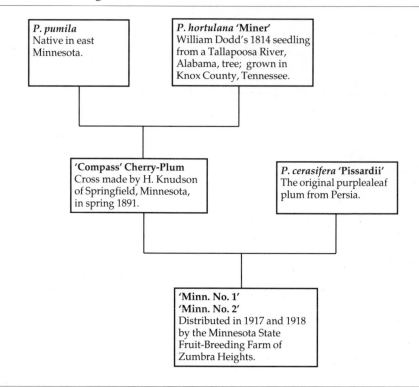

P. pumila
Native in east
Minnesota.

P. hortulana **'Miner'**
William Dodd's 1814 seedling
from a Tallapoosa River,
Alabama, tree; grown in
Knox County, Tennessee.

'Compass' Cherry-Plum
Cross made by H. Knudson
of Springfield, Minnesota,
in spring 1891.

P. cerasifera **'Pissardii'**
The original purplealeaf
plum from Persia.

'Minn. No. 1'
'Minn. No. 2'
Distributed in 1917 and 1918
by the Minnesota State
Fruit-Breeding Farm of
Zumbra Heights.

TABLE 4. Parentage of 'Newport'.

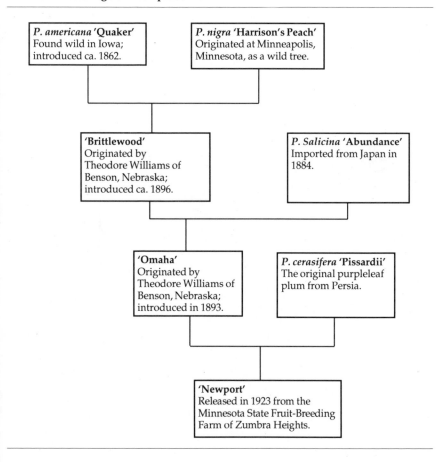

TABLE 5. Parentage of 'Trailblazer'.

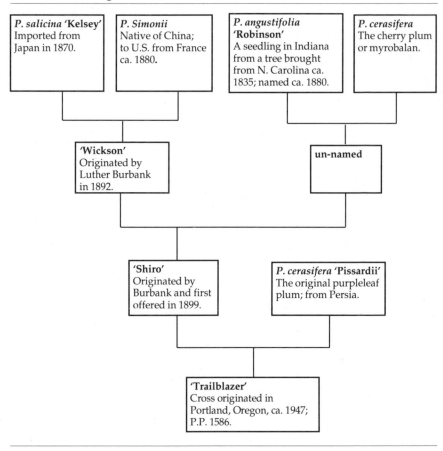

9 Culture

"Hands off!" is the plea trees would make if they could talk. Human malpractice does more harm to purpleleaf plums than insect and animal pests, diseases, or occasional acts of God such as floods, fires, earthquakes, and killer freezes. Of course, intelligent care is better than the "touch-me-not" policy, but misguided action is the deplorable norm. Having begun this chapter with such scolding, I now offer concrete advice on how to do right by your tree.

Initital Selection

First, choose the right variety. Know the characteristics of the varieties available, and do not, for example, acquire a 'Hollywood' plum if you do not care for the fruit it will inevitably yield. Learn the mature size of the tree and make sure you have room for it.

At the nursery, buy small specimens rather than large ones, because small trees are less set in their ways, have proportionately better root systems, and are easier to transport and plant. You will also be able to buy more trees with your budgeted money. If given a choice, choose bare-root or dormant-season stock rather than balled and burlapped or containerized (summertime) stock. Not only will you get a tree with a better root system (in this case, a less crowded, bruised one), but the tree roots will be exposed for your inspection. Purpleleaf plums transplant easily, so do not make it harder on yourself than necessary—small, healthy specimens transplant without requiring special precautions. With the new nursery methods of growing trees in containers, excellent containerized trees will soon be the norm.

Proper Planting

Select a sunny site. Plant the tree in ordinary, unamended native soil. Amending soil is now a discredited practice for general tree planting because of interface problems, so add no manure, no compost, no peat or sand. Choose trees that perform well in your soil. If purpleleaf plums refuse to grow well in your soil, so be it. They are easily satisfied as to soil conditions, however.

Always excepted to these admonitions are those locations where experience has proved that altering the soil is indispensable for successful tree growth. If you loosen the earth thoroughly at the planting site by forking or plowing it, and add certain amendments evenly and judiciously, the tree will grow faster and perhaps be healthier. But since so often the job is done poorly,

I hate to suggest this. Too often people dig a too-small hole, fill it with loose, rich soil, then stick the new tree in it. This is undesirable, and results in the "pot-bound" root syndrome. A wider, shallower, craterlike excavation is better than a deep shaftlike pit, because it permits the tree to send its roots broadly around the native soil instead of concentrating them in a pocket of specially formulated mix.

Plant the tree upon a slight mound. The problem with level planting is that the soil settles, thereby sinking the tree's rootcrown. Such shallow depressions invite root-rot because of insufficient drainage. To make the mound, add a bucket or two of soil from somewhere else. Try to match the existing soil texture. The slight mound above the soil line will settle back to normal, or nearly so.

Do not stake the tree. If you must stake it, do so loosely. The goal is to let the wind move the tree, thus encouraging it to root more firmly. Besides insufficient mobility, another deplorable problem with tight staking is that the ties too often are belatedly or never removed, thus they strangle the trunk. If you plant a *large* tree it must be staked or it risks falling over.

When planting purpleleaf plums fresh from nurseries, always remove a few branches that are too erect or ingrown. Nurseries and garden centers generally sell trees with too many closely spaced, strictly upright branches (see Chapter 7). Remove the worst offenders, then gently bend outwards the remaining branches. Bend them with ties and weights, or branch-spreader devices. This will impart to the branches a stronger trunk attachment, and give the whole tree a less dense, more pleasing shape.

The First Summer

Water deeply, as necessary. It makes a giant difference whether you live in an area of high or low summer rainfall. The common practice of watering lawns automatically is often injurious to trees. Usually, overwatering is more of a trouble to plums than is stress from dryness. The cherry plum evolved in a dry-summer climate and even in dry California gets by without water except while it is young and not yet established.

Whether your young plum is planted in a lawn area or not, a mulch around it helps retain a more evenly moist and congenial root environment, and keeps weeds, grass, and mowers back for a while. But mulches are sometimes problematic: they can keep your tree growing so long that insufficient "hardening off" of its new growth occurs, thereby inviting winter damage. Mulches can also encourage a shocking temperature imbalance in winter. The study of mulches for different plants and climates is a field needing much more attention. At present, I think the advantages justify the use of mulches, but, as usual, the rich complexity of nature bewilders our attempts to seek simple solutions. In any case, do not mulch too close to the trunk—stay several inches away or use only a thin layer near the tree's base. Too thick a mulch touching the bark at the base of the trunk encourages rot.

Fertilize sparingly or not at all, except with compost. Trees cannot be grown like market vegetables. Only fertilize if there is a specific reason to, and then do whatever is required and no more. For example, if an analysis of your soil shows it is deficient in manganese, add some. Simple N–P–K fertilizers (i.e., nitrogen, phosphorus, and potassium) used exclusively in chemical form will eventually deplete the soil, and it is soil conditions that chiefly affect the success of the tree. On the other hand, adding rotted plant material and manure not only supplies some N–P–K macronutrients, but also adds trace minerals, and makes the soil more water-retentive and lively with beneficial organisms such as earthworms. In short, our old view was to feed the plant–a simple mechanical operation much like filling a fuel tank; now we try to nurture the earth, returning what we take from the soil. The chemical method, at least when recurrently relied upon to the exclusion of organic proceedings, actually destroys soil, and its effects are shockingly similar to the results of steroids in humans: namely, short-term vigor and increased productivity paid for with long-term negative side effects.

Summer Pruning

During the early summer (May or June) take out about 10–20% of the branches and twigs to create a lighter form, emphasizing horizontal and weeping tendencies, and suppressing overcharged vertical aspirations—but do not cut the tree's leading shoot. This type of thinning changes opaque dark blobs of trees into specimens that artfully reveal some of their branch structure, and provides a chance for sunlight to filter through in an attractive way. Summer pruning strikes a balance between root energy and top growth: neither gets out of control or too domineering. Winter or dormant season pruning causes a major flush of energetic spring growth that is apt to encourage upright suckers (watershoots). Thus the tree looks unnatural and graceless. While winter pruning is traditional and usual because it is convenient for workers and fruit-production schedules, it is not right for ornamental deciduous tree pruning. In fact, many fruit growers now prefer summer pruning. Anyone insisting on heavy winter pruning should accompany it by root pruning to compensate for the imbalance inflicted. Root pruning is rarely done, but not for lack of advantages.

The best time to prune purpleleaf plums is during summer, although a light amount of pruning can be done right after flowering. Fall pruning while the leaves are still on the tree is not as advisable as summer pruning, but is better than winter pruning. In fall, as in winter, the pruning wounds have no opportunity to callus over (they must wait until the next spring), and yet many decay-causing fungal spores are liberated during these months. The raw wounds and eager fungal spores are not what we wish to have in conjunction.

Summer pruning is more work than winter pruning. There is no question that it is harder to view the structure of the tree and that there is more to clean up. Maneuvering so as to minimize damage to the foliage and twigs is also awkward, but I am sold on the benefits of summer pruning, and refuse to touch my trees in winter. Trees well pruned in the summer look natural and attractive as opposed to heavily winter-pruned trees, which look wounded and scarred to the sensitive eye. Summer pruning is like cleaning a glass window with a sponge; winter pruning is like scrubbing a window with sandpaper. Summer pruning helps a tree, winter pruning hurts it.

Sometimes hard freezes and snow breakage damage a tree badly in winter. Then in spring suckers shoot up like pins on a pincushion. Thin these suckers ruthlessly, but do not remove all of them. A new structure needs to begin partly from suckers, so while most are removed, some are merely shortened or bent.

Overhaul

It takes years to right the wrongs inflicted by an hour of nature's wrath or brutal human malpruning. Even strong-hearted tree lovers succumb into morose silence when surveying such shocking scenes. If you have a tree damaged by previous malpruning or some other cause, and want to recuperate it, a formidable job awaits you. In fact, sometimes you can never undo the damage. A thorough understanding of the tree's natural growth habits and knowledge of proper pruning cuts must accompany diligent, recurrent summer pruning. Make sure the tree is worth the effort.

Sometimes chopping down a ruined tree is better than trying to fix it. If it is on its own roots—that is, not grafted onto some other kind of rootstock—you can chop the tree down and a new one will replace it from the roots. This procedure is best done in winter, so that in spring the stump is ringed by a horde of suckers. Save one or two (at most three) of the strongest suckers on opposite sides of the stump and cut the rest away. The two you saved should grow as tall as a person or higher by the end of the growing season, and should begin branching. The following winter, remove the weakest of the two suckers. In a few years you will have an attractive, thriving tree.

This violent but profound way of restarting a tree from its roots is useful not only for damaged trees, but is also good for weak, aged trees. In such cases, a careful forking of the soil and a liberal topdressing of manure or compost assists the rejuvenating process. A third reason for resorting to the axe occurs when a tree has grown too big for its space. In this case, do not fertilize the stump. Most deciduous broadleaf trees and broadleaf evergreen trees resprout from their stumps. Coniferous evergreens rarely do, some members of the yew family and a few pines and such excepted.

'Cistena' and other shrubby cultivars frequently grow better if they are occasionally chopped back to the soil line and restarted. Such pruning is best done in late winter or earliest spring, right before the roots send their surge of energy for new growth.

Suckers from purpleleaf plum trunks or roots or rootstocks should be cut when they are about as long as they will get in the summer. Cut them close. If you consistently prune suckers in summer, soon the problem may be gone. Usually suckers only appear on leaning, suffering trees, though the grafted 'Spencer Hollywood' almost always suckers much at its base.

Pruning Cuts and Wound Dressing

Whenever pruning is done, there is a right way and wrong way to make cuts. It is critical to preserve the ring collar—to take off the branch, no more (i.e., a piece of the trunk) and no less (i.e., leaving a stub of branch). Painting pruning cuts or other wounds with any sort of material is another old habit now shown by study to be unnecessary and sometimes harmful. Healthy trees do not need and are not helped by the seal, and no trees are kept free from fungal invasion by such seals. Pruning cuts can be unsightly because the new wood is so light in color. If you desire to darken the raw wound, daub some harmless dark stain or charcoal over it.

Branch Structure and Balance

Some purpleleaf plums are prone to having large forks or limbs tear off, leaving gaping holes in the tree canopy and unsightly gash wounds on the trunk. To minimize such breakage, study the tree's form in winter, noting where the weight and stress points are located. Pruning to mitigate unequal weight loads is desirable, though requires more knowledge of tree growth and structure than can be communicated in this volume. As Shakespeare said, "In nature's infinite book of secrecy a little I can read." So get thee to the trees to read. World-famous tree-pruning expert Alex Shigo advises those who would treat trees right to touch them. By this he means to observe trees thoughtfully, so as to direct your actions in accordance with the best interest of the tree.

Compared to pruning, mechanical bracing of stressed limbs or forks is a less desirable option. This, too, is not as simply done (the right way) as we might hope. If you have, however, a large old purpleleaf plum whose form could be ruined by splitting, or if splitting could cause serious damage, consult a tree surgeon.

'Spencer Hollywood' is a natural dwarf purpleleaf plum that sometimes breaks its limbs with the weight of fruit. It stands like an child loaded down with a 50-pound sack of potatoes. Thinning the fruit and carefully bracing the branches are necessary or the tree could be a broken, weird-looking object.

Hedges

In England, and doubtless to a lesser extent elsewhere, purpleleaf plums are used in hedges, both informal or formal. The smaller-growing, smaller-leaved cultivars work best for most properties. 'Cistena' is very small, too small for certain uses. If you choose, then, a real tree, train it from the start, and try to be consistent. For example, prune it annually soon after its flowering period.

Pests, Diseases, Vermin

Compared to many trees, purpleleaf plums are not seriously affected by bugs and diseases, though most of them harbor scale insects, aphids, occasional caterpillars, borers and other hungry little creatures. These pests sometimes make a mess or render the tree unsightly, but they rarely threaten its survival. Fungal, viral, and bacterial diseases such as brown rot and shot-hole fungus are also common but usually not serious. Occasionally they render the trees very gaunt and diseased-looking in late spring or early summer. Small mammals such as mice and rabbits can chew the bark, girdling the tree fatally. Sparrows, bullfinches, and other birds eat the flowerbuds, thus ruining the floral display, and some birds such as crows attack the fruit itself. The lichens, moss, and algae, that grow on the bark may be unsightly to some people, but otherwise are harmless. These problems pale into insignificance compared with the problems beleaguering certain other trees. Citrus trees, for example, are loaded with troubles, elms battle for existence, and peach trees are positively finicky. With purpleleaf plums, most of the insects and diseases are not insufferable problems, but slight imperfections, ugly though they be.

Purpleleaf plums require minimal or no spray programs. Some regions cannot grow certain of these trees successfully unless such interference is practiced, but the trees had better be well worth growing if they require out-of-the-ordinary care year after year. Most trees, especially in home gardens, should not need annual pesticide sprays. Instead, homeowners should insist on growing varieties that thrive in their area. Large-scale commercial growing, of course, is another matter—to not spray in such cases is to invite bankruptcy. Of the clones known to me firsthand, the most disease-prone in Seattle are 'Blireiana', 'Cistena', and 'Trailblazer'.

Fruit Harvest

During July or August, many purpleleaf plums drop fruit. As far as I am concerned, it should be eaten, but if you do not think so, add it to a compost pile. Letting fruit collect beneath the tree may be acceptable if the tree is not by a sidewalk, street, or patio, but numerous seedlings may sprout from the stones or pits.

Fall Leaf Clean-up

The best landscapes have recycling plans, so the leaves either lie where they fall, or are gathered, composted, and applied as a mulch. To bag leaves and call them garbage is an ecologic crime. In bygone times, people practiced garden sanitation by burning old leaves, so as to minimize overwintering of pests or diseases. The new ecologic awareness bids us put up with a few blemishes in appearance for the sake of better overall health and balance.

10 Propagation and Availability

Plum trees in general are easily reproduced, and purpleleaf plums are no exception. Nurseries raise new trees from grafting, cuttings, or seeds.

Grafting is used customarily, since this method is most expedient. To graft a plum variety, a twig (at most) or a bud (at least) of the desired cultivar is carefully attached to a rootstock. The rootstock is either a seedling or a rooted cutting. The overall size of the tree is determined by the roots, therefore a dwarf rootstock makes a dwarf tree. Grafting accounts for an occasional purpleleaf plum tree that throws up green suckers from its base. Some peaches and the peach-plum hybrid 'Citation' are the only cloned purpleleaved rootstocks I know. Ordinary cherry plum seedlings, which are often purple, accept grafts of cherry plum seedlings and hybrids as well as European and Japanese plums. Nursery workers sometimes call the cherry plum "myro" (short for myrobalan). Grafting of woody parts is done in winter or earliest spring; budding is done in summer.

Cuttings are easier but less certain. Simply cut a healthy, stout twig about as long as your forearm, during late summer or autumn, slip it halfway into the ground, and next spring it may take root and grow. Its prosperity depends on several factors, including the exact twig size and constitution, whether or not you dust the end with root-promoting hormones, the nature of the soil, and the weather that winter and spring. If the tree does establish, any suckers it throws up will be the same color as the rest of the tree, since the tree is growing on its own roots. Plant-propagation specialists know many techniques to strike cuttings.

Seeds are rarely exact replicators of their parents' genetic make-up; they almost always give rise to variable individuals. Hence, a seedling of 'Thundercloud' plum is just that, it is not a 'Thundercloud' plum. A cutting-grown or grafted offspring, however is a 'Thundercloud' plum. The same principle holds true for apple pippins: apple seedlings rarely bear fruit matching the fruit on the original tree. Many cherry plum seedlings are used for grafting. Other plum seedlings are very rarely used for purpleleaf plums. The Damson plum from Europe is one example. Peach seedlings can be used, surprisingly enough.

Tissue-culture, softwood cuttings, layering, and other propagative means are certainly possible with purpleleaf plums, but few or no nurseries use these means. With our present elaborate technology, the production of virus-free stock is possible. Virus-free stock grows more vigorously and looks better.

Some kinds of purpleleaf plums are easier to propagate than others, but as far as I know none pose any serious problems. A possible exception is 'Purple Pigmy': cuttings have failed but I have not tried grafting it.

Availability

Of the 50 cultivars known to me, at least 42 are still extant or believed to be. Some cultivars are extinct under their own names in the nursery trade. The following list summarizes the present availability of the various cultivars.

'**Allred**': Easily acquired. Various U.S. nurseries offer it. It is especially common in Texas. Probably more than one clone goes under this name.

'**Atherton**': Never introduced into the general nursery trade, probably because it was not worth the honor. I have a specimen and assume that a few others exist in California.

'**Big Cis**': Easily acquired from nurseries that carry stock from the nursery of origin: J. Frank Schmidt & Son Company, Boring, Oregon 97009; telephone (503) 663-4128. Schmidt is a wholesale nursery, so neither institutions nor individuals can order single specimens.

'**Blireiana**': Easily acquired. One of the best known clones, internationally distributed. Sometimes topgrafted, which is to say it is grafted on a long clean trunk to avoid the ugly, knobby warts of its own trunk.

'**Cistena**': Easily acquired. Sold both in bush and tree form, the latter rarer.

'**Citation**': Can be acquired through some U.S. commercial rootstock dealers.

'**Clark Hill Redleaf**': Small quantities of budwood can be acquired from W. R. Okie, Southeastern Fruit and Tree Nut Laboratory, P.O. Box 87, Byron, Georgia 31008.

'**Cocheco**': Barely in the trade at present, though thousands were sold in the United States during the late 1970s and early 1980s. Present in some collections. Available via mail order from Michael McConkley's Edible Landscaping Nursery, P.O. Box 77, Afton, Virginia 22920; telephone (804) 361-9134.

'**Coleus**': Presumed extinct, or is being grown under another name. Probably it was little grown or never made it into the nursery trade.

'**Diversifolia**': For decades, Hillier Nurseries of England and some other outlets offered it, but I do not know of a contemporary source. Hillier Nurseries Ltd, Ampfield House, Ampfield, Romsey, Hants SO51 9PA, England.

'**Elsie**': A few California nurseries specializing in fruit trees retail this cultivar. With 'Gerth' and 'Shalom', 'Elsie' is in the 1991 plant list of the Exotica Rare Fruit Nursery, P.O. Box 160, 2508-B East Vista Way, Vista, California 92083; telephone (619) 724-9093.

'Festeri': Presumably still available in Australia and New Zealand. No Northern Hemisphere sources known.

'Garnet': Presumed extinct, at least under its own name. Probably little grown or never made it into the nursery trade.

'Gaujardii': Very obscure. Exists in Ireland, and possibly in Italy or elsewhere in Europe in some collections.

'Gerth': Available from a few outlets in California, such as Exotica Rare Fruit Nursery (see 'Elsie' for address) and from Robert Hartman's Fruit Tree Nursery, 713 21st Street SE, Puyallup, Washington 98372.

'Hazeldene Variety': Presumably extinct under its own name. May exist under its name in some English collections.

'Hessei': Hesse of Germany, Hillier of England, and other European nurseries have long carried this cultivar.

'Hollywood': Three or more tree clones are sold under this name. No doubt at least some of them are the original 'Hollywood'. Probably California nurseries (such as L. E. Cooke Company, Visalia) are more likely to have the original 'Hollywood' than are Oregon nurseries. Beware of various trees called by this name.

'Knaus': Unavailable. It is a southern California selection named by Paul Thomson.

'Krauter's Vesuvius': Easily acquired in the United States from California, Oregon, and Washington nurseries. Some midwestern and eastern nurseries also offer it.

'Minn. No. 1' and 'Minn. No. 2': Presumed extinct under these names, though one of the two is possibly still sold by a few midwestern U.S. nurseries as 'Minnesota Red' or 'Minnesota Purple'.

'Mirage': A brand-new clone from England. The 1990 edition of *The Plant Finder* lists one source: Bridgemere Nurseries, Bridgemere, North Nantwich, Cheshire CW5 7QB, England.

'Moseri': Difficult to find under this name in the United States. It has been often sold as 'Blireiana' or 'Veitchii' and is quite common in landscapes despite its rarity in catalogs. Overseas it may be easier to acquire.

'Mt. St. Helens': Easily acquired from nurseries that carry stock from the nursery of origin: J. Frank Schmidt & Son Company (see 'Big Cis' for address).

'Newport': Easily acquired in U.S. nurseries.

'Nigra': Easily acquired in most countries where purpleleaf plums are sold, although rarely offered in the United States.

'Oaks': Not in the nursery trade, but it exists in California in the collections of a few plum enthusiasts.

'Othello': No sources known today, although I am nearly certain that collections in the central or eastern United States have specimens. For decades it was available there.

'Pallet': In some European collections probably.

'Paul's Pink': Presumably extinct. Possibly persists in some English collections.

'Pissardii': Easily acquired. However, many clones masquerade under this name. No one knows what the original introduction looked like or where it can be obtained today.

'Purple C': Extinct.

'Purple Flame': No present sources known, but it was offered by Stark Bro's Nurseries (of Missouri) in the United States until the 1970s, so doubtless it is still found in collections.

'Purpleleaf Kelsey': Extinct under this name. Never seen in any catalogs. Since it was a Burbank introduction, it may still exist somewhere in California.

'Purple Pigmy': The type specimen is at the Washington Park Arboretum in Seattle.

'Purple Pony': Available from the L. E. Cooke Nursery, 26333 Road 140, Visalia, California 93277; telephone (209) 732-9146; and from retailers who purchase that wholesale company's stock.

'Purpurea': Available in Europe, and to a lesser degree elsewhere. Sold as *Prunus spinosa* 'Purpurea'.

'Purpusii': From Hesse nurseries of Germany. Also present at the USDA Plant Introduction Station, Glenn Dale, Maryland.

'Roebuck Castle': Present in Ireland, but not known in the nursery trade.

'Rosea': Hillier nurseries of England. Probably in Europe, also.

'R. W. Hodgins': May be extant in some old collections in New Zealand or Australia.

'Shalom': Sparingly available in California from nurseries such as Exotica Rare Fruit Nursery (see 'Elsie' for address).

'Spencer Hollywood': Wholesaled by the Samuel J. Rich Nursery, 9803 Yergen Road NE, Aurora, Oregon, 97002; telephone (503) 678-2828; and other Pacific Northwest outlets. Often sold as "Hollywood", by nurseries such as Biringer (wholesale) Nursery, 1561 Dunbar Road, Mount Vernon, Washington 98273; telephone (206) 424-6727.

'**Stanapa**': Extinct unless it still exists in some old midwestern U.S. plantings.

'**Thundercloud**': Easily acquired. Quite likely more than one clone goes under this title, however.

'**Trailblazer**': Can be acquired with a bit of looking; sometimes sold as 'Hollywood'. The nursery of origin still carries it: Samuel J. Rich (see 'Spencer' for address).

'**Vesuvius**': Can be acquired from some California and Oregon nurseries. Beware of getting 'Krauter's Vesuvius' instead.

'**Woodii**': Difficult to locate in the United States, but has been sparingly offered. Can be found in Europe.

'**Wrightii**': May be sparingly available in New Zealand or Australia. Almost certainly exists still, even if it is out of the trade.

Of the 50 cultivars, I think only 8 are almost certainly lost irretrievably: 'Coleus', 'Garnet', 'Hazeldene Variety', 'Minn. No. 2', 'Paul's Pink', 'Purple C', 'Purpleleaf Kelsey', and 'R. W. Hodgins'. By lost I mean at least under their original names. Probably some of these trees are still extant under other names.

Is it important to assemble in one location as complete as possible a collection of the different kinds? Growing many cultivars together would enable critical comparisons, provide a source for propagation material, and, if artfully designed, would make a flamboyant landscape. If anyone desires to make such a collection, I will cooperate with them.

11 Identification Keys

As it stands now, a large number of cultivars travel under a few names. Misidentification is understandably common considering the numerous varieties and the paucity of documentation.

Certain identification should be based on tree form, foliage, flowers, and fruit. To begin with, a supra-cultivar classifactory division is needed to include the numerous cherry plum (*Prunus cerasifera*) seedlings which are not referable definitely to a given cultivar/clone. As suggested in Chapter 12 (see 'Pissardii'), a *single* name should be available to include under its mantle every sort of nonhybrid purpleleaved cherry plum variant. *Prunus cerasifera* f. *purpurascens* is my proposal. *Prunus cerasifera* var. *atropurpurea* is no good because it means literally dark purple, and historically has been used largely as a synonym in a cultivar sense for 'Pissardii'.

An additional refinement to sort the various cherry plum cultivars and unnamed seedlings would be something like this:

1. Bronzy foliage, white or palest pink flowers belong to the 'Pissardii' group (grex): 'Pallet', 'Pissardii', 'Roebuck Castle'?.
2. Purplish foliage, white or palest pink flowers belong to the 'Othello' group (grex): 'Knaus'?, 'Othello', 'Purple Flame'?, 'Shalom'?.
3. Purplish foliage, clearly pink flowers belong to the 'Woodii' group (grex): 'Hazeldene Variety', 'Krauter's Vesuvius', 'Nigra', 'Paul's Pink', 'Purple Pony', 'R. W. Hodgins', 'Thundercloud', 'Woodii'.
4. Variegated or otherwise unusual foliage, usually or always white flowers, belong to the 'Purpusii' group (grex): 'Diversifolia', 'Hessei', 'Mirage', 'Purpusii'.

Group 3 differs not only in pigmentation, but these dark-leaved, pink-flowered trees (e.g., 'Nigra', 'Thundercloud', 'Woodii') are smaller and less vigorous than the trees in groups 1 and 2, they bloom later in spring, they are less hardy to winter cold, and they have more stamens—averaging 29 instead of 25.

In using the flower key below, note that the flowers examined must be representative. Do not assume that a single flower plucked at random from a twig will be identical to all the other blossoms. Look at various twigs and observe whether any obvious distinctions exist. The fragrance will be strongest as the tree comes into full bloom, then gradually decreases in strength, and sometimes in quality. Many petals are clearly pink when the tree begins blooming, but two weeks later they are a washed-out off-white. Some trees in the rose family vary the pinkness of their flowers from year to year. For example, a mazzard cherry is usually pure white; in some years the same tree can be pale pink. The same holds true with some 'Pissardii' plums, and accounts partly for the flower color being described variously as "white" or "pink." The pedicels (flowerstalks) generally lengthen as pollination occurs and the ovary begins developing into a fruit. In brief: using a flower key to identify varieties requires care and the results are merely suggestive, by no means infallible.

Rare trees are included in the keys if I have examined their flowers; commoner cultivars are excluded if I have not seen their flowers, although 'Clark Hill Redleaf' and others are included because information written by others about the flowers was sufficiently detailed to incorporate into the keys.

Flower Key

a. Flowers always with more than 10 petals; fragrant
  b. Ovary not hairy (about 20 palest pink petals) . . . . a mystery tree[3]
  b. Ovary hairy
    c. Very double (20–24 petals), deep pink . . . . 'Blireiana'
    c. Double (13–17 petals), pale pink . . . . 'Moseri'
a. Flowers usually with 5 petals, (a few with up to 8 or 10); not invariably fragrant
  b. Ovary hairy . . . . 'Atherton'
  b. Ovary not hairy
    c. Petals at full bloom appear white (or faintest possible tinge of pink)
      d. Sepals reflex strongly
        e. Stamens 17–20 . . . . 'Cistena'
        e. Stamens 22–27 . . . . *Prunus cerasifera* nonhybridized seedlings:
                    'Diversifolia', 'Hessei', 'Othello', 'Pissardii', 'Purpusii', etc.
      d. Sepals largely but not completely reflexed strongly . . . . 'Trailblazer'
      d. Sepals remain more or less horizontal
        e. Sepals acute . . . . 'Vesuvius'
        e. Sepals more or less blunt
          f. Most flowers 1 inch (25 mm) or more wide,
            very fragrant, early . . . . 'Hollywood'
          f. Most flowers 1 inch (25 mm) or less wide,
            not markedly fragrant, usually not early
            g. Twigs and pedicels glabrous . . . . 'Newport'
            g. Twigs glabrous, pedicels pubescent . . . . 'Allred'
            g. Twigs minutely, inconspicuously pubescent,
               pedicels glabrous . . . . 'Trailblazer'
            g. Twigs very pubescent, pedicels glabrous . . . . 'Hollywood'
            g. Twigs and pedicels pubescent
               h. 17–19 stamens . . . . 'Purple Pigmy'
               h. 30–36 stamens . . . . 'Gerth'

[The following cultivars also have white petals but are not included in the preceding "white-petal" key because of inadequate information: 'Big Cis' (should key-out to its parent 'Cistena', as will perhaps 'Purple C' and 'Stanapa'), 'Cocheco', 'Coleus', 'Elsie'(?), 'Garnet', 'Knaus', 'Minn. No. 1', 'Minn. No. 2', 'Mt. St. Helens' (presuambly it will key-out to its parent 'Newport'), 'Oaks', 'Pallet', 'Purple Flame', 'Purpleleaf Kelsey', 'Roebuck Castle'(?), and 'Shalom'(?).]

    c. Petals at full bloom appear obviously pink

    1. *Prunus cerasifera* purebred seedlings with pink petals have (25) 27–31 (32) stamens, sepals that are almost invariably reflexed strongly, and red ovaries. They cannot be distinguished by examining only flowering twigs alone. 'Purple Pony' stands out: its flowers appear with the leaves rather than before them, its sepals are not reflexed, and its flowers are very few. Likely it is a hybrid after all. The other cultivars (I have not seen those marked with a star) are: *'Hazeldene Variety'—extinct under this name; English. 'Krauter's Vesuvius'—common in the western United States. 'Nigra'—common. *'Paul's Pink'—extinct under this name; English. *'R. W. Hodgins'—Australian; may be extinct, at least nominally. 'Thundercloud'—common in North America. 'Woodii'—rare now, but can be located; possibly synonymous with 'Nigra'.

    2. Hybrids differ from purebred cherry plum stock in varied but nearly always prominent ways: the time of bloom can be much earlier or later, the flowers are often much larger or smaller, there may be more than the obligatory five petals, and the sepals are little reflexed, if at all (or, if reflexed strongly, other characteristics clearly indicate hybridity). The stamens may be any number.

      d. Ovary hairy; flowers quite large, short stalked
        e. A rare New Zealand ornamental tree, decades old . . . . 'Wrightii'
        e. A North American rootstock, from the 1980s . . . . 'Citation'
      d. Ovary hairy only at the top; flowers small, stalked as usual . . . . 'Atherton'
      d. Ovary not hairy
        e. Flowers 0.62 inch (15 mm) wide,
          on 0.25 inch (5 mm) pedicels . . . . 'Clark Hill Redleaf'
        e. Flowers usually larger, always on longer pedicels
          f. Flowers markedly fragrant,
            with conspicuously short, crowded stamens . . . . . 'Spencer Hollywood'
          f. Flowers not so
            g. Flowers 1.19 inches (30 mm) wide, later blooming . . . . 'Festeri'
            g. Flowers 0.5–.075 inch (13–19 mm) wide,
              earlier blooming . . . . 'Purpurea', 'Rosea'

Leaf Key

a. Leaves variegated or deformed or both
  b. Deformed only, diverse in shape and toothing; a tree . . . . 'Diversifolia'
  b. Deformed and variegated; shrubby . . . . 'Hessei'
  b. Variegated shrubby tree; new cultivar . . . . 'Mirage'
  b. Variegated tree; old cultivar . . . . 'Purpusii'
a. Leaves neither variegated nor deformed
  b. Leaves markedly long (3–5 inches; 76–126 mm) and slender compared to most
    c. Old ornamental tree; finer-toothed, less glandular,
      darker, less hairy, teeth blunter . . . . 'Vesuvius'
    c. New rootstock; less finely toothed, more glandular, lighter,
      more hairy, teeth sharper . . . . 'Citation'
  b. Leaves markedly broad compared to most; usually comparatively hairy
    (apricot hybrids)

      c. Largest, least hairy leaves; usually more than 3 inches (76 mm) long;
         common . . . . 'Moseri'

      c. Intermediate-sized, hairier leaves; usually less than 3 inches
         (76 mm) long; very common . . . . 'Blireiana'

      c. Smallest, hairiest leaves; less than 2.25 inches
         (57 mm) long; rare Californian . . . . 'Atherton'

   b. Leaves of "normal" plum-leaf shape

      c. Greenish on top, bronzy to purplish undersides; shape broad near tip,
        narrow near base (obovate)

         d. Leaf 3–4.87 inches (76–123 mm); petiole up to 0.75 inches (19 mm);
           hairier, teeth blunter . . . . 'Allred'

         d. Leaf 2.5–4.5 inches (63–114 mm); petiole up to 0.5 inches
           (13 mm); darker; teeth sharp . . . . 'Trailblazer'

      c. Greenish on top, bronzy to purplish undersides; shape widest near middle,
        broader, rounder near base (elliptic)

         d. Leaf 3–5.12 inches (76–29.5 mm); petiole up to 0.81 inches
           (20.5 mm); teeth sharp . . . . 'Hollywood'

         d. Leaf 2.5–3.5 inches (63–89 mm);
           petiole up to 0.62 inches (15.5 mm) . . . . 'Pissardii', 'Pallet', etc.

         d. Leaf 2–3 inches (50.5–76 mm); petiole up to 0.5 inches
           (13 mm); dark; glossy; teeth very fine . . . . 'Spencer Hollywood'
           (similar but with sharper teeth, hairier petioles;
           often convex on long shoots; hairier twigs) . . . . 'Gerth'

      c. Purplish, or very dark green-purplish on both leaf surfaces

         d. Leaf 2.5–4 inches (63–101 mm); petiole up to 0.62 inches (15.5 mm) . . . .
           . . . . Krauter's Vesuvius', 'Nigra','Othello', 'Paul's Pink', 'Pissardii',
                      'Purple Pony', 'R. W. Hodgins',
                      'Thundercloud', 'Woodii', etc.

         d. Leaf 2–3 inches (50.5–76 mm); almost hairless; prominent stipules;
           shrub . . . . Cistena'
           (similar but with leaves averaging 3.62 inches; 92 mm; small tree) . . . . . . 'Big Cis'

         d. Leaf 2–3 inches (50.5–76 mm); bluntish; quickly falling stipules;
           puckery or bullate . . . . 'Newport'
           (similar but with leaves averaging 3.62 inches; 92 mm) . . . . 'Mt. St. Helens'

         d. Leaf 2.37 inches (60 mm); bluntish; rootstock of rarity . . . . . . 'Clark Hill Redleaf'

Leaf color is variable to a significant degree, changing from spring through autumn. The leaf measurements above were based mostly on the larger leaves of elongated shoots, not on the comparatively small, scarce leaves found on short fruit spurs. With much labor, refinements might be made to distinguish by leaf alone the various cherry plum darkleaf cultivars such as 'Nigra', 'Thundercloud', or 'Krauter's 'Vesuvius', for example. 'Pissardii' trees vary in hairiness, leaf color, shape, and size. Although the 50 cultivars treated in this book may seem shockingly numerous, more clones than 50 have been grown and distributed over the decades. Who knows how many variations have been called 'Pissardii' in the last 100 years?

'Pissardii'

'Thundercloud'

'Krauter's Vesuvius'

'Purple Pony'

'Woodii'

'Nigra'

Figure 11a. Leaves of 6 nonhybrid purpleleaf cherry plum cultivars. Half of actual size.

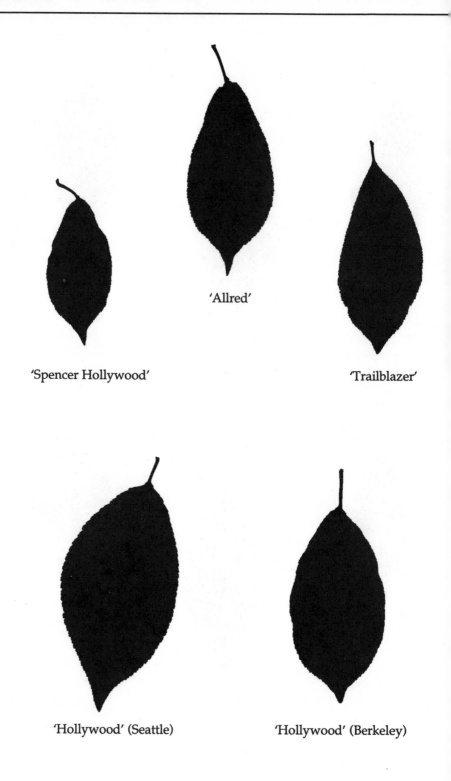

'Allred'

'Spencer Hollywood'

'Trailblazer'

'Hollywood' (Seattle)

'Hollywood' (Berkeley)

Figure 11b. Leaves of 5 *fruitful* hybrid purpleleaf plum cultivars. Half of actual size.

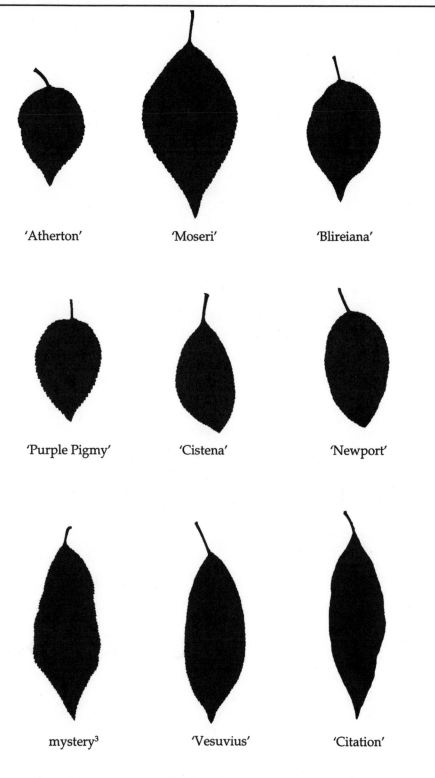

'Atherton' 'Moseri' 'Blireiana'

'Purple Pigmy' 'Cistena' 'Newport'

mystery[3] 'Vesuvius' 'Citation'

Figure 11c. Leaves of 9 hybrid purpleleaf plum cultivars.
Half of actual size.

Part II

Cultivar Descriptions

1. Cherry plum (*Prunus cerasifera*) tree in bloom. The ancestor of purpleleaf plums, shown in its floral glory, thrives without being watered, sprayed, or pruned.

2. 'Allred' attractive autumn reddish leaf color on a young tree. The leaves are late to drop.

3. 'Allred' foliage and plum in summer. The younger leaves are purplish. This cultivar is prized for its fruit, above all.

4. 'Atherton' in late September, suffering from dry conditions.

5. 'Atherton' foliage. Close examination reveals the leaves coated with fine hairs; it is a hybrid from California, of little redeeming value.

6. 'Blireiana' in bloom, electrifying pink and fragrant. No other plum is so beloved in bloom.

7.'Blireiana' in autumn: "King of Ugly Trees."

8. 'Cistena' in bloom. Normally bushy, it is rarely a small tree.

9. 'Cistena' during summer, dark and motley. By itself, it is less ornamental than when it is integrated tastefully with companion plants. Excellent tolerance of severe cold is one of its strengths.

10. 'Gerth' foliage and plum in summer. The plums of this California cultivar are as good to eat as they are dark.

11. 'Hollywood' blooming in Seattle, on March 5th. Noteworthy for the earliness of its flowers and for its early ripening crop of delicious fruit.

12. 'Hollywood' blooming in Seattle, showing the largest plum flowers.

13. 'Hollywood' trees in Berkeley, bearing dark fruit well hidden in the leaves. The flowers are smaller than those on the Seattle 'Hollywood', but they appear as early, and the fruit is as excellent.

14. 'Moseri' in bloom, supremely beautiful. The tree is confused with 'Blireiana', but is larger, less dense, and bears paler flowers.

15. 'Moseri' trees with one bright 'Blireiana' stealing the show.

16. 'Moseri' fall color. A sugar maple it is not.

17. 'Newport' in bloom—flowers are its weakest point—small, dull, and late in spring.

18. 'Newport' backlit in the summer. A specimen more than 60 years old.

19. 'Newport' in full sunshine in the summer. An attractive, rugged habit.

20. 'Newport' foliage against the blue sky. Its leaves are less pointed than those of most purpleleaf plums.

21. 'Nigra' street trees during late summer. As dark, if not darker, than any cultivar.

22. 'Pissardii' in bloom. The flowers can be paler. 'Pissardii' was the first purpleleaf plum to originate.

23. 'Pissardii' in a cemetery during late summer.

24. 'Pissardii' foliage. Foliage alone will not suffice to identify with certainty some cultivars; the flower color, too must be known. The tree pictured here bears white flowers.

25. 'Purple Pigmy' flowering despite its shaded locale in the arboretum at Seattle. It is a unique hybrid between *Prunus microcarpa* and a purpleleaf plum.

26. 'Purple Pony' characteristic scant blooms on a young specimen. Not content to bear few flowers, it is sterile.

27. 'Purple Pony' in its summer garb. This cultivar is distinguished less by leaf color than by its natural dwarfhood.

28. 'Spencer Hollywood' in bloom. A cultivar much confused with the original 'Hollywood', but differing in major points, including size.

29. 'Spencer Hollywood' plums and leaves in July. The weight of fruit often breaks branches on this cultivar. [R. Brightman photo]

30. 'Thundercloud' in bloom. Several nearly identical cultivars exist, such as 'Krauter's Vesuvius' and 'Woodii'. 'Thundercloud' is the most widely sold purpleleaf plum in the United States.

31. 'Thundercloud' foliage. Small fruit hides well, being the same color as the leaves.

32. 'Thundercloud' foliage. Luther Burbank originated this cultivar in 1919.

33. 'Thundercloud' street tree in summer.

34. 'Trailblazer' in bloom. An airy, open, broad cultivar, with the background of several species contributing to it.

35. 'Trailblazer' in bloom. Off-white, small flowers are not as pretty as those on many other cultivars.

36. 'Trailblazer' summer foliage. Hard pruning causes long, dark shoots, and reduces fruit yield.

37. 'Trailblazer' tree heavy with with ripe red fruit, which is among the last to ripen.

38. 'Vesuvius' blooming with 'Blireiana' street trees. Worthless as a flowering tree, this cultivar is prized for its branching habit and rich foliage.

39. 'Vesuvius' with murky 'Blireiana' street trees. The former has splendid blossoms but wretched summer foliage; the latter is the other way around.

40. 'Vesuvius' foliage, rich and lustrous. Luther Burbank created 'Vesuvius' and sold it in 1907.

Allred   Plates 2, 3

The 'Allred' cultivar, one of the best for fruit, is almost unheard outside the
United States. "Alfred" is an amusing misspelling of its name, rarely seen. The
most complete account of 'Allred' is by Brooks and Olmo (1972, 488):

> Originated in Amity, Arkansas, by Russ Wolfe, Wolfe Nursery, Inc.,
> Stephenville, Texas. Introduced in 1941. Parentage unknown; selection
> of myrobalan (*Prunus cerasifera* Ehrh.); discovered in 1939. Fruit: small,
> up to 1¼ inches in diameter; skin and flesh red, quality good, but very
> high in acidity; makes a delicious jelly. Tree: leaves and bark red;
> produces well; adapted over a wide area; a colorful ornamental, resem-
> bling Vesuvius.

Professor George Ray McEachern of the Texas Agricultural Extension
Service, wrote of Allred: "*Allred* plum is a large tree that has red leaves, bark,
and fruit. It makes a beautiful landscape specimen and also produces good
fruit" (McEachern 1990, 32).

The only other book to report substantially on 'Allred' is *Sunset New
Western Garden Book* (Sunset 1979, 432), which describes the cultivar as an
"upright, slightly spreading" tree "20' tall and 12–15' wide," with "red"
leaves, "white" flowers, and plums "red, 1¼ inches wide; good."

Trees sold under this name are still in the nursery trade in parts of the
United States (for example, in California, Texas, Indiana, Iowa) and are
available through Henry Field's of Shenandoah, Iowa, national mail-order
nursery. Field's spring 1989 catalog (p. 61) says this of 'Allred':

> Allred. Extremely ornamental. The name says it all! Gorgeous Japanese
> cherry-plum is red from trunk to tree-top. Fruit, flower buds, foliage
> and bark all sport the same fiery, scarlet color. Prized as much for its
> appearance as for its delectable harvest of freestone fruit. Sweet, juicy
> and perfect for preserves. Fruit ripens in early August. Use Santa Rosa
> as a pollinator.

Another mail-order source is Womack's Nursery Company of De Leon,
Texas. Its catalog describes 'Allred' thus: "ALL RED—Red leaves, red fruit. A
nice ornamental shade tree. Fine fruit."

David Ulmer (1989, 10) reports:

> Allred—Primarily a purple leaf landscape selection but has proved to
> be a prolific, tasty, disease free variety that is the only plum I have that
> has not missed a crop in the last five years. It was rated highly by many
> who saw it during the summer Southern Fruit Fellowship meeting in

June '88. A decided advantage is that the fruit hides under the foliage and escapes the birds. Ripens early in June.

How many clones are circulating under the name 'Allred'? If only one, I will be surprised. A specimen I purchased in Santa Rosa, California, in 1987, bore 18 plums in the summer of 1990 that ripened during mid- to late July. In 1991 it produced over 70 plums. The tree bears white flowers (with the barest tinge of pale pink) in March followed by reddish unfolding foliage. However, in May, the overall foliage color becomes bronzy green, and the abundant red plums in July are an impressive color contrast. In fall, the leaves again redden and are attractive as they drop off the branches.

The large leaves (3–4.87 inches long; 76–123 mm) are narrowed near the leafstalk and markedly wider above the middle nearing the tip of the leaf; and slightly bronzy, with scattered hairs on both the upper and lower surfaces; the fruit is dark in its powdery bloom, its skin, and its flesh, and has a reticulated stone of sharp edges. The tree shows what I am inclined to describe as "hybrid vigor." The branches are stout, distant, and lengthy, unlike *P. cerasifera* stock. The tree's bright fall color, too, is uncharacteristic. The flowerstalks or pedicels are hairy, unlike the pedicels of nearly all other plum varieties. I believe it is a hybrid with some *P. salicina* blood in it, but cannot prove as much with the means at my disposal.

This tree is productive and handsome when blossoming, when laden with fruit, and in autumn, but in the months after the fruit falls yet before the leaves turn red and drop, the tree is bronzy green and does not deserve the name 'Allred'. Yet Brooks and Olmo, Sunset, and some nursery catalogs claim that 'Allred' has red foliage. What is going on, then? Is my specimen an imposter? I learned that stock of 'Allred' was grown at the New York Agricultural Experiment Station at Geneva, so I wrote for information. John Watson, the station's recently retired plum breeder, had this to say about 'Allred' (letter of 9 December 1987):

> [Its] leaves tend to be rather light purple in color, especially as [the] season progresses, but [are] still distinctive from green leafed types. ['Allred' makes] excessively vigorous, large upright trees; crop usually light, small, early.

This description sounds like the 'Allred' I bought in California, so I think the proper clone 'Allred' is not all red, but only partly red. As for the books and nursery catalogs that call the foliage an unqualified red, there may be such a clone or the descriptions may be wrong. If anyone can put forth an 'Allred' worthy of its name, please step forward. In the meantime, 'Allred' can be considered a strong, productive tree, with large leaves whose summer color is neither red nor purple, but bronzy.

Asplenifolia—see Diversifolia

Atherton   Plates 4, 5

By chance I learned of the out-of-the-way clone 'Atherton' in September 1987, when I made an unplanned visit to the North Willamette Agricultural Experiment Station, Aurora (not far south of Portland), Oregon. While at this facility, I heard of a project that involved planting landscape trees for evaluation. The official in charge, Dr. Robert L. Ticknor, explained that 'Atherton' was a new purpleleaf plum that had been obtained from the Saratoga Horticultural Foundation, California, and planted in November 1977. The two specimens I saw at the Aurora Station were 10 years old. They were small, crooked, and showed signs of having suffered in the summer dryness. There was no evidence of fruit. Dr. Ticknor said he had never seen any, and believed the flowers were doubled. He said it did not strike him as a worthy ornamental and I readily agreed.

Examination suggested the affinity of 'Atherton' to 'Blireiana' and 'Moseri'; the influence of the Japanese apricot (*Prunus Mume* [Sieb.] S. & Z.) was clear. I took photographs and gathered leafy shoots. On 17 March 1988, Dr. Ticknor wrote that "during a wind storm last fall the trees were blown over as were some other trees in the tree trial. The crew cleaning up the storm damage removed them and took them to the burn pile."

One of the shoots I planted as a cutting took root and bloomed at the time of Ticknor's bad news. The cutting became the only example I could refer to. On 23 March I examined its first flower. It had 5 pink petals, 5 nondescript green sepals, about 30 stamens (with pink stalks or filaments tipped by yellow anthers), and no ovary. A second flower, on 1 April, was exactly the same except it had an ovary, minutely hairy at its top, below the narrow beak or style. This hairy ovary confirmed my hunch that *Prunus Mume* is involved, since *Prunus cerasifera* ovaries are hairless. My cutting was killed to the ground in the hard winter of 1988–89, but came back strongly in the ensuing summers, although it has not flowered again. Its leaves range in size from 1.25–2.25 inches (32–57 mm) long, by 0.75–1.87 inches (19–47 mm) wide, on petioles 0.25–0.62 inches (6–15.5 mm) long. The leaves are markedly smaller than those of most purpleleaf plums, and resemble those of 'Blireiana' and 'Moseri' in shape, but are smaller, hairier, and have scattered persistent hairs on both the upper and lower surfaces.

In subsequent communication with the Saratoga Horticultural Foundation, San Martin, California, no one was sure when or where the tree originated. (Atherton is about 25 miles south of San Francisco.) Lowell Cordas, in a letter of 27 June 1988, reported that Richard Hildreth, former director of the Saratoga Horticultural Foundation, remembered only the following about 'Atherton':

> It was a branch sport that flowered earlier and heavier than the other *Prunus* in Atherton, CA at that time (about the mid 1970's). It was grown at the Foundation in the Research Division. Plants were given out for testing but the tree was never formally introduced. He did not recall the location of the original tree except to say that it came from a residential site. I have not been able to locate anything in our records as to where it may have been planted.

Evidently 'Atherton' never impressed anyone enough to champion it as a worthwhile addition to the ornamental tree population, nor does it show promise in fruit breeding. Nonetheless, in case it may have interest, my specimen shall be preserved.

Atropurpurea—see Pissardii

Big Cis™

'Big Cis'™ is a sport of 'Cistena' that was found and put into commerce by the very large wholesale tree nursery J. Frank Schmidt & Son Company, Boring, Oregon. All the information regarding this cultivar is in the records of this company. In Schmidt's standard catalogs:

> *Prunus × cistena* 'Big Cis' P.P. No. 5003 (*Big Cis Plum*) [Zone 2]   This exciting new tree greatly broadens the potential use of Cistena Plum in the landscape. Discovered as a branch sport of Cistena, Big Cis exhibits a growth rate twice as rapid as its parent's, producing a tree intermediate in size between Cistena and Newport. In addition the leaves are larger and new growth continues to be produced longer, giving this tree a fresh, clean appearance later into the season. The trunk is heavier and stronger than Cistena, making this a much sturdier tree. It shares the same beautiful pink flowers with its parent.

According to its patent documents, 'Big Cis' was discovered "around 1975" by J. Frank Schmidt III, and the patent was applied for in June 1981 and awarded 22 March 1983. Keith Warren, the company horticulturist, wrote in a letter dated 21 September 1987 that 'Big Cis' is propagated from cuttings, and that thousands are sold annually, mostly in the United States east of the Rocky Mountains. Warren further reports: "'Big Cis', like 'Cistena', is not very well adapted to the northwest because of brown rot susceptibility."

This cultivar should succeed as a useful small tree in residential landscaping.

The name 'Big Cis' is technically a registered trademark, while 'Schmidtcis' is the tree's official cultivar name. Nurseries understandably coin deplorable garbage names for registration requirements, since trademark names are granted longer exclusive-use rights than are the official cultivar names.

Blaze—see Nigra

Blireiana
Plates 6, 7

'Blireiana' is among the best-known purpleleaf plums.

It originated as a chance seedling raised on the property of Edouard André, at La Croix, in France, about 1895. It first flowered in April, 1901, and was put into commerce four years later. La Croix is near Bléré, and it is from this town that it takes its name (Bean & Henrey 1944, 21).

It may be added that Bléré is near La Croix en Touraine, which is east of Tours, and Édouard André (1840–1911), who was prominent in French horticulture, was the first publisher of *Revue Horticole* magazine, and also named *Prunus spinosa* 'Purpurea' and numerous other plants. He gave 'Blireiana' the scientific name *Prunus × blireiana* (in the *Revue Horticole*, 1905). The spelling used here is correct as far as I can determine, but no fewer than seven alternate spellings have been noted in books and nursery catalogs.

The parentage of 'Blireiana' is thought to be 'Pissardii' and a Japanese apricot, *Prunus Mum*e 'Alphandii' (a cultivar with doubled, rosy-colored flowers; also known as 'Roseo-plena'). Another cultivar of the same or very similar parentage is 'Moseri' (which see). 'Atherton' and 'Boehmeri' also are similar; indeed 'Boehmeri' is probably a synonym of 'Moseri'.

The great value of 'Blireiana' is in its flowers: early, vivid pink, fragrant, double, and profuse. No other purpleleaf plum cultivar has flowers with so many petals and stamens. The leaves unfold deep reddish purple, turn bronze at maturity, and ultimately green with purplish spots on top. Thus the summer and early fall aspect is mottled with three gradations of color. The leaves are proportionately broader and duller than those of pure *Prunus cerasifera* stock.

The form of 'Blireiana' is chaotic, congested, twiggy, and lacks a

81

balanced, elegant presence. The trunk develops unsightly warts and burls. It is as if the tree's cream-of-the-crop genetics went into flowers, leaving only the dregs for the rest of the tree. It is naturally dwarf. I have never seen a trunk more than 10 inches (25.3 cm) thick, or more than 20 feet (6 m) tall, and both these figures are the rare exception. Since the trunk is so short and ugly, some propagators topgraft 'Blireiana' on cherry plum trunks.

Fruit is almost never set, which is unfortunate because it is not as wretched as are the trunk, form, and foliage. The plums are lightly fuzzy-skinned, deep purple inside and out, and when ripe in late July or early August are soft, juicy, and flavored like slightly bitter red wine or very strong grape juice. The flesh clings to the somewhat hairy stone, which is also less sharp than stones of pure *Prunus cerasifera* stock.

'Blireiana' has never been out of commerce and is sold wherever ornamental plum trees are available. It was given various awards by the Royal Horticultural Society of England: an Award of Merit on 7 April 1914; a First Class Certificate on 27 March 1923; an Award of Garden Merit on 13 March 1928. It has been called double-pink Japanese plum, double-rose cherry plum, Blireiana flowering-plum, double cherry-plum, and pink paradise. It is curiously appropriate how all the names emphasize the flowers—no mention is made of the muddy purplish leaves. Indeed the best employment for 'Blireiana' may be to bring its blossoming twigs indoors, for a twig of opened flowers is joyous in its rich fragrance, its bright pink color, and its ebullient fullness. As for the tree that produces these gorgeous flowers, I call it the "bleary" plum.

Boehmeri

According to Rehder's *Bibliography of Cultivated Trees and Shrubs* (1949, 321a) the name *Prunus Boehmeri* Koehne is a supposed but uncertain synonym of 'Moseri':

> *Prunus Boehmeri* Koehne in Mitteilungen der Deutschen Dendrologischen Gesellschaft. Bonn-Popelsdorf etc., 1917 (26): 69, fig. 16c [1918] "*P. cerasifera?* × *mume*"

The original German source treats 'Blireiana' on the same page (p. 69). 'Boehmeri' has long been an unused name buried in absolute obscurity. Until someone unearths evidence to the contrary, we must presume it is either a synonym of 'Moseri' or a very similar clone. Probably the name commemorated Louis Boehmer, a German who operated a nursery in Japan from 1882–1908.

Burbank® Purple Leaf Plum

Before 1988, catalogs of the Stark Brothers mail-order nursery of Missouri offered 'Thundercloud' under the title "Burbank® purple leaf plum." The heading was insufficient, however, because Luther Burbank developed at least five purpleleaf plums: 'Purpleleaf Kelsey', 'Vesuvius', 'Othello', 'Thundercloud', and 'Purple Flame'. Since 1988 Stark has sold 'Thundercloud' under its own name. However, over the decades other nurseries have sold 'Vesuvius' under the name "Burbank Purpleleaf Plum."

Cistena   Plates 8, 9

Shortly after 1895 when he joined the South Dakota State Agricultural Experiment Station at Brookings (where he stayed to work for decades), Dr. Niels E. Hansen began hybridizing the native Western sand-cherry (*Prunus Besseyi* Bailey), a bush with tiny fruit. In spite of the small size of the cherries, the Sioux and other Great Plains tribes valued the plant, which was common and produced fruit copiously. Hansen determined to make it even better by hybridization. Selecting superior sand cherry seedlings, he crossed them with other kinds of cherries, plums, and apricots. Pollinating sand cherry with the purpleleaf plum 'Pissardii' resulted in two seedlings (out of at least a dozen) deemed worthy of naming and releasing: 'Cistena' or Purple A, which was successful, and 'Stanapa' or Purple B, which was scarcely grown. A third seedling, named 'Purple C', evidently never got into general cultivation.

'Cistena', meaning "baby" in the Sioux language, arose before 1906 and was named when released in 1910. Hansen was very careful while recording his plant introductions and breeding results. Yet somehow the accomplished plant taxonomist Alfred Rehder (1863–1949) mistakenly attributed the parentage of 'Cistena' to *Prunus pumila* L. (Rehder 1927, 466; see also his later writings). Common around the Great Lakes, *P. pumila* is the eastern counterpart of *P. Besseyi*, to which it is closely related. (Full details about 'Cistena' as reported by Hansen are in various bulletins issued by the South Dakota State Agricultural Experiment Station: numbers 87, 88, 92, 130, 224, 263.)

'Cistena' is a dwarf and differs from the great number of other purpleleaf plum cultivars primarily in two respects: none are hardier in severely cold climates, and none are bushier. The nearest competition for cold hardiness is 'Newport', and for bushiness, 'Purple Pigmy'. In fact, 'Cistena' is so adapted to a continental climate that it does not perform well in milder areas. Both Carlton and Schmidt nurseries assign it USDA Zone 2, while Bailey and Sheridan nurseries give it Zone 3. Regardless of where it is grown, for the most attractive plants, it is advisable to do heavy pruning right after flowering.

'Cistena' which is sometimes spelled 'Cistina', has never been out of the nursery trade. Vernacularisms or trade names include dwarf red sand-cherry, purpleleaf sand-cherry, Hansen's purple plum, purple bush-plum, dwarf redleaf plum, and ruby tree (this latter name also applied to 'Thundercloud').

The name "Crimson Dwarf" which is almost exclusively seen in recent English literature, and which no doubt originated in Great Britain, is also used. Does it represent a distinct selection of 'Cistena' or is it merely a nursery name for 'Cistena'? Noël Prockter treated "Crimson Dwarf" as a synonym (1960, 81); so did Peter Seabrook (1982, 105), who wrote: "The lower growing *Prunus* 'Cistena', commonly called 'Crimson Dwarf', produces rich copper foliage after the blush-pink star-like flowers in April." Roy Lancaster, one of England's most knowledgeable tree and shrub experts, states, "As far as I am aware, it is an alternate name for 'Cistena' " (letter of 20 March 1988). I agree that the name "Crimson Dwarf" is a British nursery synonym of 'Cistena', even as "Purple Flash" is a British synonym of 'Pissardii', "Blaze" is of 'Nigra', and "Pink Paradise" is of 'Blireiana'.

The scientific name of 'Cistena' is *Prunus × cistena* (Hansen) Koehne. To be precise and go by the rules, any cultivars of the taxon, such as 'Big Cis' or 'Crimson Dwarf', should be written after the Latinized binomial, as was done in Bush (1964, 91):

> For colourful hedges suitable for the smaller garden a selection from the flowering plums is suggested. *Prunus cerasifera nigra (pissardii nigra),* the purple-leafed sloe, *P. spinosa purpurea,* and, best of all, *Prunus cistena* 'Crimson Dwarf,' with its crimson foliage and almost blood-red tips, will all make a wonderful show of colour. These hedges can be maintained at 3–6 ft. high by a light clipping in early spring and another in late summer.

Besides being dwarf and very hardy, 'Cistena' has two other remarkable features: it blooms late, and has small leaves. The only other purpleleaf plum which blooms as late in spring is 'Newport', which, like 'Cistena', has the blood of American species in its background. The only cultivars which rival 'Cistena' for smallness of leaves are 'Atherton', 'Newport', and 'Purple Pigmy'.

The leaves of 'Cistena' are without hairs except for a trace of fuzz by the base of the midrib on the underside. They are usually 1.87–3 inches (47–76 mm) long, and 1.06–1.87 inches (27–47 mm) wide; the leafstalk is 0.37–0.5 inches (9–13 mm) long. Two tiny dots (glands) mark where the leafstalk joins the leaf. The stipules (appendages at the base of the leafstalk) are unusually persistent, very long, and slender; stalked glands line the margins.

The flowers are fragrant and borne two per "joint," with a leaf-bud in between, or 3–4 from "fruit spur" buds without leaves. The flowerstalks or pedicels average an inch (25 mm) in length. The sepals are less than half as long as the petals, which are white (slightly pink in the bud stage) and number 5 or rarely 10. When there are 10 petals, there are also two styles and additional sepals. Stamens number 15, 20, or rarely 25, and are tipped by orange anthers.

Seattle specimens have not produced fruit, but others describe the fruit as dark purple, small and of poor quality. Hansen (*Bulletin* no. 237, 3) wrote "fruits of no value and sparingly produced."

The J. Frank Schmidt & Son Company of Boring, Oregon, one of North America's largest wholesale tree nurseries, sells 'Cistena' in three versions: (1) regular bush form; (2) treelike or standard; (3) the sport 'Big Cis' (which see). All are grown by cuttings. Canada's largest nursery (Sheridan, in Ontario) also supplies 'Cistena' in standard form.

Citation

Unlike the other purpleleaf plum cultivars, 'Citation' is used exclusively as a rootstock for stone fruits. It is a peach-plum hybrid introduced by the well-known plant breeder (Chris) Floyd Zaiger, of Modesto, California, and released to public trial on 27 September 1983. Its patent number is 5112. More than likely 'Citation' derived its purplish color from the 'Rutgers Redleaf' peach that Zaiger used in breeding. Its maternal parent, an open-pollinated plum called 'Red Beaut' (P.P. 2539) arose as an open-pollinated cross ('El Dorado' × 'Burmosa') and is a major plum cultivar in California, with thousands of acres planted to it.

The young unfolding leaves of 'Citation' are bright reddish, quickly turning coppery, then bronze, then mottled green—or the foliage remains reddish all summer, even into October. Probably the leaf color is affected markedly by the amount of sunshine. The leaves droop less than normal peach leaves, are wider and less narrow at the base, and have obvious hairs along the midrib beneath. They are sharply and finely toothed. An average leaf is 4.5 inches (114 mm) long and 1.5 inches (38 mm) wide, with a stalk or petiole studded with 2–5 prominent glands. The largest leaves can measure 5.75 inches (145 mm) long by 1.87 inches (47 mm) wide, with the leafstalk up to 0.5 inch (13 mm) long. The twigs are reddish and covered with short, light-colored hairs. The flowers are pink and short stalked. 'Citation' is propagated by cuttings.

Whealy (1989, 198) said of it:

> Peach-plum hybrid rootstock for dwarfing stone fruits. Reduces tree size 50–66% of standard on peaches and nectarines; 75% of standard on apricots and plums. Nematode resistant. Tolerant of wet soils. Induces early dormancy and cold hardiness. Induces early and heavy bearing, often in the second year. Does not sucker. Tree life comparable to standard. Strong and well anchored. Excellent compatibility. Developed by Floyd Zaiger, U.S. Plant Patent Pending.

Kourik (1986, 171) reported:

> Compatible with all peach, nectarine, plum, prune, and apricot varieties tested to date. Does not sucker. Reduces the canopy more than the height, by 30 to 40%, for better light penetration with less attention to pruning. (Watch for sunscald in canopy if overthinned.) Susceptible to crown gall. Well-anchored, does not need staking. Appears to be pest and disease resistant, except for some susceptibility to crown gall. Very tolerant of wet/heavy soils. Induces early defoliation, dormancy, and hardiness. Developed by Floyd Zaiger, Modesto, CA. Still being evaluated for commercial applications.

Kourik added (pers. com. 1991) that 'Citation' has proved to be not as useful as he, Whealy, and others had initially reported. 'Citation' dwarfs peaches and nectarines, but "plums and apricots show very slight or negligible dwarfing." The early defoliation also applies only to the peach and nectarine.

Therefore, 'Citation' is not so much a purpleleaf plum tree per se, as a somewhat purplish rootstock that is used for plums and other related fruit trees. It resembles a peach far more than it does a plum.

Clark Hill Redleaf

The 'Clark Hill Redleaf' cultivar is featured in an article by W. R. Okie and J. M. Thompson (1989). During 1973 or 1974 the tree was found wild not far from the Clark Hill Dam of the Savannah River, northwest of Augusta, Georgia. It has been tested for possible use as a rootstock. The leaves are nondescript, though relatively small, averaging 2.37 inches (6 cm); the flowers are "light pink" and "about 15 mm [0.62 inch] diameter, on a 5 mm [0.25 inch] pedicel." This is unusually small for purpleleaf plum flowers. The fruit "are round, 2–3 cm [0.76–1.2 inches] in diameter, red with yellow to yellow-red flesh. Quality is insipid and rated only fair."

From the information given, I conclude that 'Clark Hill Redleaf' is a hybrid cherry plum. The shortness of the flowerstalks or pedicels, a mere one-fifth (.2) of an inch (5 mm), is most remarkable, and may be a misprint. The clone is not likely to be used except as a rootstock.

Cocheco

Most of my information about 'Cocheco' comes from Professor Elwyn M. Meader, of Rochester, New Hampshire, a well-known plant breeder and the originator of 'Cocheco'. Meader received from Forest Colby (now deceased), of Enfield, New Hampshire, a plum called 'Purple Heart'. This mysterious Japanese plum tree is an extremely obscure clone (not a corruption or a synonym of a better-known cultivar such as 'Elephant Heart', 'Ox Heart', or 'Red Heart') with round plums. It became the seed parent of 'Cocheco'. The presumed pollen parent of 'Cocheco' was obtained by Meader from a cousin in Denisport, Massachusetts, who marveled at the fruits produced on what she called a red leaf cherry tree. Meader took scionwood, grafted it, and let it grow up into a fruiting tree, which he called 'Denisport'.

In the spring of 1962 a chance purplish seedling of 'Purple Heart' sprouted. Meader had done no intentional cross-pollinating. The new seedling grew vigorously, was handsome and productive. By 1968 the *Maine Sunday Telegram* extolled its virtues in an article titled "Lovely to Look At— and to Eat: New Plum Has Landscape Possibilities" (8 September: 10D). The newspaper reported how the tree was showy in flower, in leaf, and in fruit; hardy to -25°F (-31.7°C); and had plums ripening in mid-August that were orange-red skinned, yellow-fleshed, nearly freestone, and averaged 1.25 inches (32 mm) in diameter. Meader sent stock to Farmer Seed & Nursery Company for testing in Minnesota, but "as it was not fully hardy in all of the area that they served" they lost interest in it. Undeterred and still convinced of the clone's value, Meader named it 'Cocheco' in May 1971: "Cocheco is an Indian (native American) word meaning *red*. Also the Cocheco River flows through Rochester, thus giving it a name associated with the place of origin" (Meader, pers. com. 1987).

Finally, on 27 September 1976, Meader signed an exclusive propagation rights agreement with Bountiful Ridge Nurseries, of Princess Anne, Maryland. According to the agreement, no one else could market 'Cocheco' for 10 years. Bountiful Ridge Nurseries first offered 'Cocheco' on page 37 of their 1976–77 mail-order catalog:

> A magnificent new very hardy red leafed plum variety which produces full-sized delicious fruits when properly pollinated by another Japanese type plum. Fruits are similar to Methley and are fine for eating fresh or in canned products. If you don't want fruit for any reason, plant only

the Cocheco tree and it will be a very pretty ornamental tree for your yard. Cocheco was originated by Prof. E. M. Meader of Rochester, N.H. We are pleased to introduce this new find to the horticultural world.

The same description appeared in successive editions until Bountiful Ridge Nurseries went bankrupt–after having been in business for over 100 years and going through four generations. The nursery's last advertisement in *Fruit Varieties Journal* appeared in October 1985. Nonetheless, thousands of 'Cocheco' trees had been sold.

'Cocheco' is self sterile and produces white flowers. Meader says, "It can be stated as a fact that 'Cocheco' has no pollen of its own." The "Denisport" scionwood that he sent me produced flowers and looks like 'Pissardii' or a very similar clone. Surely what Meader called "Denisport" was the male parent of 'Cocheco', so the only question remaining is what is the obscure 'Purple Heart' parent and where did it come from?

'Cocheco' has been scarcely mentioned in books, although it is included in Rosalind Creasy's *The Gardener's Handbook of Edible Plants* (1986). 'Cocheco' is available mail-order from Michael McConkley's Edible Landscaping Nursery, P.O. Box 77, Afton, VA 22920; telephone (804) 361-9134.

Coleus

'Coleus' originated in 1891 and is known from one source. In his monumental book *Plums and Plum Culture*, Frank Waugh (1901, 206–207) wrote of 'Coleus':

> Coleus.—*P. triflora* × *P. cerasifera*, perhaps. Fruit globular; size small; cavity shallow, abrupt; suture hardly visible; color dark dull deep red; dots hardly visible; bloom bluish; skin thick and tough; flesh medium firm, red; stone small; considerably flattened, cling; flavor flat or a trifle musky; quality poor. Leaf large, broad oval, abruptly acute-pointed, rounded at base, double-crenulate, dark, fine red, conspicuously veined underneath with some pubescence along the principal veins.
>
> Specimens from the originator, J. S. Breece. The fruit of this plum is of no value, but the foliage is remarkably fine. It is larger, richer, glossier, more deeply and richly colored than the foliage of any tree of Pissard plum ever seen by the writer. Mr. Breece says that the tree is also a fine grower. It seems probable that this will prove worth propagation as an ornamental plant. Not yet introduced.

Later in the same book Waugh (1901, 361) treats 'Pissardii', 'Coleus', and 'Garnet':

Probably the plum which is most planted by the landscape gardeners of this country is Pissard. It has beautiful pink flowers, but its chief value is in its rich red foliage. A well-grown tree of Pissard is a specimen for any tree collector to be proud of. This variety might well be planted oftener, though a single specimen is usually all that any one place will require. Mr. J. S. Breece of North Carolina has grown some new varieties within the last few years which are possibly mixed with the blood of Pissard, and which certainly have better foliage than that well-known variety. The leaves are larger, better in texture, and a great deal richer in color. The most promising of these varieties are Coleus and Garnet, especially the former.

An 1898 *Vermont Agricultural Experiment Station Bulletin* (67:10) refers to 'Coleus', and Hedrick (1910, 421) simply paraphrases Waugh.

Lastly, it must be noted that the exact spelling of the originator's name is uncertain. A title issued by the Office of Foreign Seed and Plant Introduction, Bureau of Plant Industry, United States Department of Agriculture, mentions a "J. C. Breese of Fayetteville, North Carolina" (*Plant Immigrants*, no. 122, June 1916, p. 1020).

I believe that 'Coleus' is lost to cultivation or survived under a different name, and that it was a hybrid, because (1) except for 'Citation', all the other purpleleaf plums known have at least some *Prunus cerasifera* blood in them; and (2) the foliage of 'Kelsey' is markedly narrow, while that of 'Coleus' is broad.

Crimson Dwarf—see Cistena

Diversifolia

For decades 'Diversifolia' was offered almost exclusively by Hillier's nurseries of Winchester, England, under one of the following descriptions: "The cut-leaf *P. Pissardii*, leaves narrow and deeply lobed" or "Leaves bronze-purple, varying in shape from ovate to lanceolate, often irregularly lobed or toothed. Flowers white. A sport of 'Pissardii'."

'Diversifolia' was once sold as 'Asplenifolia' by Van Gauntlett & Sons nursery, of England, and maybe by others. The description in Richard Sudell's *The New Illustrated Gardening Encyclopædia* (1933, 742) is unreliably incomplete: "A form with narrow leaves." The name 'Diversifolia' appears in a meaningless, confused context in a book by Hériteau (1990, 219).

The clone has always been extremely rare in North America. Its date of origin is possibly 1925, but the plant could easily be older.

Dwarf Purple Pony—see **Purple Pony**

Elsie

'Elsie' is one of Paul Thomson's four purpleleaved plums from San Diego County, California. The others are 'Gerth', 'Knaus', and 'Oaks' (which see). Thomson was one of the founders of the California Rare Fruit Growers, a nonprofit organization dating from 1968. He has greatly encouraged the awareness and appreciation of many valuable but lesser-known fruits. 'Elsie' is sometimes misspelled 'Elsey'. Facciola describes the plum this way (1990, 178):

> Medium to large fruit; skin dark purplish-red; flesh deep dark red, quality excellent, one of the best red leaf plums; resembles Santa Rosa. Tree self-sterile, somewhat of a shy bearer, should be planted with Gerth as a pollinator. Originated in Duarte, California.

Thomson sent me a letter (20 April 1991) in which he gave much information about 'Elsie':

> The original tree was (is?) on the property of Mrs. Elsie Dement, 3708 Strang Avenue, Rosemead, California 91770. I propagated it around 1967, and again only saw the tree once. It was at that time towering over the house and I had to go up on the roof to get budwood. It was practically breaking down with the heavy crop at the time but has never produced much for me or for others that have tried it. It is self-sterile, yet I could find no other plums in the vicinity for pollination. Where it got its pollen remains a mystery to me. If I could find the pollinator it would be very well worth propagating for commercial purposes. Description of the tree, fruit and flowers are the same as for 'Gerth'. Fruit is a little larger, up to 2", and I like the flavor a little better.

Later when we spoke, Thomson clarified the tree's location by pointing out that Duarte and Rosemead were near to each other. He also said the fruit on the original tree was as large as 2.5 inches (63 mm). In a second letter (24 April 1991) Thompson added:

> [The] leaves are a lighter green than the 'Gerth' on top and are a bright red on the bottom giving the tree more of a red appearance. Fruits are oval and a shiny, bright red and mature to a more or less reddish-maroon color.

'Elsie' once was available from Pacific Tree Farms, Chula Vista, California, but has not been offered by that nursery since 1986. A contemporary nursery source is Exotica Rare Fruit Nursery, P.O. Box 160, Vista, California 92083.

Whether 'Elsie' originated as a unique seedling, or as a cloned tree planted long ago under another name, remains unknown, but we do know to whom the name 'Elsie' refers. Since 'Elsie' looks much like Gerth', which is a hybrid, I believe 'Elsie' is probably also a hybrid. The large size of the fruit is otherwise quite inexplicable.

Festeri

Harrison (1959), Krüssman (1962), and Lord (1970) contend that the Australian clone 'Festeri' is like 'Nigra' yet with larger leaves and flowers. A far more detailed account is given by Hazlewood (1968, 181), a nurseryman of Epping, New South Wales:

> P. vesuvius variety festeri. This variety originated as a chance seedling of P. vesuvius found at Kenmore Hospital, near Goulburn, New South Wales, and named after the Head Gardener who first discovered it. It has the large leaves of P. vesuvius, but with richer coloring, especially when the sun is shining on them. The flowers are single pink and open when the P. cerasifera varieties have finished blooming. Do not plant P. vesuvius or its variety Festeri in the same group or row as P. cerasifera varieties, since it would make a gap in the flowering and spoil the effect.

Hazlewood's description makes it clear that 'Festeri' is either a hybrid or a seedling of one, assuming the 'Vesuvius' in question is Luther Burbank's. I believe 'Festeri' is a hybrid because the 'Vesuvius' trees I have seen have never had fruit, which suggests they need to be cross-pollinated, quite probably with Japanese plums (P. salicina). Of course, there is no guarantee that the Australian trees called 'Vesuvius' are identical to the trees I know under that name, for the trees I know as 'Vesuvius' begin blooming very early—before or with the cerasifera clan—not after as Hazlewood writes.

Rowell (1980, 173) wrote of 'Festeri': "[It] is a seedling variant raised at Goulburn, NSW, with large, single, pale-pink flowers to 3 cm. across, and a slightly more open, less-erect habit of growth than most other clonal forms." Of 'Vesuvius' he said: "[It] has large but paler reddish-purple foliage than 'Festeri' and slightly later, white to blush-pink flowers but otherwise is not significantly different."

So, 'Festeri' may be a rare, recent introduction to Europe, to judge by its mention in Krüssman (1962), but it is not cited in any North American literature. In addition to the Australian plum called 'Festeri', there is also a 'Festeri' Sweet-Gum tree (Liquidambar Styraciflua).

Frankthrees—see Mt. St. Helens

Garnet

'Garnet' is much like 'Coleus' (which see). It originated in 1891 and the first account of the cultivar was given in the USDA *Report of the Pomologist*, 1895 (Heiges 1897, 45):

> *Garnet* (J. S. Breece, Fayetteville, N. C.).—came up in the spring of 1891 under a Kelsey tree; in 1892 it bore four plums. Its characteristics indicate that it is a chance cross between Pissardi, that grew near, and the Kelsey under which it grew. Roundish oval; large; smooth; dark garnet red; dots minute, russet; bloom bluish; cavity small, regular, of medium depth, flaring, marked with blue bloom; stem short, of medium caliper; suture very shallow, almost obscure, its length from cavity to apex; apex a yellow russet dot in a very slight depression; skin thin, moderately tenacious, bitter; stone medium size, oval, cling; flesh yellowish, translucent, stained with red on one side of fruit; mild, almost sweet; good. Season June 25 to 30 [in North Carolina].

Frank Waugh (1901, 211) gives the origin of 'Garnet' as follows: "Garnet × Kelsey × Pissard? Kelsey seed. This would be *P. triflora* × *P. cerasifera*." He then repeats Heiges' account of its origin, arguing in a footnote that the evidence supporting a chance cross between 'Pissardii' and 'Kelsey' "does not seem to have much value of itself."

> Several cases have come to light in which hybridity has been suspected on the evidence of reddish-colored foliage. But red-leaved seedlings occur rather frequently without any possible antecedent cross. They are especially common from Kelsey, though not rare from other Japanese varieties. Pissard itself is probably only another such sport, and J. W. Kerr has produced a red-leaved seedling from DeCaradeuc.

Hedrick (1950, 457) reports that 'DeCaradeuc' itself was a *Prunus cerasifera* cultivar that arose in Aiken, South Carolina, about 1850. So, for a cherry plum to give rise to a "red-leaved seedling" is no surprise.

To Heiges' description of the fruit, Waugh (1901, 211) adds the following:

> Leaves round oval, quite broad, abruptly tapering above, tapering or rounded below, roughly double-serrate, slightly glandular margins, glabrous above, slightly tomentous on the mid-nerve beneath, petiole short and stout, with inconspicuous glands or glandless, large, feathery, deciduous stipules.

The history and parentage of this plum are exactly the same as of Coleus. The foliage is much the same and appears to be the most valuable feature of the variety. The fruit resembles Satsuma in color and flesh, but appears to be of small promise. Season early. Has not been introduced to the trade. Mr. Breece says, "The fruit is quite satisfactory, but too sparingly produced."

Waugh based his conclusions on specimens of the foliage which he saw, not having seen the tree and fruit: "I must, for the present, consider this variety subject to removal from the list of hybrids" (Waugh 1901, 211).

Hedrick (1910, 450), a third source of information about 'Garnet', simply paraphrased Heiges.

Was 'Garnet' a chance purplish seedling of 'Kelsey' that did not result from pollen of 'Pissardii'? I doubt it. For the record, a description of 'Kelsey' is in order. It is a *Prunus salicina* (= *P. triflora*) cultivar that was imported from Japan in 1870. Well known, it has been much used in plum breeding and is ancestor to several standard varieties. The plums are large, yellow-green, sometimes with a purplish blush underneath the white powdery bloom, heart-shaped with unequal parts; the stone is small; the flesh is yellow or has a yellow-red blush and is firm and meaty. The crop ripens late, in September for the most part, with some in August or early October, depending on the locale. Edward Wickson (1921, 283–284), describes 'Kelsey' and includes this statement: "Tree willowy, leaves narrow, twigs brownish gray." In October 1990 I examined a 'Kelsey' specimen obtained from the L. E. Cooke nursery of California. It had remarkably narrow, hairless leaves, and was rather strictly upright.

Luther Burbank also released a plum called 'Garnet' (Howard 1945, 23):

> Garnet.—About 1898. "Cross between Wickson and Satsuma." Named by H. E. Van Deman, Pomologist of the U.S. Department of Agriculture. "Ripens a month earlier than Satsuma."

Thus Burbank's 'Garnet' ripens in late June. Moreover, it has green leaves. Hedrick (1910, 296) reports that this 'Garnet' was renamed 'Sultan' for a short time, until someone pointed out that an English seedling dating from about 1871 already had that name—Burbank's tree next was named 'Occident'. In other words, Breece's 'Garnet' is a now-lost purpleleaf plum; Burbank's 'Garnet' was a greenleaf plum properly called 'Occident'.

Since Breece's 'Coleus' and 'Garnet' are seedlings of 'Kelsey', it is necessary to remember that Burbank, too, had a plum called 'Purpleleaf Kelsey' (which see). Alas, the available information on Burbank's tree is minimal. All three purplish seedlings of 'Kelsey'—'Coleus', 'Garnet' and

'Purpleleaf Kelsey'—are no longer grown under their original names. Possibly they never were except to a limited extent almost 100 years ago.

Gaujardii

'Gaujardii' is mentioned in only one source—for a study by George W. Cochran (1962, 64) of cultivated ornamental members of the genus *Prunus*, the National Botanic Garden, Glasnevin, Ireland, reported having "*Prunus cerasifera ganjardii*" in its collection.

In *Trees and Shrubs Cultivated in Ireland* (1985), Mary Forrest lists the following purpleleaf plums: 'Blireiana', 'Cistena', 'Hessei', 'Nigra', 'Pissardii', 'Purpurea', 'Trailblazer', and 'Woodii'. On 3 April 1991, I wrote Ms. Forrest and requested any information she might have on 'Ganjardii' or 'Roebuck Castle' plum trees. In her 17 April reply, Ms. Forrest wrote: "*Prunus cerasifera blireiana 'Gaujardii'* was planted [at the National Botanic Gardens, Glasnevin] in 1927 from material supplied from the Gaujard nursery [of] Rome." Dr. E. Charles Nelson at the Botanic Gardens confirmed (pers. com. 1991) that 'Gaujardii' was still present at the Gardens.

About the Gaujard nursery I know nothing. The name 'Gaujardii' is evidently scarce in treedom, and any purpleleaf plum known under that name is certainly far off the well-traveled path. Possibly the name merely referred to 'Blireiana' in a slightly different guise, such as 'Moseri'. To discover what (if anything) makes 'Gaujardii' distinctive from other purpleleaf plum cultivars, awaits investigation at Glasnevin.

Gerth

Plate 10

'Gerth', a purpleleaf plum that produces good fruit, is cultivated in California to a limited extent. I first encountered the name in a 1987 catalog issued by the Exotica Rare Fruit Nursery, Vista, California. 'Gerth' was described as a "red leaf plum." In July 1990, a nurseryman in Puyallup, Washington, told me he had received 'Gerth' scionwood from California. I examined Robert Hartman's specimen at his fruit tree nursery on 6 August 1990. It was a unique entity. The ripe plums were round, dark purple inside and out, and measured about 1.5 inches (38 mm). The leaves resembled those of 'Spencer Hollywood' but had finer, sharper teeth, and hairier petioles, were less hairy on the midrib of the upper side of the leaf, and were often convex on long shoots. The twigs were more hairy, also. The flowers, seen on 18 March 1991, were pink in the bud stage, opening palest possible pink. They look superficially like those of many *Prunus cerasifera* flowers, but a minute examination showed they differ in having pedicels covered with short hairs, and they bear unusually numerous (30–36) stamens. Some have 8 or 9 petals.

Mr. Hartman has a letter dated 2 February 1987, that he received from Mark Albert, of Ukiah, California. Of 'Gerth' the letter says:

> It is a selection of Paul Thomson, founder of the California Rare Fruit Growers association. It has very beautiful purple foliage like the Hollywood, and the fruits are darn good, 1¼", dark purple inside and out, firm texture, not juicy, sweet & sour near [the] pit, flavor a little like Santa Rosa but lacking that exquisite perfume. Flavor of naturally sundried fruit like the classic cerasifera purple leaf myro but better, sweeter, larger [sic]. Ripe here early July. On the ground by 7-15 last year. Very vigorous grower like myro seedling or 29C. (So good I'm going to try rooting cuttings for rootstock.)

Paul Thomson, of Bonsall (40 miles north of San Diego), California, originated this plum as well as 'Elsie', 'Knaus', and 'Oaks'. An article in the 1980 *Yearbook* of the California Rare Fruit Growers association (Neitzel 1980, 27) mentions 'Gerth':

> Paul Thomson has selected many promising seedlings from North (San Diego) County. He has grafted scion wood from them on trees on his Bonsall property. He has three very interesting red-leafed and -fleshed plums that provide big crops of quite large and enjoyable fruit. 'Elsie,' 'Oaks,' and 'Gerth' are three of these. 'Oaks' needs the latter to pollinate it. These should be good fruiting-flowering cultivars and preferable to the non-productive 'Bleirianna,' 'Krauter Vesuvius,' etc.

Mr. Hartman reports that 'Gerth' is the most vigorous of the 12 kinds of plums he grows. It does not bear heavily, although the plums are good and the tree handsome, and, along with 'Spencer Hollywood', blooms first of all his plums except cherry plum.

Facciola (1990, 178) wrote of 'Gerth':

> Medium to large fruit, 1½" inches in diameter; skin dark deep purple; quality very good; resembles Santa Rosa but somewhat smaller; ripens 7 to 14 days before Santa Rosa. Tree self-fertile, has a relatively low chilling requirement. Originated in Vista, California by Otto Gerth.

Exotica Rare Fruit Nursery lists three "red leaf" plums in its spring 1991 inventory: 'Elsie', 'Gerth', and 'Shalom'. Paul Thomson (pers. com. 1991) wrote of 'Gerth':

> The original tree was located on the property of Otto Gerth, a lawyer long since deceased, on Mar Vista Road, Vista, California 92083.This

was a large, old tree in 1962, or thereabouts, when I went to get graftwood from it. I had heard of it from a Surveyor with whom I worked who said it had excellent flavored plums on it. I only saw the tree this once and it was dormant at the time so I will describe it from the grafted tree on my property. Tree is fast-growing, large, spreading, a heavy bearer and is self-fertile. Leaves are not a dark purple but more of a red or maroon-red, green on the underside ["upperside" meant?]. The tree is spectacular when in flower with its rose-pink blossoms and is worthwhile as an ornamental. Fruit is a very dark maroon color both outside and in, 1½ to 1¾" in diameter, oval, but almost round, with a cling-stone (not a free-stone). It looks very much like a small 'Santa Rosa' and could be sold for that with very few people knowing the difference. Flesh is firm, juicy and of an excellent flavor when fully ripe.

In a second letter (pers. com. 1991) Thomson added, "Leaves are dark-green on the top and a rose-pink on the bottom and give the tree a dark appearance. Fruits are oval and a shiny, maroon-red which darkens to a maroon when ripe."

In conclusion, it appears we have a firm account of 'Gerth'.

Hazeldene Variety

'Hazeldene Variety' is mentioned in only one source: "A dark-leaved form of Pissard's plum is var. *nigra*; the best of all, perhaps, is one known as the 'Hazeldene Variety' " (Bean 1950–1951, 2: 542).

It probably was an improved 'Pissardii' or 'Nigra' seedling grown only in England, whose estimated date of origin is 1940 or earlier. The Ordnance Survey Gazetteer of Great Britain (1989, 343) lists five Hazeldene localities in Great Britain, ranging approximately from Plymouth in the southwest and Hastings in the southeast, to near Blyth (north of Newcastle) in the north. It is impossible to tell which, if any of these, Hazeldenes originated the tree clone. Maybe a person named Hazeldene was responsible.

Hessei

Even among purpleleaf plums 'Hessei' is a freak. Krüssman (1986, 21) best describes it: "Shrub, small, slow growing; leaves narrow, irregularly incised and partly deformed, usually dark brown, teeth usually yellow or greenish, occasionally also yellow on a portion of the leaf blade. Developed around 1906 by Hesse of Weener, W. Germany."

Hillier's Manual of Trees and Shrubs says this of it (1971, 235): "A medium-sized shrubby form with leaves pale green on emerging, becoming bronze-purple and mottled creamy white. Flowers snow-white, crowding the slender purple shoots in late March."

The few additional books to mention 'Hessei' (e.g., Schneider 1904–1912, 2: 991; Bailey 1914–1917, 1930, 1935, 1941; Sudell 1933, 742; Bean 1988, 396–397) offer no new information.

This plum has been rare but available in Europe, and virtually unknown in North America. A comparatively early North American nursery reference to it is the 1931 catalog of Leonard Coates Nurseries, of San Jose, California (24): "A dwarf slow growing plum with purple leaves margined white." Besides 'Hessei', the two other variegated purpleleaf plum cultivars are 'Mirage' (also bushy) and 'Purpusii' (a tree).

Hermann Albrecht Hesse (1852–1937) had an important nursery career and distributed numerous plants.

Hollywood

Plates 11, 12, 13

Three (or more!) clones are confusingly called 'Hollywood': (1) the original clone; (2) 'Spencer Hollywood'; (3) 'Trailblazer'. Table 6 compares the various 'Hollywood' trees; the Samuel J. Rich nursery of Oregon introduced both 'Spencer' and 'Trailblazer'. This account is about the original claimant to the name.

The first usage of the name 'Hollywood' dates from California during the 1930s, as detailed by Brooks and Olmo (1952, 127; 1972, 502):

> Hollywood.—Originated in Modesto, California, by L. L. Brooks. Introduced commercially in 1936. *Prunus pissardi* × *P. salicina* (direction of cross unknown); discovered about 1932; first commercially propagated by Ralph S. Moore, Visalia, California. Fruit: flesh red, like a giant cherry, quality good; ripens early, in Beauty season; hangs well on tree; used for jelly and canning; most nearly resembles Satsuma. Tree: most nearly resembles *Prunus pissardi*.

Modesto is about 80 miles east of San Francisco, and Visalia is closer to Los Angeles than to San Francisco, being in the San Joaquin Valley 40 miles southeast of Fresno. Any connection with Hollywood (which is just north of Los Angeles) needs to be brought to my attention. As for L. L. Brooks, there is no information on him. There was a Lenard L. Brooks who obtained patents for 12 azaleas between 1952 and 1963, but his whereabouts are not known.

TABLE 6. Attributes of various trees called 'Hollywood'.

Name	Size/Form	Foliage	Twigs	Flowers	Fruit
'Hollywood' (Seattle)	Very large, vigorous	Very large; greenish tops and bronzy underneath	Scarcely or not hairy	Early; large, 1.12" (28.5 mm) wide, white, fragrant	Roundish; red skin, red flesh; late June to mid-July
'Hollywood' (Berkeley)	Medium	Smaller than Seattle tree but darker-colored	Clearly hairy	Early; small	Roundish; red skin, red flesh; late June to mid-July
'Spencer'	Compact natural dwarf	Small; dark shiny green top, deep purple beneath	Hairy	1–1.12" (25–28.5 mm) wide; pink fading to white; fragrant; pedicels 0.5"–0.87" (13–22 mm) long; stamens short and crowded	Egg-shaped; red-skinned, pale red-fleshed; late July or August
'Trailblazer'	Medium; broad; not compact	Similar to Seattle 'Hollywood' but smaller, darker-colored; shaped more like leaves of 'Spencer'	Hairless or weakly hairy	Small, 0.62–1" (15.5–25 mm) wide; white; pedicels 0.25–0.75" (6–19 mm) long; stamens long and uncrowded	Egg-shaped; red-skinned; yellow to deep pink flesh; August to early September

Ralph S. Moore, however, the nurseryman who introduced 'Hollywood', is a world-famous breeder of miniature roses, having introduced over a hundred varieties. He founded Sequoia Nursery in 1931, which is still in business, but no longer has 'Hollywood' for sale, and he supplied the above-quoted information to Brooks and Olmo in April 1947. Dr. Olmo (pers. com. 1991) noted that 'Hollywood' was discovered as a chance seedling.

The clone has been little grown outside its home state, though Oregon, Washington, and British Columbia nurseries have stocked it. California nurseries which have carried 'Hollywood' include Armstrong, W. B. Clarke, Leonard Coates, L. E. Cooke, Orange County, Select, and Stribling. Ed Scanlon in Ohio and Baier Lustgarten in New York have also listed it. Searching on a national or international level, the question is whether the "Hollywood" cited in nursery catalogs is the original clone or one of the two later cultivars. Some European nursery catalogs (e.g., F. J. Grootendorst & Sons) equate 'Hollywood' and 'Trailblazer' as synonyms; more than likely the tree for sale is 'Trailblazer'. References to 'Hollywood' dating before the mid- to late 1940s certainly refer to the original tree, because 'Trailblazer' and 'Spencer Hollywood' were unheard of then.

The Brooks and Olmo account of 'Hollywood' is weak on diagnostic features. Sunset (1979, 432) gives a more complete account of this cultivar:

Hybrid between *P. c.* 'Atropurpurea' and Japanese plum 'Duarte'. Upright grower to 30–40 ft., 25 ft. wide. Leaves dark green above, red beneath. Flowers are light pink to white. February-March. Good quality red plums 2–2½ in. wide.

Earlier editions of the same book (1954, 1940) ignore the clone, though they list some others which are rarer in California ('Nigra', and 'Purpusii'—as "Purpurea"), and show thus an inadequate understanding of the purpleleaf plum world. *Sunset Garden Trees* (1975, 54) repeats the 'Hollywood' information just quoted except the plums are "tasty, 2-inch red plums." This size makes more sense than does the size in the 1979 account, because plums fully 2.5 inches (63 mm) wide are extraordinary. No other cherry plum hybrid fruit that I have seen is near so big, although Paul Thomson reported this size for 'Elsie' plums. Some greenleaf plums, such as Luther Burbank's 'Great Yellow', can be 3 inches (76 mm) wide. Quite a mouthful.

California nurseryman W. B. Clarke's 1940 catalog declares: "This is a combination ornamental and fruit tree. The leaves are green above and red beneath. Flowers single white. The fruit is sweet."

An Oregon State Agricultural Extension *Bulletin* (Zielinski 1961, 16) stated that 'Hollywood' blooms 23 February through 13 March, peaking about 5 March. This is very early in the season for a plum tree. A study of plum blossoming dates in Mississippi between 1959 and 1960 (Overcash 1963) cites the dates of full blooming for 37 cultivars: 'Hollywood' is second, 5 March (the greenleaf 'Mariposa' is first, 4 March). How remarkable that two independent studies found 'Hollywood' in full bloom on 5 March.

The Del Rancho Fortuna Nurseries, of McFarland, California, placed an advertisement in the December 1955 *Pacific Coast Nurseryman* magazine that reports (7):

Prunus Hollywood Plum. Past sales emphasis on the lovely white blossoms and purple leaf foliage of this variety has somewhat masked the fact that it has a really fine fruit. The crisp blood red fruit is truly delicious, ripening in early June.

At the time, the nursery also was selling 'Pissardii', 'Thundercloud', and 'Vesuvius'.

Apparently it was Donald Wyman who started the much-quoted assertion that the leaves of 'Hollywood' are green at first, then darken. In his article, which treats 13 cultivars of purpleleaf plums, Wyman (1964, 97) writes of 'Hollywood': "This is unique since the foliage first appears green as it opens, then turns a deep purple." That is all he says, thus implying that nothing more is needed by way of description. He repeats that description in the revised edition of his book *Trees for American Gardens* (1965, 380), although he did not include the tree in the original edition (1951), and he included the same little statement in his 1971 and 1990 books. His assertion is repeated unquestioningly in other writings, such as in Dirr, Krüssman, and Everett. In truth, it is such a fast color change as to be unworthy of noting, and certainly no ornamental consideration. Other hybrid purpleleaf plums do the very same thing. By contrast, the 'Schubert' cultivar of the choke cherry *Prunus virginiana* is commanding in its dramatic color switch.

Which of the several possible clones is the original 'Hollywood' tree? For the time being, a tree at the University of Washington Medicinal Herb Garden fits the (rather vague) criteria best. This tree is of unknown age, stands on its own roots, is almost 40 feet (12.2 m) tall and a bit wider, with a 4.5 foot (1.4 m) trunk girth. In late February the first of its palest pink flower buds open to pure white, fragrant flowers 1.12 inches (28.5 mm) across (which is relatively large), on a flowerstalk or pedicel 0.56–0.62 inches (14–5.5 mm) long. There are 5 rounded sepals and 5 unnotched petals (but some blossoms have 6, 7, or 8 sepals and petals). The stamens number 29–34 (or 45 when there are 8 petals and 2 ovaries). The leaves are unequaled in their large size, 3.5–5.6 inches (89–143 mm) long by 1.5–3 inches (38–76 mm) wide on petioles 0.5–0.7 inches (13–7.5 mm). Their color is greenish on top and weakly bronzy beneath after an early spring phase of more uniform redness. The leaves of 'Allred' are similar, though slightly smaller, more narrowed near the base, broader near the tip, hairier, blunter-toothed, and with stalks as long as 0.75 inches (19 mm). The plums of this 'Hollywood' tree are the first to ripen in Seattle, during the last week of June or in early to mid-July (usually the latter). They are red-skinned, roundish, 1.5 inches (38 mm) thick or so, with deep red flesh.

This Herb Garden tree does not fit 'Purpleleaf Kelsey' or any other described clone. It does have large leaves and large, fragrant flowers that are not mentioned in the quoted descriptions above, but then the quotes are anything but complete. Until a better candidate is identified to serve as an example of authentic 'Hollywood', this specimen cannot be ruled out. It has dropped many stones or pits, but no seedlings have come up, even though other trees around it regularly bring forth seedlings (*Cornus sanguinea*, blood-twig dogwood; *Juglans nigra*, black walnut; *Koelreuteria paniculata*, golden rain tree; *Prunus serotina*, black cherry; *Rhamnus Purshiana*, cascara; *Styrax japonicus*, Japanese snowbell; *Ulmus pumila*, Siberian elm). Even if it turns out not to be the original 'Hollywood', it is worth preserving.

An equally strong contender for the title of authentic type has two specimens at the University of California, Berkeley, on the west side of Oxford Street, north of Hearst Avenue. These two purpleleaf plum trees are grafted, unlike the Seattle tree. They also bloom very early, being quite fully flowered in mid-February, yet their flowers are small, and rarely or never have extra petals. Twenty-eight or twenty-nine stamens are present. The twigs are conspicuously hairy, unlike the Seattle tree. The leaves are the same shape, but smaller and darker. The fruit is very similar, and ripens mid- to late June.

Assuming that Sunset correctly identified 'Duarte' as a parent of 'Hollywood', the background of 'Hollywood' includes four species of *Prunus: P. angustifolia, P. cerasifera, P. salicina,* and *P. Simonii.* Most remarkable in the pedigree chart (see Table 2 in Chapter 8) is the impressively fast breeding of Luther Burbank who offered 'Duarte' in 1900 as a seedling of 'America' (which he had introduced in 1898) that had been pollinated by a 'Climax' (which he had offered in 1899). By quickly budding seedling hybrids, Burbank sped up the results enormously. The dates of introduction are not to be confused with the dates of origin.

'Duarte' plums are medium or (usually) large sized and dark red-purple skinned with a dull silvery aspect. They have deep red flesh and ripen early to midseason. Another red-skinned, red-fleshed comparatively early ripening "blood" plum is 'Satsuma'. To compare the leaves of 'Duarte' and 'Satsuma' would be useful. One of them, or a similar tree, is probably a parent of 'Hollywood'.

Knaus

'Knaus' is one of the four fruitful southern California purpleleaf plums named by Paul Thomson. The other three—'Elsie', 'Gerth', and 'Oaks'—are better known. Regarding 'Knaus', Thomson wrote me 20 April 1991:

> The original tree is located on the property of Mr. Heimo A. Knaus, 1219 Via Sendero, Escondido, California, 92025. This is a true "purpleleaved" plum with very dark leaves. I have never seen the tree but was given graftwood of it in or about 1980. It is one of 6 or 7 similar plums on his property and bears heavily for him since it gets plenty of pollen from the other trees. It seems to have an even lower chilling requirement than the 'Oaks' and I have had very few fruits off of it except one year when it had a light crop. It always blooms ahead of all the others and it is about through when the others start. I guess I should get wood of one of his other trees for pollination and graft it on the same tree if I ever want fruit as it is self-sterile. My grafted tree is tall, narrow, moderately fast in growth with flowers that are a deep rose in color. Fruits are a shiny-maroon in color, as contrasted to the dull-maroon of the others ['Elsie', 'Gerth', and 'Oaks'], oval, 1½" or slightly more in diameter and are freestone. It is definitely a different species than the

above three and that might be a factor in the poor pollination even when flowering does overlap. Flavor is very good.

Four days later Thomson examined his specimen of 'Knaus' and clarified his earlier statements:

> This is not a "true purple-leaved plum" as previously stated but when it first leafs out it is the darkest of the four. Later, right now-this date, the leaves are turning a very dark green on top and a rose on the bottom. The flowers are a very pale pink and appear white from a distance. The fruits are oval, dull-purple in color maturing to a darker purple. The tree is the darkest of the four in appearance and is a slow, to moderate grower. Right now it has died back some 4 or 5 feet due to our drought and subsequent curtailed water supply.

Although the tree is not available in nurseries, it justly deserves additional testing. It may be worthwhile as a fruit tree, if a pollinator can be located, or as an ornamental.

Krauter's Vesuvius

Like 'Hollywood', the name 'Vesuvius' has been applied to at least three clones. However, when a nursery lists 'Krauter's Vesuvius' it means just that. No other tree gets so-called. Here is the story of 'Krauter's Vesuvius'.

Practically anything purple might have been called 'Vesuvius', so when Carl Krauter of Krauter Nurseries, Bakersfield, California (three generations involved; in business since 1923; one of the largest nurseries in the San Joaquin Valley), found a superior purpleleaf plum, he called it *Krauter's* Vesuvius to distinguish it from the others. Exactly when Mr. Krauter found his version is unrecorded, as is the date he began selling it commercially. The earliest mention of the tree is in the May 1956 *Pacific Coast Nurseryman* magazine (p. 30), where an advertisement says:

> Del Rancho Fortuna [Nursery, of McFarland, California] presents for 1956–57 *Krauter Vesuvius*—A selected strain of Prunus vesuvius, purple-leaf plum. Has prolific display of pink blossoms. Deeper red foliage than regular Vesuvius. Holds color better throughout the summer. Superior in all respects.

Another ad appears in September 1956. Then in May 1957 an anonymous article titled "Here's the Newest in Flowering Trees for 1958" (pp. 20, 36,) says:

> Flowering plum *Krauter Vesuvius* (Del Rancho Fortuna)—Selected by Carl Krauter, Krauter Nurseries in Bakersfield, this variety is a threefold improvement over Vesuvius. It is more vigorous, foliage is darker

and more uniformly held through the season. The flowers, produced in abundance, are pinkish-white.

W. B. Clarke's nursery catalog for 1957–1958 listed the following: "Krauter's Vesuvius. Large-leaved, purple." Quickly the clone spread in cultivation, so that dozens of wholesale nurseries on the West Coast have grown it over the last several decades. It has become not only far more widely planted than the original 'Vesuvius' of Burbank, but is the single most commonly grown purpleleaf plum in the southwestern United States

Gross, widespread confusion has occurred in books and catalogs by writers failing to understand or articulate the great differences between the original 'Vesuvius' and Krauter's version. The two trees have nothing in common except their name.

'Krauter's Vesuvius' looks like 'Thundercloud'. There is no doubt of its genetic validity as a separate individual clone, but seeing one or the other, it is impossible to know which it is. The youngest leaves of 'Krauter's Vesuvius' are deeper red and less bronzy-purple than those of 'Thundercloud', but this identifying difference is observable only for a week or two in a nursery where both trees are together for comparison.

If 'Thundercloud' and 'Krauter's Vesuvius' look identical, why grow both? Because 'Krauter's Vesuvius' thrives better in the hot, dry Southwest. A second reason is that 'Krauter's Vesuvius' may be somewhat narrower and more upright, and/or differ in size, fruit yield, or some other comparatively subtle attribute. Such attributes are parroted in nursery catalogs, but with time and comparative study, the truth will be clear and we will know whether there are any significant differences besides climatic adaptability.

It is disheartening that writers tend to copy one another without verifiying accuracy, or even simply qualifying their cribbing with "said to be" or "reportedly." In all my research, not a single book-writer and very few nursery owners have articulated in an honest, first-hand fashion, the distinguishing characteristics of Krauter's clone compared to the other 'Vesuvius' or other purpleleaf plums. The 1983–1984 catalog of Handy Nursery Company of Portland, Oregon, gives the best account: "'Krauter's Vesuvius' is vase-shaped, more upright than 'Thundercloud.' Flowers single pink. Leaves deep purple, possibly darker than 'Thundercloud.' To 40'. Zone 4." This description is honest in describing the tree as "possibly" darker and in allowing a 40-foot (12.2 m) height instead of the unreasonably small 18-feet (5.5 m) more commonly cited. It also acknowledges that Krauter was the originator, by giving the possessive spelling. Disregarding those nurseries which merely call this clone 'Vesuvius' (for example, Boething Treeland, Oregon Bulb Farm, Portland Wholesale), other nursery catalogs often cite it as Kroter Vesuvius, Krauteri Vesuvius, *Prunus vesuvius* 'Krauteri' or even "Vesuvious."

Being perplexingly similar to 'Thundercloud' in appearance and to Burbank's 'Vesuvius' in name probably dooms 'Krauter's Vesuvius' to a future as confused as its past. If Krauter had been comparing his find to the original 'Vesuvius' it is easy to imagine why he called it such an improvement: its flowers are incalculably superior, the tree is larger and faster growing, and its leaves are more uniform in color throughout the growing season. But, we do not know what his idea of 'Vesuvius' was—it might have been something totally different from Burbank's—and unfortunately Krauter died late in 1985 so we cannot get his input.

The third clone to which the name 'Vesuvius' has been applied is typified by a tree at the Washington Park Arboretum in Seattle. The tree was received (in March 1945) under the name 'Vesuvius' before 'Krauter's Vesuvius' was known. It definitely is not Burbank's clone. What is it? It looks like 'Thundercloud' or 'Krauter's Vesuvius' and serves as an example of what may be widespread: calling virtually any purpleleaf plum *Prunus vesuvius!* The specimen should be labeled 'Thundercloud' with an indication of doubt on the label.

Minn. No. 1
Minn. No. 2
(and Minnesota Purple and Minnesota Red)

The Minnesota State Fruit-Breeding Farm of Zumbra Heights, five miles from Excelsior, is responsible for introducing three purpleleaf plum hybrids: 'Minn. No. 1', 'Minn. No. 2', and 'Newport' or 'Minn. No. 116'. The names 'Minnesota Red' and 'Minnesota Purple' refer variously to these hybrids, unless 'Cistena', too, sometimes was or is so designated. The *Minnesota Horticulturist* (also called *Trees, Fruits and Flowers of Minnesota*) explains the origin of these cultivars as follows (Haralson 1915, 19–20):

> "Minnesota State Fruit-Breeding Farm in 1914" by Charles Haralson, the Superintendent: Several seedlings, the results of crossing the Compass cherry with apricots and peaches are growing and look promising; also some fifty seedlings of Compass cherry and native plums crossed with Prunus pissardi. These seedlings have proved hardy so far and will make fine ornamental shrubs or trees, on account of their dark purple foliage. They resemble Prunus pissardi with its purple bark and leaves. They are good growers and sometimes make a growth of five or six feet the first year in the nursery row.

Speaking of the Compass cherry used as the mother parent, and peach, apricot and Prunus pissardi as male parent, we find in almost every instance the seedlings have the peach, apricot and Prunus pissardi leaves and resemble the male parent to a marked degree. These are new creations of trees as far as I know. What we can expect of these seedlings we cannot say at present, but in case of success in this new line of plant-breeding the range of possibilities will become almost inexhaustible.

Table 3 (in Chapter 8) depicts the parentage of these Minnesota hybrids. Two of the seedlings resulting from the 'Pissardii' cross were "distributed in 1917 and 1918 as Minn. No. 1 and Minn. No. 2," but "[n]either of them proved hardy and they are not to be confused with Newport" (Alderman 1926, 47).

The other references to Minn. No. 1 and Minn. No. 2 deal with a greenleaf hybrid of 'Burbank' × 'Wolf'. This cross came later, after the purpleleaf pair had been written off.

The first edition of Brooks and Olmo (1952, 130) gives an account of 'Newport' with nothing said of 'Minnesota Purple', but the 2nd edition (1972, 508) gives the following account in which only the name and last two sentences refer to 'Minnesota Purple'—the rest refers to 'Newport':

Minnesota Purple.—Originated in Excelsior, Minnesota, by University of Minnesota Agricultural Experiment Station. Introduced in 1920's. Omaha × *P. cerasifera Pissardi*; selected about 1920. Fruit: ¾ in. in diameter; round; skin purplish-black, thin bloom, tender; flesh purplish-black, tender, moderately juicy, sour, quality poor, clingstone; ripens early August. Tree: small, bushy, spreading; not hardy in Minnesota. Variety perished and no longer growing in the trials at the above station.

Where did the name "Minnesota Purple" come from? It may be shorthand for "Minnesota Purpleleaf Plum." What does it refer to specifically? Probably either 'Minn. No. 1' or 'Minn. No. 2'. The name appears (or appeared) in some Midwest U. S. nursery catalogs, and in Manning's 6th edition (1958) it appears (along with 'Newport' and 'Hollywood'), albeit under the peach section. Manning cites two nursery sources.

The Morton Arboretum of Lisle, Illinois, grew 'Minnesota Purple' (Floyd Swink, pers. com. 1987):

Our plants have long since died, but we can give you historical information.

In 1947 we obtained 5 cuttings from Hinsdale Nursery, Hinsdale, Illinois. Most died early, and the last one died in 1974.

In 1958 we obtained 30 plants for hedge purposes from the Sherman Nursery, Charles City, Iowa. This hedge was gone by 1975.

In 1958 we obtained 5 plants from Matt Tures Nursery in Des Plaines, Illinois. These had gone by 1968.

The 1979–1980 catalog of Matt Tures Sons Nursery of Huntley, Illinois, offered 'Minnesota Red'. John M. Tures (pers. com. 1987) wrote:

> Regarding the Prunus Minnesota Red. I don't know what you think Minnesota Red is. As far as we know, Minnesota Red is a cultivar of Prunus Cistina. We are unaware of anyone who could send you a specimen.
>
> The plant does best as a bush, as stems of trees scald badly.
>
> We do not grow it anymore, but started plants from root cuttings and bench grafts. We have found the plant not worth growing anymore, borers and cankers insurmountable problems.
>
> The first plants were obtained so long ago we can't remember where they came from.

Michael Dirr (1990, pp. 653–654) writes that 'Minnesota Red' is a cultivar of 'Cistena' with "deeper reddish purple leaf coloration that persists into fall."

That is all the available information on these Minnesota hybrids. Either 'Minn. No. 1' or 'Minn. No. 2' was propagated in Iowa and Illinois, when Minnesota proved too cold for the plant(s). Whichever clone was grown, it was called not by its dull numerical name, but by the more descriptive 'Minnesota Purple' or 'Minnesota Red' names, which identifies its state of origin and leaf color. The consensus is that the plants have insufficient merit to be still cultivated. I propose using 'Minnesota Purple' as the name of choice and citing the other names as synonyms of it.

As for the suggestion of 'Cistena' going under the name 'Minnesota Red', it is possible but not probable. Both Hansen at South Dakota and the Minnesota State Fruit-Breeding program publicized their new introductions well, and probably nurseries would not have called a Hansen selection "Minnesota" anything. Moreover, 'Cistena' is a strong and well known-clone under its own name. The 1983 catalog of the Valley Nursery, Poulsbo, Washington, which listed eight different purpleleaf plum cultivars, cited one of the eight as "Cistena bush or Minnesota Purple Leaf." Five years later the nursery was sold and the details of what had been for sale in 1983 were lost.

Mirage

'Mirage' is a brand-new clone, which Alan Mitchell brought to my attention in a conversation early in 1989. Mitchell, the world's foremost tree-measurer, lives in England. He recalled seeing this new cultivar in south England, and it appeared to be a variegated 'Pissardii', presumably other than 'Hessei' or 'Purpusii'. Mitchell hates purpleleaf plums, but thought this one not as bad as most. In a letter of 28 March 1991, Mitchell informed me that 'Mirage' was

> discovered and entered for patent rights, by Brinkham Brothers, Walton Farm Nurseries, Bosham, W. Sussex. It was granted rights in the UK (No. 3164) on 20 October 1986. On trial it was classed as "a weak grower with semi-upright to horizontal shoots." When growing freely it becomes semi-weeping with the longer shoots drooping. Leaves small and crumpled. New leaf, yellowish white. Develops on expanding, a central part of greenish tones, the margin remaining whitish yellow, then the whole is overlain by red-purple patches. It then looks variegated cream-pink-purple.

Apparently it is only recently in commerce. The most recent edition of *The Plant Finder* (Philip 1990) lists one source: Bridgemere Nurseries, Bridgemere, North Nantwich, Cheshire, CW5 7QB England. The Bridgemere 1988–1989 catalog doesn't list 'Mirage' so the 1989–1990 edition would be the first offering. Two other variegated purpleleaf plums to which 'Mirage' might well be compared are 'Hessei' and 'Purpusii'.

Moseri

Plates 14, 15, 16

Prunus × *blireiana* 'Moseri' is the technically correct way to write this tree's name and shows its close relation to 'Blireiana', its better-known associate.

Rehder (1927, 455) says 'Moseri' originated in 1894 and 'Blireiana' in 1895. According to Bean and Henrey (1944, 21), 'Blireiana' originated as a chance seedling (see 'Blireiana' in the present volume). 'Moseri' might have had a similar beginning. The Moser nursery family at Versailles has played a prominent role in horticulture. Besides the 'Moseri' plum, there are plenty of other plants whose names commemorate the family name—for example: *Clematis* 'Nelly Moser', *Hypericum* × *Moseranum, Mahonia aquifolium* 'Moseri', *Picea* × *Moseri, Pinus sylvestris* 'Moseri', and *Rhododendron* 'Moser's Maroon'. The purpleleaf plum name may refer to Jean Jacques Moser (1846–1934) or to some other member of the family.

During its long history, the 'Moseri' plum's names have usually been given as *Prunus Pissardi Moseri* fl. pl., *Prunus Moseri* fl. pl., *Prunus cerasifera atropurpurea Moseri* fl. pl., or the like, with *fl. pl.* meaning *flore pleno*, referring to the tree's flowers being doubled. Very often it also has been sold as *Prunus Veitchi(i)* or *Prunus Pissardi Veitchi*. Why? Because the clone received an Award of Merit when it was exhibited in 1912 by Sir Harry James Veitch to the Royal

Horticultural Society of England (Royal Horticultural Society 1912, 38: lx). Nonetheless, the name *Prunus Veitchii* should not be used for 'Moseri' because in 1912 Emil Koehne applied it to a cherry: *Prunus serrulata* var. *pubescens*. Koehne's name was invalid and has been buried, however. More importantly, another ornamental cherry (properly called 'Fugenzo') was once (as early as 1902) called *Prunus* 'James H. Veitch'. So the Veitch name is too confusing in the genus *Prunus*.

Other synonyms for 'Moseri' are "Light-" or "Pale-pink Blireiana," and *Prunus Boehmeri* of Koehne probably is 'Moseri' (see 'Boehmeri' in this volume). In the United States, at least, the correct *Prunus* × *blireiana* 'Moseri' or plain *Prunus* 'Moseri' is less often used. Henry Kohankie & Son Nursery of Ohio, Leonard Coates Nurseries of San Jose, California, and some other nurseries, have sold the clone under its proper name. As *Prunus Veitchi*, the tree was available from Wayside Gardens Company, of Mentor, Ohio, from at least 1947 through 1957. West Coast nurseries have sold it under various names, including often ordinary *Prunus blireiana*. Contemporary North American sources for the clone are few, if any.

Turning from its twisted nomenclature to its description, we can do no better than compare 'Moseri' to 'Blireiana'. 'Moseri' is a larger and more open tree, while 'Blireiana' is invariably a congested dwarf. 'Moseri' flowers are palest pink, while 'Blireiana' flowers are deep pink. 'Moseri' leaves are usually over 3 inches (76 mm) long, while those of 'Blireiana' are usually less than 3 inches (76 mm) long. Some twigs of 'Moseri' are microscopically hairy, while those of 'Blireiana' are essentially hairless except near the buds. Rehder (1927, 455) says of 'Moseri': "Leaves less purple; petiole and midrib above glabrous (pubescent at first in 'Blireiana'): flowers slightly smaller and paler." The pubescence on 'Moseri' is indeed less than the pubescence of 'Blireiana', but the word "glabrous" (that is, absolutely without hairiness or fuzz) is too unforgiving to be accurate. 'Moseri' flowers have fewer petals and stamens than those of 'Blireiana', and bloom a bit later in the season.

'Moseri' sets fruit more readily than 'Blireiana' does. Ripe during late July or early August, 'Moseri' plums are reddish with a sheen of fine fuzz covering their skin. They measure about 1.5 inches (38 mm) long, almost or as wide, without being round: they are "squished sideways" in effect. The flesh is red, soft, and better to eat than the flesh of *Prunus Mume*, the Japanese apricot, which served as one of the parents of 'Blireiana' and presumably of 'Moseri', too. The stones or pits of 'Moseri' are larger than those of 'Blireiana' and equal in size to those of *P. Mume*, though they are less hairy.

The largest 'Moseri' tree I knew was cut down before it could be measured, but with the help of a photograph its height can be estimated at 15 feet (4.5 m), its spread of branches at nearly 30 feet (9.1 m), and its trunk 4 feet (1.2 m) around. Other examples measured about 20 feet (6.1 m) tall, though not as wide or as stout-trunked. No 'Blireiana' is anywhere near so large. By size and form alone, mature specimens of these two clones can be distinguished even in winter.

Mt. St. Helens™

'Mt. St. Helens' is an improved version of 'Newport' which was discovered, named, patented (1 March 1988), and put into commerce by the J. Frank Schmidt & Son Company nursery, of Boring, Oregon. Everything we know about this cultivar comes from the company, which also originated 'Big Cis' at the same time. The Schmidt catalog says:

> *Prunus cerasifera* 'Mt. St. Helens' P.P. No. 4987 (*Mt. St. Helens Plum*) [Zone 3] This small, ornamental plum is very hardy and does well where extremes of climate are encountered—such as Chicago. It has attractive dark purple foliage when grown in full sun. It develops a dense head. They should be thinned judiciously so that a shapely basic branch skeleton is formed. Selected as a sport from 'Newport' this cultivar grows faster, develops a stronger, sturdier trunk with a better caliper. St. Helens leafs out earlier, has a richer darker purple color in the spring and holds it longer into late summer under most conditions. The leaves are not only larger but are wider in proportion to their length than those of 'Newport'.

Keith Warren, the staff horticulturist with the company, supplied more details in a letter of 21 September 1987:

> Both 'Big Cis' and 'Mount Saint Helens' were discovered around 1975 by J. Frank Schmidt III. Frank found 'Mt. St. Helens' growing in a budded field of 'Newports'. He noticed it because of its faster growth and brighter reddish color. It was found at our Milton-Freewater growing area.
>
> 'Mt. St. Helens' was introduced in 1981 and was named by myself after the recent eruption of the mountain, which dusted our nursery with ash at the time we were choosing the name.

The patent document details with measurements how the sport indeed outgrows ordinary 'Newport' and how its leaves are larger.

	Length of leaf	Width of leaf
'Mt. St. Helens'	3.62 inches (92 mm)	1.87 inches (47 mm)
'Newport'	2.75 inches (70 mm)	1.31 inches (33 mm)

Specimens are rarely offered by Seattle-area nurseries. If 'Mt. St. Helens' is truly better than 'Newport', it should be planted widely. Its correct name is *Prunus* 'Mt. St. Helens' because of its hybrid background; its incorrect citation as a cultivar of *Prunus cerasifera* should be stopped. The name 'Mt. St. Helens' is technically a registered trademark, while the crudely contrived 'Frankthrees' is the tree's official cultivar name.

Newport   Plates 17, 18, 19, 20

Few purpleleaf plums have had an origin that is better recorded, yet for decades 'Newport' has been mistakenly cited as a cultivar of *Prunus cerasifera*, *P. americana*, *P.* × *blireiana* or even the peach tree *P. Persica*! U.S. books and catalogs usually cite it by one of the following erroneous formulas: *Prunus Newportii*, *Prunus* × *blireiana* 'Newport', *Prunus americana* 'Newport', or *Prunus cerasifera* 'Newport'. It is long overdue to stop this nonsense. Table 4 (in Chapter 8) displays the hybrid background of 'Newport'. The botanically correct name is *Prunus* 'Newport'. Its story is as follows (Alderman 1926, 47):

Newport (Minn. No. 116)

(Prunus salicina × *Prunus americana)* × *Prunus cerasifera*

Newport is a hardy ornamental plum of the Pissardi type. The fruit is of little or no value, but the highly colored purplish red foliage makes it a striking and valuable tree for landscape work.

The variety originated from a cross made in 1913 of the hybrid variety Omaha by Pissardi. The hope that an ornamental variety bearing valuable fruit might be produced was not realized, but the colored foliage seemed to be worth retaining, so the variety was marked for propagation in 1920 and was named and introduced in the spring of 1923.

Newport is a medium sized, upright growing tree, reaching a height of about 12 to 15 feet [3.66–4.57 m]. It is hardy enough for all but the northern district of Minnesota. The foliage is a deep purplish red while young, but changes to a bronze or greenish red as it becomes older. Under favorable growing conditions it is of strikingly high color until the middle of August, after which time it becomes slightly dull, but is still a beautiful plant. The flowers are small, pinkish white, and blend well with the foliage. The fruit is small, roundish ovate, suture lacking or a line, stem long, slender; color rich magenta red with a light bloom; dots minute or lacking; skin thin; flesh light red, tender, juicy, sour, quality poor, of little value; stone medium size, oval, smooth, red, semi-cling. Late mid-season.

The name 'Newport' refers to a town in Minnesota—many new fruit varieties raised at the time were given Minnesota geographic names. The 'Omaha' parent of 'Newport' mentioned above had three (not merely two) species in its background (see Table 4 in Chapter 8) and is described in Vermont (1900–1901). The location of 'Newport' plum's birth was near Excelsior, Minnesota, at the University of Minnesota State Fruit-Breeding Farm of Zumbra Heights.

In the nursery trade, a common name for 'Newport' is "Purpleleaf American Plum." It has been available commercially, under one name or another, since its release, and long with 'Thundercloud', is one of the most widely available clones. It is most common in the Midwest and Southeast.

'Newport' is remarkable for its cold hardiness. 'Cistena' is more cold hardy, but no other cultivars are known to be hardier. Of course, presumably the 'Big Cis' sport of 'Cistena' is as hardy as its parent, and the 'Mt. St. Helens' sport of 'Newport' as hardy as its parent.

No purpleleaf plum tree has a more handsome crown of branches when left to its own natural pattern. It grows wider than tall, unless forced up by competition, pruning, or shade. The tallest Seattle tree is 23 feet (7 m). The largest specimen was 18.5 feet (5.6 m) tall, 34.5 feet (10.5 m) wide, with its trunk more than 5 feet (1.5 m) around—possibly planted about 1927. The largest 'Newport' trunk known to me measures 6.3 feet (1.92 m) around.

The foliage unfolds bronzy-red in April but by July is dark reddish purple. Most leaves are 2–3.5 inches (50.5–88.5 mm) long, and are often "puckery" (bullate) near the lower part of the midrib. The leaves are definitely folded lengthwise rather than rolled up in the bud stage, and the stipules fall away quickly. The leaves turn an attractive reddish color in autumn while those of the straight *Prunus cerasifera* cultivars ('Krauter's Vesuvius', 'Nigra', 'Thundercloud', and so on) remain deep purple. Not only do the autumn leaves color brightly, they drop much earlier than those of the *P. cerasifera* clan.

Excepting 'Cistena', 'Newport' is the last purpleleaf plum to flower, beginning in late March and lasting into the first week of May. But, except for Burbank's 'Vesuvius', it is the least ornamental when blooming. Its flowers are small, 0.62 inch (15.5 mm) or less, pale, and compete for attention with the emerging leaves. The petals are dull white to dirty pink, 5–8 (presumably 10, too). When doubled, the flowers have 2 (rarely 3) styles, 8–10 sepals, and up to nearly 50 stamens. Normally there are 18–27 stamens. The anthers are yellow. The sepals are erect and spreading or somewhat recurved in age, and more than half as long as the short-clawed petals. The flowerstalks or pedicels are about 0.75 inch (19 mm) long. The ovary is greenish, red-tipped, with the beak or style pale pink.

Fruit is rarely set on Seattle trees, and nearly all of its aborts before ripening; I have never seen it ripened here. Dirr (1983, 552) describes the fruit as "dull purple 1" thick." The 1929 mail-order catalog of the Storrs and Harrison Company of Painesville, Ohio, described the plums as "magenta red" (p. 13).

The twigs are essentially hairless and have prominent speckles or lenticels. The buds are blunt and short, more hairy than those of other cultivars.

The young trees are vigorous and have better floral displays. Older trees, pruned hard in winter, also have better flowers than average mature specimens, but their graceful branch pattern is ruined by such pruning, and replaced with congested vertical shoots of ugly appearance. In general, the tree lacks the vigor of many other clones. Whether this is due to its desiring a more continental climate than Seattle affords, or is always the case, I do not know. Aside from its dirty-looking flower display, it is a truly superb selection.

'Newport' has been confused with 'Minnesota Purple' and 'Minnesota Red', which see. *Prunus* 'Mt. St. Helens' (which see) is an improved sport of 'Newport'.

Nigra   Plate 21

The first printed work containing the cultivar name 'Nigra' was the 1916 *Standard Cyclopedia of Horticulture* by Liberty Hyde Bailey. Unless Bailey coined the name (a practice he tried to minimize in his encyclopedia), either a North American or European nursery catalog had used the epithet. Since his purpose was to discuss North American horticulture, Bailey would not have listed European clones if they were neither present in the New World nor soon to be introduced. Bailey's encyclopedia treated species, using garden varieties only as illustrative matter rather than cataloging them completely. The other purpleleaf plums Bailey cited are 'Blireiana', 'Hessei', 'Moseri', 'Pissardii', 'Purpurea', 'Purpusii', and 'Woodii'. The sole extent of Bailey's treatment of 'Nigra', however, is "Very dark purple leaves" (p. 2825). The brevity and vagueness of this mention makes it worthless, because many clones have "very dark purple leaves." It leaves us with an unsatisfactory, cloudy origin for the name.

Bailey's failure to mention 'Vesuvius' (released in 1907), 'Cistena', and 'Othello' (both released in 1910), makes me wonder if the name 'Nigra' was intended to account for one of those clones—most likely 'Othello'. If North American nurseries offered 'Nigra' at all during 1909–1915, the clone was at least as rare as 'Othello' and 'Vesuvius'. Only 'Pissardii' was commonly available then. In brief, we have no certain idea what 'Nigra' was to Bailey. Whether contemporary nursery stock dubbed 'Nigra' is the same as stock that Bailey (et al.?) originally intended is impossible to certify. We can, perhaps, show that the contemporary 'Nigra' is not a mere synonym of any other clone, possibly excepting 'Woodii' in part.

'Nigra', as described and sold currently, represents *P. cerasifera* with some of the darkest leaves, but it also differs in bearing pink flowers which open some two or three weeks later in spring than those of 'Pissardii'. If the West Coast North American stock of 'Nigra' is representative of the East Coast and overseas stock, then we can add that the cultivar is relatively densely compact compared to its otherwise similar kin 'Thundercloud', 'Krauter's Vesuvius', and 'Woodii'. It may also differ from these similar taxa in bearing fewer plums. Krüssman (1986) says it is "similar to 'Woodii' but with larger leaves." Both Krüssman and Bean assert its U.S. origin, though they do not substantiate this claim with details. Oddly enough, though 'Nigra' is a major clone (or name, anyway) in Canada, Europe, and Australia, it has been relatively little grown in the United States. This trend continues even today. In England, a fancy nursery name for 'Nigra' is "Blaze."

A tree called 'Nigra' was awarded a First Class Certificate in England on 21 March 1939, when exhibited by Lionel de Rothschild (Royal Horticultural Society 1939, 64: 231). Dr. B. K. Boom (1903–1980) suggested (Boom 1956–1958, 146–149) that the "Nigra" of European commerce was really 'Woodii' and that the authentic 'Nigra' of U.S. origin was rarely grown (for further discussion see 'Woodii' in the present volume).

To standardize the ambiguous name 'Nigra' so that it applies strictly to only one clone, we must order specimens from various nurseries and reach a consensus as to which are (is) best entitled to the name. Failing this ideal solution, all that can be done is to write a more complete set of distinguishing marks for 'Nigra' and hope they prove meaningful: leaves as dark if not darker than most; flowers pink, appearing later than those of 'Pissardii; fruit few; tree with a compact head. This description rules out all clones but 'Woodii', or perhaps the 'Hazeldene Variety', or 'Paul's Pink', and so forth.

If cultivar names were treated according to the rigorous rules applied to scientific names, 'Nigra' would be instantly disallowed as ambiguous, or a type specimen would be selected and set up as the comparative standard. If the latter course is chosen, I elect as "typical" the North American clone called 'Nigra', if that clone should differ from overseas stock grown under the name, because Bailey's 1916 reference is the oldest known citation of the name. If research uncovers an older citation in an overseas catalog, then the whole outlook would shift accordingly.

Oaks

Like 'Elsie', 'Knaus', and 'Gerth', 'Oaks' is a fruitful introduction by Paul Thomson, of Bonsall, California. It has received less publicity, however. Thomson supplied the following information (pers. com. 1991):

> The original tree was (is?) on the property of Mr. William Oaks, 2608 Roca Verde Drive, Spring Valley, California 92077. In 1977 when I propagated it, it was a multi-trunked tree, some 15 feet [4.57 m] tall with an umbrella shape. I was told it did not produce every year, perhaps every 5 or 6 years, but when it did bear the plums were of excellent flavor. I figured all it needed was a pollinator so I grafted it on a rootstock sucker of the 'Gerth' tree. The graft grew like a weed and was 15 feet [4.57 m] tall in one year. The next year was a cold winter and the two trees flowered at the same time. The 'Oaks' plum flowered heavily and I think every flower must have set fruit. Just about the time it started to ripen the whole graft broke off at around ground level and I lost it. Later I went back and got more wood and grafted it on another tree but it never had more than a few fruits on the other rootstock. The reason is that the 'Oaks' has a rather low chilling requirement and blooms ahead of the above two ['Elsie' and 'Gerth'] except in a cold winter when they all break dormancy at once and it gets pollinated. Foliage is like the above two but slightly darker, the leaves are smaller as is the fruit, up to 1¼" [32 mm] in diameter. The redeeming factor is that it is free-stone.

Later Thomson added (pers. com. 1991): "Leaves are a little smaller than the two above ['Elsie' and 'Gerth'] and are more of a greenish-brown on top and pink on the bottom. Fruits are round and a shiny, chestnut-brown in color maturing to a reddish-brown."

'Oaks' is not in the nursery trade, but is included in this book in case it ever should become available.

Oregon Trail

The purpleleaf plum tree called 'Oregon Trail' is properly known as 'Trailblazer'. Because an obscure green-leaved Japanese plum had been named 'Oregon Trail' first, the purpleleaf clone originally called 'Oregon Trail' was renamed 'Trailblazer' (Samuel J. Rich, pers. com. 1987).

Fortunately, few books mention 'Oregon Trail' at all, regardless of its leaf color; only two books refer to the purpleleaf version (McClintock and Leiser 1979, 95; Everett 1980, 8: 2827). The name has also appeared in inventories of the collections at certain botanic gardens, agricultural research stations, and arboreta.

Othello

'Othello' is a 'Pissardii' seedling with darker leaves whose fruit ripens earlier than normal. Luther Burbank of Santa Rosa, California, originated it and later sold the rights in 1905 to Vaughan's Seed Store. Burbank wrote of it:

> The European plums have also contributed largely to the production of new races of fruit trees that are highly ornamental. A whole race of plum trees beautiful enough for lawn decoration has sprung into being in my open air laboratory.
>
> The French plum with purple leaves, *Prunus pissardi*, formed the basis for the development of these ornamental fruit trees. The methods used in developing these hybrids are the same as with the others, and the results are similar, although the fruits have not proven so generally valuable as certain varieties raised solely for fruit.
>
> The main use of the purple-leaved plum is for decorative purposes, but the fruits of the two varieties introduced are good enough for home use and in some cases are sold in near-by markets. This refers more especially to the very early purple-leaved plum, the Othello (Burbank et al., 1914–1915: 222).

Burbank's description, written in 1913 but published a year later, refers to "the *two* varieties introduced" (emphasis mine)—likely 'Vesuvius' and 'Othello'. Presumably Burbank's 1893 'Purpleleaf Kelsey' was, as Walter Howard (1945, 27) suggested, "probably never sold or disseminated except at retail by Burbank."

Howard's reference (1945, 26) to 'Othello' is quoted here in its entirety: "Othello.-1914(?). Selected *Prunus Pissardii* seedling. Fruit large; very early, but soft. No information as to when it was introduced." The dates Howard cites in variety descriptions are "the dates they were first announced in print"—not necessarily the date of origin or introduction (Howard 1945, 9).

Evidently, Howard missed the 1910 Vaughan catalog (outlets in Chicago and New York), which announces 'Othello' on page 125, and illustrates the tree in full color on an insert between pages 16 and 17. It describes "Othello Plum" as "a purple-leaved Burbank plum" that is "a useful fruit with splendid foliage":

> Our own introduction. A rare combination of the useful and the beautiful. A wonderful new fruit and ornamental tree, one of Luther

Burbank's creations, of which we purchased the first and only rights in 1905.

The tree is an upright grower, and a prolific bearer; fruit deep crimson, about one inch [25 mm] in diameter, ripening before the very earliest of ordinary plums.

The foliage is of the most brilliant reddish purple, and holds its color throughout the season.

The colored illustration shows a leafy shoot, and a plum section revealing pale flesh. It is clearly a *P. cerasifera* selection rather than a hybrid. The 1915 Vaughan catalog description (129) of 'Othello' changed somewhat from the earlier versions:

Introduced by us many years ago, having purchased the first and only tree from the originator, Luther Burbank.

It is an ornamental shrub of rare beauty, the growth is vigorous and upright. The white flowers appear early in spring before the leaves and literally cover the tree. The foliage is deep crimson purple, lighter on the under side of leaves, holds well into the fall, forming a grand contrast with the lighter tints of other shrubs. It is very similar to Prunus Pissardi, but much hardier.

From 1912 until 1930, the Storrs and Harrison Company of Painesville, Ohio, retailed 'Othello' in its national mail-order catalog. Alfred Carl Hottes (1928, 275) wrote: "Another purpleleaf Plum is Othello, a variety of the Burbank Plum which has larger leaves of a deeper purple and early fruit of a deep crimson color." Where did Hottes get the idea of "larger" leaves?

Bay State Nurseries of North Abington, Massachusetts, listed the tree in their 1929 catalog: "Prunus cerasifera, Othello. (Improved Pissard.) A handsome, small tree with deeper color than the original Purple-leaved Plum, of which it is an improved variety." Manning's *The Plant Buyer's Index* (1931) cites two sources for 'Othello': Bay State Nurseries, and Swain Nelson & Sons Co., of Glenview, Illinois. Manning's 1939 edition mentions two additional sources: Princeton Nurseries in New Jersey, and Storrs & Harrison Co. in Painesville, Ohio. The first edition of *Standardized Plant Names* (1923) does not mention 'Othello', but the second edition (1942, 501) places it under *Prunus* × *blireiana* (along with 'Newport' and 'Moseri'). P. J. Van Melle, (1943, 223) believes 'Othello' is "a darker-leaved variant" of 'Pissardii', and John C. Wister (1947, 240) mentions it with six other purpleleaf plum cultivars.

That is the extent of published data on this clone. From this information it appears 'Othello' is at least an extra-dark, fecund 'Pissardii' whose fruits ripen earlier. No mention is made of tree size, so we can presume it is of average growth and form. On the basis of Burbank's use of the word "hybrid" in the quote above; Howard saying the fruit was "large" (unlike *P. cerasifera* plums which are small); Hottes' calling the leaves "larger"; and the early ripening of the plums which might be partly attributable to the influence of a Japanese plum, I (Jacobson 1990, 110) wrote of 'Othello': "I have a hunch it is a hybrid." But a hunch is no proof, and subsequently I learned of the Vaughan catalog, and became firmly convinced that 'Othello' is no hybrid.

In the last decade or two this clone has been little or not offered for sale, at least under its proper name. If someone locates a labeled tree of 'Othello' in a collection, please inform me. I probably have seen 'Othello' specimens, but did not know them; the black Moor of Venice blends in well with the swarthy seedlings of 'Pissardii'!

Oval Crimson

One source only mentions 'Oval Crimson': a caption accompanying a color plate in *Luther Burbank, His Methods and Discoveries and Their Practical Application* (Burbank et al. 1914–1915, 5: 263). The caption reads:

> Purple Leaved Plum with Fruit. This is the so-called oval crimson variety of purple-leaved plum. It is a fruit of very attractive appearance and of rather good quality; which is by no means usual with the fruit of the purple-leaved plum. As a rule these plums are prized for their ornamental foliage rather than for their fruit.

The color plate (no. 89) shows three plums whose flesh is amber colored. In my opinion, they are neither oval nor crimson, but rather round and bright cherry-red. With the fruit is a purplish leaf, markedly wide near its upper portion, narrowing to the leafstalk or petiole, after the fashion of Japanese plum leaves. The 12-volume book set has no other reference to the name 'Oval Crimson'.

Pallet

The name 'Pallet' was given in 1912 by Lombarts Nursery of Zundert, Holland, to a 'Pissardii' derivative—seedling or otherwise sported. Krüssman (1951, 253) claimed the clone was like 'Pissardii' except the leaves were greenish red above, purplish underneath, and more coarsely toothed; the flowers were larger and white rather than pinkish; and the tree bloomed a bit later. Trees fitting this description may be hybrids. Dr. Boom (1956–1958, 147) said the name 'Pallet' was confusing and had become, in effect, a synonym of 'Pissardii'; Alfred Rehder, the great organizer and describer of trees and shrubs, ignored the 'Pallet' name. I am inclined to believe it was a valid name, applied to a tree other than the original 'Pissardii' introduction. We cannot now, perhaps, identify with certainty either the original 'Pissardii' or 'Pallet' clones. The Paillet (proper spelling) nursery in Sceaux, France, south of Paris, originally distributed 'Pissardii'.

Paul's Pink

Presumably 'Paul's Pink' was a British pink-flowered selection of 'Pissardii' as obscure as 'Hazeldene Variety'. Only one reference mentions this cultivar's name, an article titled "The Making of Lanarth" by the Right Reverend J. W. Hunkin, Bishop of Truro: "Spring next year (1925) was early. *Prunus Pissardi* ('Paul's Pink') was in full flower on February 8, so was *R. zeylandicum,* 'the best Rhododendron to-day' "(Hunkin 1945, 105). There were (still are?) several nurserymen in England named Paul: George Paul operated a nursery at High Beach, Cheshunt, from 1861 to 1921; his brother William Paul (1814–1905), commemorated in the famous 'Paul's Scarlet' Hawthorn, ran a nursery at Waltham Cross, also in Hertfordshire. Various roses are named "Paul", including 'Paul's Single White', 'Paul's Himalayan Musk Rambler', and 'Paul's Lemon Pillar'. Further research should be done in England to document the various Pauls and their plant introductions.

Pink Paradise—see Blireiana

Pissardii
Plates 22, 23, 24

'Pissardii' was the first, the "mother" of all purpleleaf plums, and its story has often been told. Around 1878, Monsieur Pissard, the head gardener to the shah of Persia (Iran), found the tree which was to immortalize his name. The tree was located in or near Tabriz (formerly known as Taurus), just over 340 miles (or almost 550 kilometers) northwest of Teheran (or Tehran).

In 1880, Pissard sent propagation material of his recent discovery to M. Chatenay of France, and soon the Paillet nursery, in Sceaux, south of Paris, offered the tree. The French horticulturist Elie Abel Carrière (1816–1896) wrote up the new find in the *Revue Horticole* (1881, 190; 1884, 396). It was from Carrière that the name *Prunus Pissardi(i)* or *Prunus Pissarti(i)* dates.

The novelty tree boomed in popularity, was sold widely, and soon the original clonal 'Pissardii' was "diluted" by an undocumented combination of seedling variants, sports, and later imports from Persia. Today it is an uncertain matter to know and describe the pure, original 'Pissardii' clone. Though dark-leaved, it was not as dark or as persistently so as were some of its seedlings. Its flowers were white, not pink. It was fruitful, with plums of red skin and flesh. The twigs were hairless. Various seedlings have exhibited darker flowers, later blooming, darker leaves, larger leaves, cut or variegated leaves, hairy twigs, darker or larger (to 1.44 inches or 36 mm) plums, sometimes with yellowish flesh.

In England, the tree won a First Class Certificate when exhibited by Veitch in 1884 (Royal Horticultural Society 13: 87), and an Award of Garden Merit on 13 March 1928 (Royal Horticultural Society 53: 328–329).

For decades after its introduction, 'Pissardii' was often thought of as a large shrub rather than a tree, and most older North American nursery catalogs included it in the shrub section, not the tree section. Time has proved that it is a tree. One specimen at 1020 St. Charles Street, Victoria, British Columbia, was 44 feet (13.4 m) tall, 47 feet (14.3 m) wide, with a trunk over 9 feet (2.8 m) in circumference when measured in 1989. A Seattle specimen measured in 1988 was 47.5 feet (14.5 m) tall, 58 feet (17.7 m) wide, with a trunk 7.3 feet (2.2 m) in circumference.

On the West Coast of North America 'Pissardii' has long been miscalled a Japanese purpleleaf plum. This misconception began decades ago and is still current in some circles, applying generally to purpleleaf plums.

According to the Cultivar Code, 'Atropurpurea' is the correct cultivar name, while 'Pissardii' is invalid. "Atropurpurea" means dark purple and can therefore literally describe many clones; 'Pissardii', by contrast, commemorates the clone sent by Pissard to France. Historically, the tree has usually been known as 'Pissardii', so for those logical and laudatory reasons I prefer to retain the technically incorrect 'Pissardii' epithet. Hermann Jaeger (Jäger) (1815–1890), a German horticulturist, published the name *Prunus cerasifera atropurpurea* in 1884, although Carrière had written in 1881 *Prunus Pissardi* instead of *Prunus cerasifera Pissardi*. We are not sure Jaeger was not describing a darker-leaved cultivar of *"Prunus Pissardii"* with his name 'Atropurpurea'.

The plants we designate today by either name constitute a *grex*—a group of various clones and seedlings. On the other hand, a *cultivar* is a plant that maintains its distinctive characteristics whether propagated vegetatively or via seed. Since we have been careless in observing and documenting distinctions in the 'Pissardii' population, the continued use of the term cultivar for what really should be a *forma* name has gone unquestioned. A slight improvement for the sake of precision is in order, however.

My suggested improvement is best illustrated by example: The European beech (*Fagus sylvatica*) has purpleleaf clones assigned cultivar names such as 'Riversii', 'Spaethiana', and 'Swat Magret'. All these cultivars, plus unnamed purplish seedlings, are included in the general name *Fagus sylvatica*

f. *purpurea* (Ait.) Schneid. Similarly, with the various bluish or silvery-needled Colorado spruces (*Picea pungens*), the name *P. pungens* f. *glauca* (Reg.) Beissn. covers such cultivars as 'Hoopsii', 'Koster', 'Moerheimii', and 'Thomsen'.

For better or worse, most gardeners and nursery operators ignore such niceties of naming and instead use the word *variety* to include any sort of named entity. This is fine—people have a right to be nonspecific. Nonetheless, we should also have the option of a group name for the nongreen *Prunus cerasifera* seedlings and cultivars. The most appropriate name may be *P. cerasifera* f. *purpurascens* (which means "purplish"), but other candidates to consider include *heteropurpurea, coloratus,* or *nonchloratus.* Until such a *forma* name is established, those who care about accuracy must designate seedling purpleleaf plums and unknown cultivars as "*Prunus cerasifera* seedling" or "*Prunus cerasifera* affin.'Pissardii'" or something along these lines.

Pissardii Rubra

The name 'Pissardii Rubra' appears in the 1939 catalog of nurseryman W. B. Clarke, of San Jose, California (10). The description only reads: "A form of ['Pissardii'] with somewhat ruddier foliage."

Purple C

Purple A was named 'Cistena' (which see), and Purple B was named 'Stanapa' (which see), but Purple C was never otherwise designated. Niels Hansen of the South Dakota Experiment Station at Brookings obtained all three as seedlings from *Prunus Besseyi* which had been intentionally pollinated by 'Pissardii'. 'Cistena' was bushy and dark, 'Stanapa' was more treelike but less dark, and Purple C was a "greenish-purple" selection. Presumably both 'Stanapa' and 'Purple C' are lost. They are mentioned here for the sake of completeness, but their names appear nowhere else except in the writings of Hansen. Brian R. Smith (pers. com. 1987) reports that nothing is known of them presently at the South Dakota Extension Service.

Purple Flame

The most complete account of 'Purple Flame' appears in Brooks and Olmo (1952, 131; an edited version appears in 1972, 514):

> Originated in Sebastopol, California, by Luther Burbank. Introduced commercially in 1931 by Stark Brothers Nurseries and Orchards Company, Louisiana, Missouri; trademarked by this company. Parentage

unknown; selected about 1922. Fruit: flesh red; quality good. Tree: foliage red; an ornamental variety.

The tree is not mentioned in the comprehensive catalog of Burbank's introductions compiled by Walter Howard (1945), possibly because Stark Brothers nurseries named and introduced the cultivar. But since the tree had been "selected about 1922" (Burbank died in 1926) possibly it was Burbank's choice, and also his name.

'Purple Flame' has been scarcely mentioned in print other than in the Stark Brothers catalogs. It is the only purpleleaf plum listeds under "Fruits and Edible Nuts" in the 1942 edition of *Standardized Plant Names* (261) though under other categories (pp. 501–502) the book mentions 11 other purpleleaf clones, some of which should also have been in the "edible" category.

Stark Brothers sold the clone "in the early 1970's", but no longer (Joyce Sherlock, pers. com. 1987). In the 1968 catalog, the tree, item no. 650, is listed as: "Burbank Purple Flame Plum: Height 15 to 20 ft. [4.57–6.10 m] Before the colorful Wine Red foliage appears, the tree is a mass of Pink blushed White blooms with deep Red at the throat. Small Red plums, which are good to eat, follow the blooms. Zones 5 to 9."

Between the two descriptions, we are left with a tenuous understanding, insufficient to pin the label 'Purple Flame' on any tree. Likely the clone has been offered exclusively by Stark Brothers, so probably only individuals scattered around the United States have obtained specimens. How this clone differs from 'Allred', 'Othello', and other purpleleaf plums whose fruit is considered a major asset is still unknown. It may be an extra-narrow tree, as is suggested by its name "flame."

Purple Flash

'Purple Flash' is possibly an English cultivar, but almost certainly is a nursery trade name of relatively recent origin. It is listed as a cultivar under *Prunus cerasifera* in the *Catalogue of Plants in the Cambridge Botanic Garden* (Yeo and King 1981, 94). Yeo (pers. com. 1988) reports the tree was received in 1961 as "*Prunus Pissardii* Purple Flash" from Pyecraft Hedges, Limited, Barnston, Dunmow: "We do not appear to have a Pyecraft catalogue in our collection. I think the nursery no longer exists. They went into business by offering under fancy names *mixtures* of *Prunus* hedging plants, each name indicating a particular selection." *The Plant Finder* (Philip), of the Hardy Plant Society, lists in the 1987, 1988, and 1989 editions only one supplier of 'Purple Flash'—Reginald Kaye Ltd. Waitham Nurseries, Silverdale, Camforth, Lancs LA5 OTY—but the 1990 edition lists no sources.

There is a mention in Peter Seabrook's *Shrubs for Your Garden* (1982, 105): "Equally popular for hedging is *Prunus cerasifera* 'Pissardii', commonly called "Purple Flash." It has dark red bark and rich dark red young foliage that turns almost black with age." So, 'Purple Flash' is a name applied by some English nurseries to a certain form of 'Pissardii'. Whether the clone is distinctive enough to warrant its own name cannot be concluded without additional study, though I think "Purple Flash" is just a nursery marketing gimmick and does not denote a distinctive clone. "Crimson Dwarf" in relation to 'Cistena' is in exactly the same situation, as is "Blaze" for 'Nigra', "Pink Paradise" for 'Blireiana', and "Sloepink" for 'Rosea'.

Purpleleaf Kelsey

'Purpleleaf Kelsey' was the first intentional purpleleaf plum hybrid, and the first selection other than 'Pissardii' to be commercially available in North America. The first (of five) purpleleaf plum cultivars by Luther Burbank, it was first offered in his 1893 catalog titled *New Creations in Fruits and Flowers*, (p. 16). The cross might have been made as early as 1888. Walter Howard wrote of it (1945, 27):

> Purple-leafed Hybrid K.P. 193.—1893. A seedling of Kelsey pollinated with *Prunus Pissardii*. The characters of the male parent predominate in the hybrid with the exception of the size and the time of ripening— later than *Pissardii*, earlier than Kelsey. Size intermediate between these two. Dark purple, with numerous white dots; thin blue bloom; flesh reddish-purple throughout; firm, subacid. "Its great value lies in its large purple leaves, which hold their color all summer, and its handsome wineglass form." Probably never sold or disseminated except at retail by Burbank.

A color photo (no. 70) in the 12-volume Burbank set (Burbank et al. 1914–1915, 5: 196) shows very red, not purplish, foliage and round fruit of the same color, but whether this picture is of 'Purpleleaf Kelsey' is unclear. The caption reads: "Seedling Red Leaved Plum. One of the most striking of plum seedlings, being the result of Kelsey, Cerasifera, and Triflora crosses. The magnificent reds of leaves and fruit make a strikingly handsome and effective combination that is as pleasing as it is unusual." Hedrick (1910, 521) wrote of 'Purpleleaf Kelsey':

> A seedling of Kelsey pollinated by Pissardi; from Luther Burbank, Santa Rosa, California. Resembles the male parent in wood, bark, leaves, flowers and fruit; very ornamental on account of its large purple leaves. Fruit larger than Pissardi, dark purple with many white dots;

bloom thin; flesh reddish-purple throughout, firm, subacid; good; ripens several weeks before Kelsey.

Rehder (1927, 456) includes this brief note following *Prunus cerasifera*: "Purple-leaved Kelsey" (*P. c. atropurpurea* × *P. salicina* 'Kelsey'). Burbank, catalog 1893." The second edition of *Standardized Plant Names* (1942) mistakenly placed 'Purple-leaf Kelsey' under *Prunus × gigantea* (that is, as *Prunus cerasifera* hybridized with the almond/peach cross). It takes a careful reading of Rehder's notes to determine exactly what parentage is attributed to each taxon mentioned.

I have found no other references to this clone and conclude that the tree has long been unknown by its original name; it may exist under other names.

It is worth remembering that two other cultivars were described as 'Kelsey' seedlings: 'Coleus' and 'Garnet'. Moreover, Frank Waugh's note (1901, 211—see 'Garnet' in this volume) is not to be ignored: "But red-leaved seedlings occur rather frequently without any possible antecedent cross. They are especially common from Kelsey." 'Kelsey', one of the very first Japanese plums imported into North America, arrived in 1870 and was named after John Kelsey, of Berkeley, California (see 'Garnet' in this volume for a description of 'Kelsey' plums). No other source claims that 'Kelsey' produces plentiful purple-leaved seedlings so I dismiss the likelihood, and yet time and again *Prunus cerasifera*—by itself or by cross-pollination—is cited as the responsible parent. Nonetheless Waugh commands respect; there probably are some cases where 'Kelsey' produced purpleleaved seedlings. After all, 'Kelsey' is self-fertile, unlike many other Japanese plums (e.g., 'Duarte' and 'Satsuma'), and can set fruit certainly, and viable seeds possibly, without needing to be fertilized with pollen from another tree.

Purple Pigmy

Plate 25

'Purple Pigmy' is my name for a hitherto undescribed clone. It is a unique seedling of what Carl Anton Meyer named *Prunus microcarpa* (= *Cerasus microcarpa* [C. A. Mey.] Boiss.), a shrub of southwest/south-central Asia in the area bounded by the Black and Caspian seas and the Persian Gulf. It makes black, red, or yellow cherries half an inch (13 mm) or less long. A good account of this species is in Browicz and Zielinski (1984, 4: 13).

On 28 December 1947, the Washington Park Arboretum in Seattle received (accession number 886–47) seeds of *Prunus microcarpa* from the Ashkabad Botanic Garden, Turkman S.S.R., USSR. In April 1951 two of the seedlings, one with purple leaves, were planted in the arboretum. Over the years both grew well and flowered beginning in early February, peaking in late February, with the last flowers in late March. The purpleleaf seedling not only had different color, but it also had larger leaves, larger fruit, greater vigor, and in short looked to be a hybrid.

On 8 July 1988, I gathered dozens of cherries, ranging from fully ripe to unripe. The smallest, quite unripe, were over 0.5 inch (13 mm) long; the ripe ones were as large as 0.69 inch (17.5 mm) long. All were red and almost as broad as long, except three which were fully as wide as long. The largest pits or stones measured 0.44 inch (11 mm) long. Of the 34 seeds I sowed on 30 July 1989, in the spring of 1990 one came up, a dark green seedling, ever so slightly mottled with purple. I have no doubt 'Purple Pigmy' is a hybrid: its characteristics do not fall within the described limits of *Prunus microcarpa*, even though that species is notably variable.

The bush is at its best in early spring, when the flowering shoots are excellent to behold and perfect in arrangements and for forcing. By midsummer the foliage is greenish bronze and of little appeal, though the red cherries are attractive as well as tasty. The flowers have palest pink or practically white petals, and measure 0.5–0.75 inches (13–19 mm) wide. The flowerstalks or pedicels are unique: they are hairy and very short—less than 0.5 inch (13 mm) long. The stamens are remarkably few, (14) 17–19 (20).

My efforts and those of a local nurseryman to strike cuttings of 'Purple Pigmy' failed. We believe, however, not only in propagating one-of-a-kind plants, but that this particular shrub may be useful, as it probably is cold-hardy, drought-hardy, and relatively disease-resistant. Bush-cherries generally do poorly in western Washington, evidently because of. the maritime climate, but 'Purple Pigmy' offers a chance of success plus the value of novelty.

Following are some of the differences between the arboretum's greenleaf *Prunus microcarpa* (which died in 1989) and the 'Purple Pigmy' on my herbarium sheets: The greenleaf shrub had hairless yellow-brown shoots and hairless leaves no more than an inch (25 mm) long; the 'Purple Pigmy' has short-haired purplish-brown shoots and both sides of the leaves, which are up to 2.5 inches (63.5 mm) long, are covered with evenly distributed short hairs. The flowers of the greenleaf specimen were pure white, while those of the hybrid have a pink blush. The greenleaf plant set no fruit. More than likely the pollen from some 'Pissardii' cousin caused the hybrid. The arboretum specimen of 'Purple Pigmy' is about 11 feet (3.3 m) tall, somewhat shaded by a dense, big *Prunus tomentosa* and 'Tai Haku' cherry trees. Released from shade, it would probably exhibit superior purplish coloration.

Purple Pony™   Plates 26, 27

'Purple Pony', frequently called 'Dwarf Purple Pony', is a trademark of a clone. The wholesale nursery catalog of the L. E. Cooke Company, of Visalia, California, describes it as a semi-dwarf tree with "[o]utstanding purple foliage that holds its color from spring to leaf drop. Observed since 1962 and believed to be sterile. Estimated height at full maturity is 10' to 12'. Has single Pale Pink bloom."

I bought a specimen in March 1988. After four years it is still not even 8 feet (2.44 m) tall, so there is no question as to its true dwarfhood. It bears regular pink *cerasifera* flowers with 30–32 pollen-bearing stamens and seemingly regular red pistils, but most of the ovaries shrivel and fall away, and it has set no fruit so far. It has had few flowers, due partly to the extremely cold winter weather, which killed some of its young shoots. In any case 'Purple Pony' is a scant producer of blossoms: one per bud, or rarely, a few pairs. The flowers are borne primarily near the tree top, and appear with rather than before the unfolding leaves. The overall display, even in full bloom, is of unappealing floral stinginess. On a more technical level, the sepals do not reflex strongly as they do on nearly all other cherry plum seedlings, and the flowerstalks or pedicels are comparatively short.

The tree's foliage is very dark and persistently so. In this respect it is like 'Nigra' and other cultivars; however, its leaves are comparatively narrower and less hairy. The form of branching and mode of growth are hideous: every branch ramificates wildly and the compact head of foliage is dense, inelegant, and floppy. Pruning is not a practical solution, wherefore I conclude it is a small, weak, very dark tree, of no use except where the goal is nothing more than a small, very dark tree. If flowers, form, fruit, or larger size are sought, 'Purple Pony' will not suffice.

The combination of features exhibited by 'Purple Pony' suggest it is a hybrid, but until still more evidence is found, I believe we should be conservative and consider it an aberrant, nonhybridized cherry plum seedling.

It is rarely seen in nurseries outside of California, and is mentioned in print practically nowhere except the Cooke catalogs and my writings. According to the Cooke nursery (pers. com. 1988)

> 'Purple Pony' is the result of a breeding experiment by Mr. Walter Krause in the late 1960's. It is an open pollinated seedling of Krauter Vesuvius. George Daniels became interested in the selection because of its small structure, full purple color in the summer, and the fact that it has never been known to bear fruit. George Daniels named it 'Purple Pony' because of the small structure and full purple color. Mr. Krause

was kind enough to present the variety to the L. E. Cooke Co. for propagation. The estimated height at full maturity is 10' to 12'. Has single Pale Pink bloom.

While the letter speaks of a breeding experiment "in the late 1960's," the Cooke catalog says 'Purple Pony' was "observed since 1962." The letter writer probably meant "late 1950s." By the way, the Cooke nursery stocks nine different purpleleaf plum cultivars, a feat not matched elsewhere. It carries 'Allred', 'Blireiana', 'Cistena', 'Hollywood', 'Krauter's Vesuvius', 'Newport', 'Pissardii', 'Purple Pony', and 'Thundercloud'.

Purpurea

The sloe or blackthorn plum (*Prunus spinosa* L.) cultivar 'Purpurea' originated in France. Its first mention is in the 1903–1904 nursery catalog of Barbier & Co., Orléans (p. 126):

> Less prickly than the type *P. spinosa*. Narrow lengthened leaves as coloured as those of *P. Pissardi*; more compact, and more branched, a little less vigorous, takes a roundish shape. Flowers small, pink, numerous. A nice variety, which will be at least as prized as *P. Pissardi*. Very hardy; offered for the first time.

Rehder (1927, 454) wrote: "*P. s. purpurea* André. Less spiny: leaves purplish, larger: flowers pink. Origin before 1903. ?Hybrid." Why did Rehder think it might have been a hybrid? Because ordinary *Prunus spinosa* is not only greenleaved, but has white flowers, smaller leaves, and is spinier. The Dutch tree expert B. K. Boom called it a hybrid in his 1949 *Flora der Cultuurgewassen van Nederland* (233), but not in his 1959 update (249).

Whether the purpleleaf tree grows larger or smaller than normal *Prunus spinosa* is disputed. Alan Mitchell reports (1985, 76), "Blackthorn (*Prunus spinosa*) is a spiny suckering shrub wild all over the British Isles, but it can be trained into a small tree and is sometimes seen in gardens in this form. The red-leafed form 'Purpurea' is more inclined to be a tree and can be eight metres tall." On the other hand, Hillier (1971, 243) contends: "A neat, compact bush with rich purple leaves and white flowers. One of the elite of purple-leaved shrubs." The New Zealand nurseryman Richmond Harrison also suggested (1959, 267) that 'Purpurea' was smaller than typical blackthorns or sloes: "In this smaller-growing form the young spring leaves are a beautiful red, becoming purple later, colouring beautifully in autumn. The masses of flowers which appear before the leaves, are pale pink." Lord (1970, 89), too, comments on the fall color, writing that the leaves turn orange. He adds that the plant is "tolerant of hot, dry conditions." Ignoring size, parentage and fall color, Bean wrote (1929, 2: 253), "Leaves a beautiful red when young, becoming purple, flowers pink."

Part of the confusion is due to more than one clone circulating under the name *Prunus spinosa* 'Purpurea'. Krüssman (1986, 3: 51) explains:

> Young leaves red-brown, later more green above with a reddish margin, purple and glabrous; flowers pink. Disseminated by Barbier, Orleans, France, 1903. More recently, a form was developed in Holland with much more intensely red leaves; both forms may occur in cultivation under the same name.

Hedrick (1910, 43) took a close look at 'Purpurea':

> *Prunus spinosa purpurea* is another horticultural group, more vigorous than the species, less thorny and with larger foliage. Its branches are erect, purplish in color, striated. The leaves and petioles are at first very pubescent but at maturity glabrous; the upper surface of the leaf is green marked with red, the under a deep reddish-violet. The flowers are a pale rose.

From the available information, it reasonable to assume the original manifestation of this clone is a hybrid of 'Pissardii' or a similar cherry plum with *Prunus spinosa*. I am confident that if I could examine specimens, this view would be borne out by the evidence. A similar clone is 'Rosea' (which see). The scientific name covering such hybrids is *Prunus × Simmleri* Palézieux. These crosses appear wild in Soviet Georgia (Stace 1975, 229).

Purpusii

'Purpusii' is best described by Krüssman (1986, 3: 26): "New growth green, then becoming red-brown, later with yellow and pink zoning along the midrib. Introduced into the trade by Hesse of Weener, W. Germany in 1908 [as *Prunus Pissardi Purpusi*]." In the 1916 *Standard Cyclopedia of Horticulture*, L. H. Bailey wrote (p. 2825) of it: "Leaves similar in shape to those of usual var. *Pissardi*, dark red and variegated with yellow and bright rose."

Bean (1988, 396) reports of 'Purpusii': "Bronze with yellow and pink variegation along the midrib, and white flowers."

'Purpusii' was named after Joseph Anton Purpus (1860–1933), who worked at the botanic gardens of Darmstadt, Hesse, Germany. The name was given by Hermann Albrecht Hesse (1852–1937) in 1906–7 on page 42 of the 15th *Mitteilungen der Deutschen Dendrologischen Gesellschaft*. Purpus was also commemorated in a name given by Alfred Rehder to a honeysuckle: *Lonicera* × *Purpusii*.

The 'Purpusii' plum has been offered by the Hesse nursery for decades. Rarely has it been imported into North America. The name is sometimes misspelled and more often mistaken for meaning "purple." In brief, 'Purpusii' is a variegated purpleleaf plum—like 'Mirage' and 'Hessei' (which see) in this respect, yet the latter two cultivars are both bushy.

Roebuck Castle

Roebuck Castle is part of the University College campus in Dublin, Ireland. For a study by George W. Cochran of cultivated ornamental members of the genus *Prunus*, the National Botanic Garden, Glasnevin, Ireland, reported having "*Prunus cerasifera atropurpurea* 'Roebuck Castle' " in its collection (Cochran 1962, 64). It is the only source to mention this clone. The other purpleleaf plums reported at the Garden were 'Blireiana', 'Hessei', 'Pissardii', 'Purpurea', and the baffling 'Ganjardii' [i.e., Gaujardii].

Mary Forrest's book called *Trees and Shrubs Cultivated in Ireland* (1985) lists the following purpleleaf plums: 'Blireiana', 'Cistena', 'Hessei', 'Nigra', 'Pissardii', 'Purpurea', 'Trailblazer', and 'Woodii'. When I wrote her about 'Roebuck Castle' plum trees, she replied (Forrest, pers. com. 1991):

> *Prunus cerasifera atropurpurea* 'Roebuck Castle variety' was planted at Glasnevin October 19th, 1925. It was supplied by Daisy Hill nursery, Newry, Co. Down. This variety was not listed in the Daisy Hill catalogues of that period. Dr. [E. C.] Nelson has spoken to Dr. Neil Murray whose family owned Roebuck Castle and Dr. Murray has no information about this plant.

No doubt the 'Roebuck' name was given to designate the locale of a certain purpleleaf plum that in some way merited unusual attention. Although the name might have continued to sleep, alone with its mute memories, it is resurrected here in hope that someone can reveal more about it. Despite the Daisy Hill Nursery being long out of business, its 'Roebuck Castle' cultivar still lives at the Glasnevin Botanic Gardens (E. C. Nelson, pers. com. 1991).

Rosea

The name 'Rosea' has been applied to various cultivars of *Prunus*, including two purpleleaf plums—one of them the true clone, the other, a wrong use.

The true clone is almost unmentioned in books, appearing chiefly in nursery catalogs. The best account is in Hillier's Manual (Hillier 1971, 235):

Leaves bronze-purple at first, becoming bronze-green, then green in late summer. Flowers of a clear salmon pink, paling with age, crowding the slender purple stems. Distributed by Messrs. B. Ruys, Ltd., of Holland, who believe the plant to be of hybrid origin (*P. cerasifera* 'Nigra' × *P. spinosa*). Sometimes found in gardens under the name *spinosa* 'Rosea'. It is looser and more open in habit that *P. spinosa* with slightly larger flowers less densely crowded on the branchlets, which are scarcely spiny.

The nursery of question in Holland is the Royal Moerheim Nurseries at Dedemsvaart. Its 1954–55 wholesale catalog (p.16) lists "*Prunus spinosa Purpurea*, brown foliage, pink flowers" and "*Prunus spinosa Rosea*, (Ruys), [n]ovelty raised in our nurseries, very charming, pink flowered sloe-variety."

In the 1961–62 catalog of the Slieve Donard Nursery Company, of Ireland, the tree is listed as "new" with rich pink flowers on 21 March. Brian Davis (1988, 61) writes that 'Rosea' is "rare in cultivation, but worthy of some research." *The Plant Finder* (Philip 1987–1990) lists only Hillier nurseries of England as a source. A British nursery name for the plant is "Sloepink."

The improper use of the 'Rosea' name started when the famous Wayside Gardens Company of Mentor, Ohio, offered *Prunus Pissardi rosea*, calling it thus from at least 1944–1972. The usual account given in the Wayside catalog was this:

> *Prunus Pissardi rosea* (Purple-Leaved Plum "Special Selection") The deep bronzy purple foliage of this small tree is its great attraction; however, the thousands of pink, single flowers in spring are not to be overlooked. Most "purple" leaved trees lose much of their color throughout the summer, but this is not the case with this special selection of ours recently imported from England. Its foliage is of the deepest shade of purplish red imaginable, almost black. It makes a fine contrast plant and helps give variety and color in the garden, easily grown and ideal for the small yard or as a special point of interest. Ultimate height about 10 feet. Occasional pruning will keep it in shape desired.

Sometimes the Wayside catalog included a color photograph of what looks like 'Nigra' or 'Woodii'. A few other references cite this 'Rosea', but in each case it is obvious the writer obtained the information from Wayside's catalog. When I wrote the company, I was told all old records were unavailable, as the company had been sold, and relocated from Ohio to South Carolina. Recent editions of the company's catalog have offered 'Thundercloud'. It would be worth knowing what clone the Wayside 'Rosea' really is.

R. W. Hodgins

The sole source for this name is Richmond E. Harrison's *Handbook of Trees and Shrubs for the Southern Hemisphere*, first published in 1959 (p. 271): "'Pissardii R. W. Hodgins' A Victorian-introduced form with larger and darker foliage, flowers pale pink." The 4th edition of Harrison's handbook also mentions 'R. W. Hodgins', but the 5th edition does not.

There are several Englishmen for whom the plant could have been named—Captain A. Hodgins, who discovered the rare Chinese conifer *Fokienia Hodginsii* in 1908, and Edward Hodgins, who founded a nursery around 1780 and for whom *Ilex × altaclerensis* 'Hodginsii' was named—but this purpleleaf plum clone did not come from England at all. It originated at Hodgins Nurseries, Essendon, Victoria, Australia, the nursery that gave rise to *Prostanthera ovalifolia* 'R. W. Hodgins', *Cupressus glabra* 'Hodginsii', and so forth.

The clone of purpleleaf plum known in Australia and New Zealand as 'R. W. Hodgins' is not likely to be significantly different from the usual, or it probably would not have remained so unknown. Certainly Harrison's description makes the tree sound like one of the various seedlings which superseded the original 'Pissardii' and assumed even its name. It was probably introduced about 1920.

Schmidtcis—see Big Cis

Shalom

'Shalom' appears with 'Gerth' and 'Elsie' in the 1991 plant list of the Exotica Rare Fruit Nursery, Vista, California. Both 'Gerth' and 'Elsie' are southern California purpleleaf plums with useful fruit which were introduced by Paul H. Thomson (pers. com. 1991), but of 'Shalom' Thomson said he knows nothing. Facciola (1990, 178) describes 'Shalom' thus: "Small to medium, roundish, deep red fruits; flesh juicy, sweet, desert quality excellent; resembles Santa Rosa. Ornamental dwarfish tree with attractive reddish leaves."

Sloepink—see Rosea

Spaethiana—see Woodii

Spencer Hollywood or Spencer

Plates 28, 29

The wholesale tree seller Samuel J. Rich, Inc., of Hillsboro, Oregon (not far from Portland), lists a plum called 'Spencer' or 'Spencer Hollywood' in its catalog which describes the tree as a natural dwarf, freestone-type plum with "light pink" or "single blush white flowers. Large delicious red fruit. Foliage reddish purple changing to garnet brown." There are no references other than the Rich catalogs. Regarding the clone's origin, Mr. Rich (pers. com. 1987) wrote:

> The Spencer Hollywood that we sold came to us from some friends who had it growing in their yard, apparently from a seedling. At the time we presumed it to be Hollywood because of its fruit but when we started growing it and later obtained the real Hollywood it was evident that our plum was different. It (our plum) was decidedly smaller and had desirable fruit. Our tree was only three to four feet [0.91–1.22 m] and produced fruit the second growing season. When compared with the Hollywood which we finally got from California it was much slower growing and a much smaller tree.
>
> The name "Spencer" is the name of the people from whom I got the original budwood. Their tree was quite small, probably not more than 4' [1.22 m] and had 15 or 20 plums on it at the time. We don't know anything more about its origin. We named the plum for the people who had it in their yard. They did not know of its origin or who planted the tree.

The specimens I have seen are alike and truly dwarfish; the oldest probably dates from about 1960. The trees are pink with fragrant blossoms in early spring, the petals fading to whitish, then the leaves come out a deep purple color, attractively shiny. By early summer the older leaves are glossy dark green on their upper sides, purplish on the undersides. Greenleaf rootsuckers come up occasionally. The branches tend to arch and bend gracefully under the weight of numerous large red plums, which ripen in late July or August. The plums are red on the inside, too, and very tasty. Obviously the clone is a hybrid.

The Rich nursery still carries 'Spencer Hollywood', in their 90th year of business (1990). Most of the trees have been sold to customers in Oregon and Washington. As Mr. Rich noted in his letter, for some years the company sold the clone under the name 'Hollywood'. The real 'Hollywood' of California origin looks nothing like 'Spencer' because it is a huge tree with large leaves whose plums ripen in late June or early July.

The Rich nursery is also the original distributor of 'Trailblazer', but 'Trailblazer' leaves do not look much like those of 'Spencer Hollywood' because they are larger, less glossy, less dark, and thinner. The flowers differ greatly: those of 'Spencer' are 1–1.12 inches (25–28.5 mm) wide, on pedicels up to 0.87 inches (22 mm) long; they are pink and fragrant—a few are semi-double—and they have 27–31 short white stamens tipped by yellow anthers; the ovary is green; the beak or style is pale yellow-green, or sometimes absent. By contrast, 'Trailblazer' flowers are little over half an inch (13 mm) wide, are white, not pleasingly fragrant, have notably long stamens, and are borne on shorter stalks. Also, 'Trailblazer' ripens its plums later, grows broader and is not such a dwarf.

Although many people do not want as much fruit as this clone produces—they prefer sterile, ornamental trees—I happily pronounce 'Spencer Hollywood' my favorite purpleleaf plum! The tree is pretty, fragrant, edible, of convenient size—what more can we ask? It deserves to be better known and more widely grown for four reasons: (1) It is a natural dwarf; most other purpleleaf plums grow larger, some getting awkwardly gigantic in small yards. (2) Its flowers, besides being beautiful, are fragrant—unlike those of almost all other plums. (3) Its plums are abundant, handsome, and delicious. (4) It is rare; planting diversely makes life more interesting and the environment healthier.

Stanapa

Like 'Cistena', the purple bush-cherry, 'Stanapa' was a seedling of *Prunus Besseyi* pollinated intentionally with 'Pissardii' pollen by Niels E. Hansen of South Dakota. Unlike 'Cistena', it was larger (semi-dwarf instead of a dwarf), less purplish, and never as popular. It was, however, named and released in the spring of 1911, so may still exist in some old sites or collections.

Hansen delivered a lecture in August 1926, in New York, where he said: "*Prunus Besseyi* × *P. Pissardi* (*P. cerasifera purpurea*). Fruits of no value and sparingly produced. But as ornamental shrubs with red leaves the varieties Cistena and Stanapa are popular in western gardens" (Hansen 1927, 229). Apart from Hansen's articles in various bulletins of the South Dakota Experiment Station, neither 'Stanapa' nor its synonym 'Purple B' appear elsewhere. The name 'Stanapa' means "purple leaf" in the Sioux (Lakota) language. See 'Cistena' for further details.

Stribling Thundercloud

From the limited information obtained from Stribling's Nurseries, Inc., of Merced, California, founded in 1911, I have concluded that 'Stribling Thundercloud' is another name for Burbank's 'Vesuvius'. Marion Ed Gardner (pers. com. 1987), the nursery president, explained how "25–30 years ago" he was disturbed how greatly different trees were sold as 'Thundercloud', so he did some research and concluded that Stribling's version needed its own name. There is some uncertainty in the matter, but T. B. Stribling, Jr., recalled that Stribling's strain was received from the W. B. Clarke nursery, of San Jose, California. Gardner's description of the clone fits what I have been calling Burbank's 'Vesuvius', but the 'Vesuvius' Gardner mentions resembles the virtually indistinguishable duo of 'Krauter's Vesuvius' and 'Thundercloud'. Gardner has not responded to two additional letters I wrote, so either I mistakenly use Burbank's 'Vesuvius' name, or 'Stribling Thundercloud' is a synonym for it.

Thundercloud   Plates 30, 31, 32, 33

The first use of this name, spelled as two words, was by Luther Burbank in 1919. The big question is: How do we know whether Burbank's original 'Thunder Cloud' is the same clone that in recent decades has become the most widely planted purpleleaf plum in North America? We cannot be sure. Early references to the tree are scarce, as apparently the use of the name was not widespread in the 1920s and 30s, but the following chronologic listing of some of the earlier references may yield a consensus on the characterization of this tree.

Manning (1934) lists only one nursery source: B. O. Case & Sons of Vancouver, Washington. His 1939 edition lists Case, plus W. B. Clarke of California, and his 1949 edition adds Carlton of California.

Donald Wyman (1964, 97; 1965, 380) attributed the clone to Housewearts Nursery of Woodbury, Oregon, 1937.

On 21 October 1948, the Washington State Agricultural Experiment Station published a list of *Woody Ornamental Plants Available in Northwest Nurseries*, compiled by J. W. Caddick and Andrew T. Leiser. 'Blireiana' had 16 Washington sources, 8 Oregon sources, and 3 California sources. 'Pissardii' had 10 Washington sources, 5 Oregon sources, and 2 California sources. 'Vesuvius' had 7 Washington sources, 5 Oregon sources, and 1 California source. The list did not mention 'Thundercloud'.

The 3rd edition of *Sunset's All-Western Garden Guide* (1934, 48) mentions only 'Blireiana', 'Pissardii', 'Purpusii', and 'Vesuvius'. *The Sunset Western*

Garden Book (1954, 274) lists 'Pissardii', 'Hollywood', 'Vesuvius', and 'Thundercloud'. The latter clone is described as having "dark, coppery foliage. More rounded form than purpleleaf plum [i.e., 'Pissardii']."

An undated nursery catalog from the 1930s of B. O. Case & Sons, of Vancouver, Washington, says (10):

> *Prunus Thunder Cloud*. This is Luther Burbank's masterpiece, with foliage leaves measuring 6 inches [152 mm] long. Dark maroon in color, which it holds though out the entire season. In color nothing equals this in the floral world. Think of it—brightest autumn foliage from March to November.

The W. B. Clarke nursery catalog of 1939 says of it, "Not strictly new although we have not offered it previously. Has splendid bronzy purple foliage; this coloring is actually held all summer. Best of all for color and duration." The 1958 catalog says of it, "flowers single white; deepest purple leaves known in plums, holding their color until they fall."

Other nursery catalogs and more-recent books cite conflicting information. The flowers are sometimes listed as white, but normally (and more recently) as pink. Obviously, more than one clone has gone under the name. Alas, all we know about Burbank's tree is this little bit written by Walter Howard (1945, 90): "A form of ornamental plum was brought out by Burbank in 1919 under the name Thunder Cloud. Probably a selected form of myrobalan or cherry plum, *Prunus cerasifera*. Commended for the metallic purple-crimson luster of its foliage." It is apparently impossible to know if the tree sold by Stark Brothers and hundreds of other nurseries today is Burbank's. The 'Thundercloud' in contemporary commerce is an unhybridized *Prunus cerasifera* form with dark leaves, pink flowers, and purplish plums, inside and out. I cannot tell it apart from 'Krauter's Vesuvius' and imagine 'Woodii', 'Paul's Pink', 'R. W. Hodgins', and so on, are very like it. It has been imported to New Zealand, Europe, Canada, and other places where the climate allows.

The tallest specimens are over 40 feet (12.2 m) and some are almost as wide. The severe winter cold of 1988–89 killed many twigs and branch ends on Seattle 'Thundercloud' trees, but 'Pissardii' specimens were scarcely damaged.

Genetic fingerprinting and/or a computer analysis of purpleleaf *P. cerasifera* cultivars should reveal minute distinguishing marks in the leaves of the following cultivars; at present, based upon leaf characteristics alone, with our present level of knowledge, these clones appear to be veritably indistinguishable:

Hazeldene Variety	Paul's Pink	R. W. Hodgins
Nigra	Pissardii	Thundercloud
Krauter's Vesuvius	Purple Flash	Woodii
Othello	Purple Pony	

Obviously, some leaves are darker, others larger, some more-or-less sharply pointed at their tips, or of varying pubescence or toothing, but we simply have no comparative data.

Trailblazer

Plates 34, 35, 36, 37

'Trailblazer' is a clone which has been much confused with 'Hollywood' and is often sold as such. By either name, it has been widely grown in Canada, the western United States, and Europe. I do not say much grown or frequently grown, but the nurseries listing it are scattered on the map. The synonymous name 'Oregon Trail' (which see) is fairly well buried. Zielinski et al. (1961, 6) say of 'Trailblazer':

> 'Trail Blazer' originated at Hillsboro, Oregon, and was introduced about 1954. The fruit is oval, 1¼ to 1½ inches in diameter, and bright cherry red, with a light bloom. The flesh is greenish yellow, fairly tart, and firm. It is a clingstone type and rated as fair to good in overall quality. The tree has very handsome bright red leaves and a profusion of blooms. It is a heavy producer and the fruit hangs well. It is an attractive ornamental tree besides producing edible fruits for fresh eating purposes. Trail Blazer ripens about August 15 at Corvallis [Oregon].

A more complete account is in Brooks and Olmo (1972, pp. 522–523):

> Orig. in Portland, Oregon, by Mrs. Mildred M. Smith. Introduced in 1955. Plant Patent 1,586; April 2, 1957; by Mrs. Smith; assigned to Samuel J. Rich, Rich & Sons Nursery, Hillsboro, Oregon. Shiro × *Prunus cerasifera* var. *atropurpurea* (purple-leafed plum); cross made in 1947; selected in 1952. Fruit: skin cherry red; flesh apricot-orange, slightly more acid than Shiro but sweeter than purple-leafed parent; ripens about 1 week later than Shiro. Tree: growth habit similar to Shiro; flowers white at anthesis, with prominent stamens; leaves when young red on both sides, at maturity dark green on upper surface, red on lower surface.

Both 'Trailblazer' and 'Spencer Hollywood' were introduced by the Rich nursery. Samuel J. Rich (pers. com. 1987) explained the origin of 'Trailblazer':

We discovered this variety in a customer's yard where it grew from seed. It is a strong grower with rather open pattern of growth. We suspect that one of the parents is the Shiro variety of fruit tree, the other is probably Pissardi, but the origin is not known other than that it grew in a customer's yard.

A typical entry in the Rich nursery catalog says only, "Open spreading growth. Blush pink flowers. New foliage cherry red gradually changing to deep green at maturity. Underside of leaf is wine colored. Good and abundant fruit." Bean (1970–1980, 3: 361) says:

P. 'Trailblazer'.—Leaves narrowly to broadly oblong-obovate, acuminate, cuneate at the base, bronzy or purplish green above when mature, undersides purplish red. Flowers pure white in sessile umbels, about ½ in. wide, cup-shaped, borne very profusely in early spring. Fruits not seen, said to be red and edible. A very attractive hybrid between *P. cerasifera* 'Nigra' and some form of *P. salicina*. According to Dr. Boom, it is the same as 'Hollywood'.

Krüssman (1978, 21), as well as many other writers and nurseries, lumps the name with 'Hollywood'. Probably this came about because 'Trailblazer' had been sold as 'Hollywood' and as 'Trailblazer', and the Europeans received the one clone under both names. The authentic 'Trailblazer' has been in Europe for at least 30 years, but possibly neither the real 'Hollywood' nor 'Spencer Hollywood' have been imported to Europe yet. Or, perhaps both 'Trailblazer' and 'Hollywood' are in Europe, but no one has noticed how different the flowers and fruit are since the leaves of the two clones can appear confusingly similar. Whatever the cause of confusion in Europe, the two clones, as described in this volume, are different.

There is no reason to continue confusing 'Trailblazer' with 'Hollywood' or any other cultivar. It is a distinctive clone. Yet, by looking only at a leafy spray, it is difficult to tell 'Trailblazer' from 'Hollywood'. The leaves of 'Trailblazer' are smaller, darker, finer-toothed, and shorter-stalked. In flower, 'Trailblazer' is unique—see Table 6 in this volume for comparisons between 'Hollywood' and 'Trailblazer'. The "open, spreading growth" of 'Trailblazer' is a pronounced feature: the tree is comparatively diffuse, with a crown that spreads widely but is not dense as are most purpleleaf plum cultivars. When artfully pruned, 'Trailblazer' rivals 'Newport' for the honor of having the most handsome pattern of branching. The trees are usually broad, not markedly upright. None are large enough to be worth measuring; perhaps the largest is 20 feet (6.1 m) tall, wider still, with its trunk less than a foot (305 mm) thick.

Whether the parentage is 'Pissardii' × 'Shiro' is unsettled. 'Shiro' is an abundant, well-known cultivar, producing yellow plums. It may be that the parentage of 'Trailblazer' is altogether different from what is generally ascribed, but in case the parentage is correctly recorded, Table 5 (in Chapter 8) shows the involved background of 'Shiro'.

From firsthand observation, the leaves of 'Trailblazer' can be up to 4.87 inches (123 mm) long and 2.25 (57 mm) inches wide on vigorous sucker shoots of established trees, but they are usually considerably smaller, 2.5–4.5 inches (63–114 mm) long and 1–1.75 (25–44.5 mm) inches wide. They are inconspicuously glandular, greenish on top, purplish beneath, and sharply toothed. The leafstalks (petioles) are proportionately short, rarely if ever more than 0.5 inch (13 mm) long. The twigs are hairless or weakly hairy and when cut show green cambium. The flowers are white, 0.62–1 inch (15.5–25 mm) wide. The (24) 28–30 stamens are notably long, surrounding a yellow-green to pink beak or style. The flowerstalks or pedicels are 0.62 of an inch (15.5 mm) or less long, or rarely up to 0.75 inch (19 mm) long. Very few flowers are semidouble. The sepals are prominently toothed and can reflex partly.

The plums, ripe in Seattle beginning in very late July but chiefly in August (even into early September), are bright red underneath the dull bloom, freckled with plentiful dark dots, 1.5–2 inches (38–50.5 mm) long, and somewhat less wide. They are usually borne abundantly.

Veitchii

The purpleleaf plum sold as 'Veitchii' is 'Moseri' (which see). The Wayside Gardens' catalogs describe 'Veitchii' as follows:

> Prunus Pissardi veitchi
> This small tree grows about 10 feet tall, but can be pruned to smaller size if desired. In early spring it is covered with thousands of large clusters of double pink blossoms not unlike those of the double-flowering Cherry or Peach. It is very hardy and should be used in place of flowering Peaches or Cherries exclusively in those localities where the latter are not hardy. In addition to the delightful display of double pink flowers you will enjoy the light bronze colored foliage which in late summer turns green.

> Veitch's Double Pink Flowering Plum
> This small tree grows about 15 feet tall. In early spring it is covered with large clusters of double pink blossoms like those of the double flowering Cherry. In fact, it is often mistaken for a flowering Cherry. It is very hardy and should be used in place of flowering Peaches or Cherries in

those localities where the latter are not hardy. In addition to the delightful display of double pink flowers you will enjoy the bronze-colored foliage as well as the delicious, small, sweet Plums which ripen in early autumn. Here is a small tree equally charming for the small garden or as a specimen on the large lawn. It is the first tree to bloom along with the Forsythia.

In the 1960s the tree's name in the catalog changed to 'Blireiana', but I think 'Moseri' was still the clone being sold. When I wrote Wayside Gardens, John E. Elsley, assistant vice president of plant product development, replied (30 November 1987):

> I am afraid that I have absolutely no information about what was offered by the old company, and I am totally unaware of their original sources. I myself have been with the company for the past 7 years and to the best of my knowledge the plant that we are now selling as Prunus blireana is, in fact, this cultivar.

The name "Veitchii" has scarcely appeared in books, despite its presence in nursery catalogs. It is mentioned with 'Moseri' in *Hortus Second* (Bailey 1941, 600), but without comment. *Trees and Shrubs for Pacific Northwest Gardens* (Grant and Grant 1943, 103) mentions it immediately after the 'Blireiana' discussion: "Other hybrids of the same parentage are sold under the name of *P. blireiana*. One of these with flowers of less gaudy pink is correctly known as *P. moseri*, or sometimes *P. veitchi*."

In conclusion, I have not even the slightest doubt that "Veitchii" is a synonym of 'Moseri'.

Vesuvius Plates 38, 39, 40

The original 'Vesuvius' was one of Luther Burbank's intentional hybrids, obviously named after the Italian volcano whose A.D. 79 eruption destroyed the Roman cities of Pompeii and Herculaneum. It was first offered for sale in 1907, as related by Walter Howard (1945, 29):

> Probably a cross between *Prunus Pissardii* and *P. triflora*. Unusually large leaves of a metallic-crimson color. Branches same color. "Its fruit is of a deep, rich color, possessing a pleasing, acid flavor." Introduced by Fancher Creek Nurseries, Fresno, California, in 1907. Chiefly valuable as an ornamental.

U. P. Hedrick, in *The Plums of New York* (1910, 559) reported: "[Vesuvius is a cross of] Pissardi and some native or Triflora sort; introduced by the Fancher Creek Nurseries in 1907. Tree vigorous, elm-like in habit of growth, not productive; fruit small, roundish, purplish-red; flesh yellow, quality fair; stone small; valuable only as an ornamental." These two quotes establish the hybridity of the cultivar. Today, *P. triflora* Roxb. is known as *P. salicina* Lindl.—the Japanese plum.

The following references to 'Vesuvius', in approximately the order they were published, give us a picture of what various writers had to say about the tree, and how they copied one another. The Fancher Creek Nurseries, of Fresno, California, first offered the tree. Their 1907–1908 catalog simply says: "Burbank's Latest Introduction. Introduced solely by us. Write for illustrated booklet." The nursery's 1912–1913 catalog is more helpful: "Burbank's latest introduction. A foliage tree like the purple-leaved Plum, but vastly superior in growth and in the size and beautiful tint of the foliage which is of a rich, metallic crimson color, with a crumpled surface like a Coleus. A splendid ornamental tree with edible purple fruit." Note that the description plays down the value of the fruit. The company's 1920 catalog has a slightly different version (14):

A foliage tree like the Purple Leaved Plum but vastly superior to it. A much more vigorous grower; branches inclined to droop; foliage very large with a very much crumpled surface with a pronounced crimson color intermingled with a lustrous green. Fruit nearly globular, three and one half inches [89 mm] around and a fair quality for cooking.

The 1915 catalog of the California Nursery Company, of Niles, describes 'Pissardii' as "*P. Pissardi* Purple-leaved Plum" and 'Vesuvius' as "*P. vesuvius* Burbank's Purple-leaved Plum:"

Differs from common Purple-Leaved Plum in its more vigorous growth, with longer, willowy branches and much larger, longer leaves. Color of foliage is very pronounced and held well throughout the season. It is of a rich, metallic crimson color, with a crumpled surface like a Coleus. Very fine.

Its 1931 catalog says: "Foliage longer and more reddish than *Prunus Pissardi*. Flowers are slightly larger and later. A very brilliant decorative tree."

The 1931 catalog of Leonard Coates Nurseries, San Jose, California, says (24): "A comparatively new introduction by the late Luther Burbank. A very graceful, small tree, with leathery leaves of a purplish color. A strikingly attractive purple-foliaged tree." *Sunset's All-Western Garden Guide* (Sunset 1934, 48) and *Sunset's Complete Garden Book* (Sunset 1940, 178) report: "large, highly colored, luminous, purple leaves." Grant and Grant (1943, p.103) maintain that: "Vesuvius, also known as Burbank's Purple-leaf plum, has the most interesting branching pattern of this group, forming a picturesque irregular head of curling branches." Buckley Nursery Company of Washington, wrote in its 1952 catalog (p.15): "Deep blood-red foliage with purple branches, the color being retained all summer. . . . One of the more dwarf growing varieties. Flowers are white, fruit dark purple." Harrison, the New Zealand nurseryman (1959, 271) declared: "*P.* 'Vesuvius' Very large foliage of a rich crimson-purple colour, and white flowers. Still grown in Australia, but not as popular in New Zealand as it was at one time. It is said to be a purple-leafed sport of the well-known Burbank fruiting plum." Walter Hazlewood (1968, 181), another Southern Hemisphere (Epping, New South Wales) nurseryman, wrote: "Said to be a sport of the Burbank fruiting Plum, this species has large leaves of a purplish-red colour and single white flowers in September. It grows to a height of about 30 feet and a width of 25 feet."

Ernest Lord (1970, 86) stated of 'Vesuvius', "leaves larger than 'Nigra', reddish purple and puckered, white flowers," and Donald Wyman (1965, 380) wrote, "the leaves are large and deep purple, one of the most colored of these varieties. It seldom blooms, but this is no defect since the pink bloom of these purple-leaved varieties is ineffective, to say the least. This was a Luther Burbank introduction before 1929."

From the above quotes, it appears that 'Vesuvius' is a hybrid, with very dark, longer if not larger leaves, often puckered, and scant white flowers which rarely produce fruit (and when they do, the plums are nothing special). The tree is vigorous but only moderately sized.

One tree fitting this picture, and called by this name, is in Luther Burbank's Santa Rosa garden. Of course, I cannot be certain that the trees I am calling 'Vesuvius' are the same trees Burbank called by that name, but my studies lead me to conclude that they are and that 'Stribling Thundercloud' (which see) is another name for 'Vesuvius'. M. E. Gardner's (pers. com. 1987) description of 'Stribling Thundercloud' follows:

> Ours is a bright copper colored leaf that is very much like a peach leaf. The tree is much smaller than Vesuvius, Pissardi or Hollywood varieties and has an inverted cone shape to it, rather than a globular shaped head as the others tend to have, especially the Vesuvius. The cambium is bright red, the bark is lighter in color than the others.

The trees I am calling 'Vesuvius' are small; the largest is about 30 feet (9.15 m) tall and wide, with its trunk more than a foot (30.5 cm) thick, measuring 3.5 feet (106 cm) in circumference. On most trees, the long branches have been trimmed back. The trees exhibit a unique flaring vase form and their crowns fork low and wide. The leaves are indeed large on the vigorous long shoots: up to 6 inches (152 mm) long, 2.62 inches (66 mm) wide; but the ordinary fruit-spur or short-shoot leaves are only 2.12–4.12 inches (53.5–104 mm) long, and 1.12–1.75 inches (28.5–44.5 mm) wide, with petioles 0.5–075 inches (13–19 mm) long. Thus the leaves are quite narrow, and many curl up their sides, having revolute margins. The color is well held, and very shining dark; the upper side can be dark greenish, but the under surface remains deep maroon. They are conspicuously glandular, often puckered, and the midrib beneath is markedly pale, often yellowish-tinged.

The flowers appear early, beginning in late February, are sparse, not showy, and pure white, against bronzy young unfolding leaves—the latter are rolled up longitudinally in the bud stage. The flowers, which keep appearing for a month, are single, in pairs, or in threes, or are borne 4–7 on fruit spurs. Each flower is 0.87–1 inch (22–25 mm) wide with 27–33 prominent wide-flung, long, white stamens and egg-yolk–colored anthers. There are usually 5, sometimes 6, sepals and petals. The sepals are hairless and red-tinted, minutely glandular toothed, and more pointed than those of other cultivars. The flowerstalk or pedicel is long, sometimes an inch (25 mm). The ovary is hairless, as are the twigs. The tree bears no plums and I suspect it needs to be cross-pollinated with early blooming Japanese types.

Overall, the clone is one of the most distinctive purpleleaf cultivars. It has no cherry plum traits. The superficial aspect is like that of a peach tree, but it is not a peach hybrid. Some sort of greenleaved Japanese plum is the most similar tree, but 'Vesuvius' is more sparing in flowers than any Japanese plum.

Woodii or Wood's Variety

Named for or by the English nurseryman W. Wood, 'Woodii' is a tree, which, like 'Nigra', has deep colored leaves and pink flowers. It was apparently raised in Wood's nursery but first put into commerce in 1910 by the German firm Späth (Spaeth), as suggested by Rehder (1949, 320) as well as B. K. Boom (1956—1958, 148): *P. cerasifera purpurea Woodii* Wood ex Spaeth, Cat., no. 143, 111 (1910). *P. cerasifera Pissartii Spaethiana* Wood ex Spaeth in Fedde, Repert. Sp. Nov. Reg. Veg. 13, 127 (1913). Bean elaborates (1970–1980, 3: 361): "The similar [to 'Nigra'] 'Woodii' was raised at Wood's nursery, Maresfield, E. Sussex, but apparently put into commerce by Späth's nurseries, Berlin, in 1910." At the time, Späth's was the world's largest nursery. Krüssman says of the tree (1986, 26), "shoots *red* in cross-section. Leaves small, like 'Atropurpurea' but remaining evenly black red from spring to fall. Flowers pink. Späth 1910." In *The Book of Trees*, Alfred Carl Hottes (1942b, 311) says: "Variety *spaethiana* has shining leaves which are said to retain their color better than *pissardi*."

'Woodii' has been rarely offered in North American nurseries. Manning's various editions list only English sources. However, Wyman included the cultivar in *Trees for American Gardens*, which he would not have done unless it was in the United States trade. What he says of it is little, but worth comparing with his comments on 'Nigra' (Wyman 1951, 284—285): "'Nigra'—Flowers single, pale pink, ⅝" diameter, leaves dark purple. 'Woodii'—Flowers single, light pink, ¾" diameter, leaves dark purple." In his second (1965) and third (1990) editions Wyman describes 'Nigra' but omits 'Woodii': "'Nigra'—the foliage color of this clone is very dark purple, slightly darker than that of 'Atropurpurea,' and is retained throughout the summer. The flowers are single, pink and ⅝ of an inch in diameter. It is called the Black Myrobalan Plum."

It appears Wyman figured that 'Woodii' was too similar to 'Nigra' to bother including it. A tree bought in the United States as 'Woodii' stands right next to a 'Thundercloud' tree at the Rhody Ridge Arboretum, 17427 Clover Road, Bothell, Washington 98012. There is no observable difference between the two trees. Only a detailed study of the leaves shows that the two are not identical clones: the 'Woodii' leaves are slightly darker, less sharply toothed, and more "pinched" near the tip. I wonder how many specimens of 'Woodii' I have seen but thought were 'Thundercloud' or 'Krauter's Vesuvius' or 'Nigra'?

Boom (1956–1958) suggests that the 'Nigra' of European commerce is really 'Woodii', and that the real 'Nigra' of L. H. Bailey is relatively rare, and sold under the name 'Atropurpurea' (as in Lombarts' nursery catalogs). I am unable to figure out his reasoning, but it may well be so. This scenario, in fact, would explain why we so often read of 'Woodii' and 'Nigra' together, and why they are called similar if not identical. Dr. Boom said the real 'Nigra' differs from 'Woodii' in having larger leaves that are less deeply colored, and more horizontally held, and in being a more vigorous tree. We can possibly typify 'Woodii' in England, but Bailey's 'Nigra' is too elusive to pin down, so it may be that in the nursery trade, at least in Europe, 'Woodii and 'Nigra' are the same.

Richard Sudell wrote about both in *The New Illustrated Encyclopædia of Gardening* (1933, 742): "Nigra: Leaves blackish-purple. Woodii: A very fine form with larger and deeper-coloured foliage and deep rose-coloured flowers."

Michael Haworth-Booth (1951, 44) wrote that the flowers of 'Nigra' were "vivid pink" yet those of 'Woodii' were only "blush-pink." And so it goes, one writer saying this, the other contradicting.

The Plant Finder (1990) lists 21 English nursery sources for 'Nigra' and none for 'Woodii', so the latter name is clearly in decline still. Possibly the attraction of the name 'Nigra' is that it palpably describes what it signifies—a darkleaf tree; on the other hand, 'Woodii' is just another person's name.

Wrightii

Richmond Harrison (1959, 271) wrote: "*P. Wrightii*. A New Zealand cross between a Flowering Prunus and the flowering almond 'Pollardii'. Attractive bright pink single flowers and shining purple-red foliage. A valuable addition."

The clone came from "The Avondale Nursery" of Hayward R. Wright of Avondale, Auckland, New Zealand. The years of operation are unknown to me, but from at least 1916 onward, Wright introduced many crab-apple, peach, nectarine and plum cultivars. He also introduced the well-known 'Hayward' kiwi-fruit (*Actinidia*); it did not derive its name from Hayward, California.

Lord (1982, 67) says: "P. c. 'Wrightii'; leaves purple; flowers large, rose-pink, as in *P. 'Pollardi'*."

In his *Manual of Trees, Shrubs and Climbers*, Stanley J. Palmers (n.d., 234), of New Zealand's leading garden center, wrote:

Prunus wrightii. A New Zealand raised hybrid of P. Pollardii and one of the flowering plums. It embraces the deeper flower colour of the almonds, and the bronzy foliage of the prunus. Flowers are large, single, saucer shaped, and bright rose pink with prominent stamens. Foliage is purple red and quite glossy. Deciduous. 3.5 × 2.5 m.

The name *Prunus* 'Wrightii' appears nowhere else, except the Washington Park Arboretum in Seattle gave nine plants of "*Prunus Wrightii*" to the Finch Arboretum in Spokane, Washington, on 19 September 1950. Neither arboretum presently has any such trees.

The 'Pollardii' parent of 'Wrightii' is an Australian cultivar of the almond/peach cross (*Prunus* × *Amygdalo-persica* [West.] Rehd.) that arose around 1864. Specimens of it in Seattle flower during late March and early April, exhibiting delicate pink blossoms of surpassing size. 'Pollardii' is vigorous, large-growing, and fruitful.

A scientific binomial exists for hybrids between the peach-almond and the cherry plum: *Prunus* × *gigantea* (Späth) Koehne. Therefore, the name 'Wrightii' should be written as a cultivar following that combination: *Prunus* × *gigantea* 'Wrightii'.

Any fruit borne by 'Wrightii' should be fascinating: it will be a mix of genes from peach, plum, and almond trees.

Concluding Remarks

This book brings much disparate information together conveniently. Some of its findings, however, are based on so little watertight evidence that they should be viewed as suggestions, not pronouncements. In this chapter we will consider a few of the inherent problems in studying purpleleaf plums.

Limited Original Names

The original descriptions of three major purpleleaf clones are so inadequate that I could not pin their identities and names with confidence: 'Nigra', 'Thundercloud', and 'Vesuvius'. Given the information available today, I cannot yet rest confident that I know to which tree clones these prominent old names were originally applied.

Local Bias

Library work aside, my first-hand observations refer almost exclusively to how purpleleaf plum trees appear and behave on the west coast of North America. Had I lived elsewhere, doubtless my observations and comments would have been different, but exactly how the emphasis would have shifted, we cannot know. Still, it would have been difficult, if not impossible, to choose another area with more kinds of purpleleaf plums available to study.

Leftover Trees

I encountered half a dozen unusual trees to which I have been unable to affix names. These trees are very rare, often unique, as far as I know, and include what may simply be unnamed seedlings. Some have nicknames: 'Hairy Pissard', 'Queen Anne Double-flower', 'Berkeley Hollywood', and so forth. Probably at least one or two of these mystery trees are examples of cultivars treated in this book. The one such tree hitherto undescribed that I did name is 'Purple Pigmy', because there is no question of its uniqueness. Should a comprehensive purpleleaf plum collection ever be assembled, I will be pleased to contribute propagating material from these unnamed but distinctive trees. Incidentally, a well-designed purpleleaf plum arboretum would be a popular, novel attraction. In bloom it would dazzle visitors, in summer its grim atmosphere would afford a rare study of color contrasts.

Both gardeners and editors delight in rendering order out of chaos, and making scenes of beauty where there was none before. The goal of this book was to report my adoption of some tree orphans, who were well known as a group, but who suffered from decades of receiving no particular care—and endured some vicious bad-mouthing. By taking the time to become acquainted with these purple trees, I was rewarded by the satisfaction available to all of us who pursue what we cherish. In the big scheme of life, this book is a mere speck, and not a scintillating one. But to tree lovers, it is another pillar gracing the house of ornamental trees. I tried to ensure its having sound structure, and beauty as well. Even so, my favorite purpleleaf plums combine pleasing beauty with fruit worth eating.

Late Addition

As this book goes to press, a 51st purpleleaf plum cultivar has come to my attention. It is called 'Kankakee Newport', and is said to be a "pyramidal 'Newport' plum." Since regular 'Newport' plum trees are broad-crowned, any pyramidal or narrow-crowned variation would be significantly different.

Appendix 1 Thumbnail Summaries

The 50 cultivars elaborated upon in this book can be summarized as follows:

'**Allred**': 1939 U.S. hybrid valued for its fruit. A vigorous tree of large bronzy leaves, white flowers, and profuse red plums.

'**Atherton**': A California hybrid related to 'Blireiana'; apparently little valued and deservedly rare.

'**Big Cis**': A treelike 'Cistena' sport introduced in Oregon in 1982.

'**Blireiana**': A familiar 1905 French dwarf hybrid with deep pink, fragrant, doubled flowers; scarce, fuzzy-skinned fruit.

'**Cistena**': 1910 North Dakota intentional hybrid bush; well known; very hardy.

'**Citation**': 1983 intentional hybrid rootstock for grafting peaches, apricots, nectarines, and plums. Patented.

'**Clark Hill Redleaf**': 1974 Georgia chance hybrid, possibly in limited use as a rootstock.

'**Cocheco**': A hybrid from New Hampshire, sold since 1976. White flowers, delicious red plums if cross-pollinated.

'**Coleus**': 19th century North Carolina chance hybrid of 'Pissardii' and 'Kelsey'; extinct or renamed. Noted more for its foliage than its fruit. Kin to 'Garnet'.

'**Diversifolia**': 1925(?) English 'Pissardii' seedling with white flowers, odd-shaped leaves.

'**Elsie**': Fruitful hybrid from southern California, named by Paul Thomson.

'**Festeri**': Pink-flowered Australian hybrid dating from perhaps 1950.

'**Garnet**': 1891 sister seedling of 'Coleus' but with better fruit. Lost under its name.

'**Gaujardii**': From Rome, about 1920, possibly a 'Blireiana' variation. Rare, but present in Ireland.

'**Gerth**': Fruitful hybrid from southern California, named by Paul Thomson. Foliage similar to that of 'Spencer Hollywood'.

'**Hazeldene Variety**': English selection from perhaps 1940; the name, at least, is now very obscure.

'**Hessei':** White-flowered, variegated, shrubby tree; about 1900 in Germany.

'**Hollywood':** 1936 California chance hybrid prized for fruit: flowers appearing very early; early ripening roundish plums, red inside and out.

'**Knaus':** Fruitful selection from southern California, named by Paul Thomson, but far rarer than 'Elsie' and 'Gerth', and a smaller tree; less likely a hybrid.

'**Krauter's Vesuvius':** 1956 California darkleaf, pink-flowered cherry plum.

'**Minn. No. 1':** Bushy 1917 Minnesota intentional hybrid. Now very rare if not extinct.

'**Minn. No. 2':** Bushy 1917 Minnesota intentional hybrid. Now probably extinct.

'**Mirage':** 1990 variegated, bushy English selection.

'**Moseri':** Like 'Blireiana', but a larger tree, larger leaved, with paler flowers; more fruitful.

'**Mt. St. Helens':** A sport of 'Newport' from Oregon in 1981.

'**Newport':** 1920 Minnesota intentional hybrid. Cold-hardy. Broad-crowned tree with small, pale flowers late in the season.

'**Nigra':** Mysterious pre-1910 name, long applied to a cherry plum of intensely dark color, lively pink flowers, few plums. Possibly just a synonym of 'Woodii'.

'**Oaks':** Fruitful selection from southern California, named by Paul Thomson, but rarer than 'Elsie' and 'Gerth'; may not be a hybrid.

'**Othello':** 1910 California 'Pissardii' seedling. White flowers, dark leaves, abundant good plums.

'**Pallet':** Pre-1910 French origin. Mysterious. White flowers; leaves green above, red beneath.

'**Paul's Pink':** United Kingdom cherry plum with dark leaves, pink flowers, from about 1920. An extinct name.

'**Pissardii':** The original 1880 introduction from Persia. Lost in a baffling flood of varied, superior and inferior seedlings. Often called 'Atropurpurea'. Almost anything may be called by these names.

'**Purple C':** 1910 North Dakota intentional hybrid bush; larger and less dark than 'Cistena'. Never introduced commercially.

'**Purple Flame':** 1931 U.S. clone with good fruit. Available descriptions deplorably inadequate. Still extant but out of the nursery trade.

'**Purpleleaf Kelsey**': 1893 California intentional hybrid with good fruit. Long extinct under that name, and possibly extinct altogether.

'**Purple Pigmy**': 1948 Seattle origin. *Prunus microcarpa* chance hybrid. Not yet propagated, but worthy of the honor.

'**Purple Pony**': 1962 California cherry plum seedling of dwarf habit; flowers few, pink, with the leaves—not showy; leaves dark.

'**Purpurea**': Pre-1900 French chance hybrid of *Prunus spinosa* and 'Pissardii'. Pink flowers. Similar to 'Rosea'.

'**Purpusii**': 1908 German white-flowered, variegated purpleleaf cherry plum.

'**Roebuck Castle**': Irish cherry plum, dating from maybe 1920. Rare, but present in Ireland.

'**Rosea**': Like 'Purpurea', from the Netherlands, about 1950(?); pink flowers.

'**R. W. Hodgins**': From Australia, about 1920. A darkleaf, pink-flowered cherry plum. Now unknown by name.

'**Shalom**': From southern California, a little-known, recent, dwarf, fruitful plum.

'**Spencer Hollywood**': Oregon chance hybrid, introduced 1956 or before. Dwarf, with pink, fragrant flowers; leaves small, deep glossy green above, dark red beneath; fruit large, abundant, egg-shaped, late July or August.

'**Stanapa**': 1910 North Dakota intentional hybrid bush; less dwarfish than 'Cistena', rarer by far, if not totally extinct.

'**Thundercloud**': 1919 California introduction. A cherry plum with dark leaves, pink flowers. The name is confusingly ambiguous.

'**Trailblazer**': 1954 Oregon hybrid. Small, dull white flowers, leaves bronzy-green above, red beneath—quite similar to those of 'Hollywood'; fruit copious, large, egg-shaped, red, in August or September.

'**Vesuvius**': 1907 California intentional hybrid. Narrow, very dark leaves. White, scant flowers of little ornament.

'**Woodii**': 1910 English cherry plum with dark leaves and pink flowers. May be the proper name for what is sold as 'Nigra'.

'**Wrightii**': New Zealand peach-almond-plum hybrid, from perhaps 1955. Pink flowers. Rare but not lost.

Appendix 2 Scientific Names

Of the 50 cultivars of purpleleaf plums described in this book, 30 have been given scientific binomials (i.e., genus/species names), leaving 20 hybrids without official specific epithet designations. Hybrids are not required to be assigned Latinized genus/species formulas, but when a botanist chooses to create such names, the rules of plant nomenclature accept the proposed names if they have been published in a valid and standard fashion. Following are the proper botanic names of the trees, as they exist in 1992.

1. *Prunus* × *blireiana*

2. *Prunus* × *blireiana* 'Atherton'

3. *Prunus* × *blireiana* 'Moseri'

4. *Prunus cerasifera* 'Diversifolia'

5. *Prunus cerasifera* 'Hazeldene Variety'

6. *Prunus cerasifera* 'Hessei'

7. *Prunus cerasifera* 'Knaus'

8. *Prunus cerasifera* 'Krauter's Vesuvius'

9. *Prunus cerasifera* 'Mirage'

10. *Prunus cerasifera* 'Nigra'

11. *Prunus cerasifera* 'Oaks'?

12. *Prunus cerasifera* 'Othello'

13. *Prunus cerasifera* 'Pallet'

14. *Prunus cerasifera* 'Paul's Pink'

15. *Prunus cerasifera* 'Pissardii'

16. *Prunus cerasifera* 'Purple Flame'

17. *Prunus cerasifera* 'Purple Pony'

18. *Prunus cerasifera* 'Purpusii'

19. *Prunus cerasifera* 'Roebuck Castle'

20. *Prunus cerasifera* 'R. W. Hodgins'

21. *Prunus cerasifera* 'Shalom'?

22. *Prunus cerasifera* 'Thundercloud'

23. *Prunus cerasifera* 'Woodii'

24. *Prunus* × *cistena* 'Big Cis'

26. *Prunus* × *cistena* 'Purple A'

27. *Prunus* × *cistena* 'Stanapa'

28. *Prunus* × *gigantea* 'Wrightii'

29. *Prunus* × *Simmleri* 'Purpurea'

30. *Prunus* × *Simmleri* 'Rosea'

31. *Prunus* 'Allred'

32. *Prunus* 'Citation'

33. *Prunus* 'Clark Hill Redleaf'

34. *Prunus* 'Cocheco'

35. *Prunus* 'Coleus'

36. *Prunus* 'Elsie'

37. *Prunus* 'Festeri'

38. *Prunus* 'Garnet'

39. *Prunus* 'Gaujardii'

40. *Prunus* 'Gerth'

41. *Prunus* 'Hollywood'

42. *Prunus* 'Minn. No. 1'

43. *Prunus* 'Minn. No. 2'

44. *Prunus* 'Mt. St. Helens'

45. *Prunus* 'Newport'

46. *Prunus* 'Purpleleaf Kelsey'

47. *Prunus* 'Purple Pigmy'

48. *Prunus* 'Spencer Hollywood'

49. *Prunus* 'Trailblazer'

50. *Prunus* 'Vesuvius'

Appendix 3 Purpleleaved Nonplum
Prunus Trees

Seventeen cultivars from four species of purpleleaved but nonplum *Prunus* trees are listed in Chapter 1. Now they receive their deserved attention.

Peaches

The peach (*Prunus Persica*) was the first *Prunus* to originate a purplish variant. U. P. Hedrick (1917, 188) relates in detail how the **'Bloodleaf'** peach arose in Mississippi during the 1860s. Either this novel North American find was exported quickly to Europe and there renamed **'Foliis Rubris'**, or a purpleleaf peach of independent origin, bearing the latter name, coincidentally arose and was marketed in Belgium under the name in 1873. Apparent synonyms include 'Foliis Rubis', 'Purpurea', 'Rubrifolia', and 'Atropurpurea'.

In 1939 the Royal Horticultural Society of England conferred an Award of Merit on a purpleleaf peach clone circulating in Europe. It had reddish young spring growth, changing to bronzy-green, with pink flowers and dark-skinned fruit.

Ackerman Nurseries of Bridgeman, Michigan, introduced the **'Royal Redleaf'** peach about 1940. 'Ackerman Redleaf' is a mere synonym. Del Rancho Fortuna Nurseries of McFarland, California, said of 'Royal Redleaf' in one of their advertisements: "Beautiful large creamy-white, single blossoms; followed by red foliage. Sweet white freestone peaches ripening in mid August" (*Pacific Coast Nurseryman*, December 1955, p. 7).

'Rancho Redleaf' was introduced by Del Rancho Fortuna Nurseries. One of their advertisements said of it: "Big, extremely double, radiant pink blossoms that swathe the branches from trunk to tip. Followed by deep-red, wine-colored foliage. Our exclusive introduction" (*Pacific Coast Nurseryman*, May 1956, p. 30). While we can rely upon the accounts of Del Rancho Fortuna, because that nursery grew and sold the two clones ('Royal' and 'Rancho'), nonetheless, confusion has ensued. Sunset (1979, 432) says: "Royal Red Leaf: Foliage red, deepening to maroon. Deep pink flowers. This might be classed as flowering-fruiting as it bears red, white-fleshed, edible fruit. Late." Probably the Rancho clone is primarily a floriferous selection, while the Royal is a fruitful one—red skin, whitish flesh.

'Rutgers Red Leaf' was introduced as related by Brooks and Olmo (1952, 110):

> Originated in New Brunswick, New Jersey, by the New Jersey Agricultural Experiment Station (M. A. Blake). Introduced commercially in 1947. Parentage unknown. Fruit: very sweet; freestone; flesh white; of no value. Flower: showy. Tree: suggested as a source of hardy seedling rootstocks; may have slight dwarfing effect; readily identified in nursery because of dark color of young leaves.

'Kingston Redleaf' was reported under one of its synonyms in Brooks and Olmo (1952, 86):

> Davidson (Redleaf, Tennessee Redleaf).—Found growing on a roadside in southwest Davidson County, Tennessee, by Joseph C. McDaniel. Introduced commercially in 1946 by Peach Ridge Farm, Clemson, South Carolina. Parentage unknown; discovered and first propagated in 1938. Fruit: flesh yellow; freestone; poor edible quality; pits give high germination without special treatment, many double kernels; for use as a rootstock variety. Most of the seedlings are red-leafed, vigorous, and well adapted to June or dormant budding.

Harrison (1959, 270) says of **'Hiawatha'** redleaf peach: "Single pink, brilliant purple-red foliage in spring. There are two forms grown, the better one also produces a good crop of edible fruit." Palmer (n.d., 234) wrote of 'Hiawatha': "Distinctive coppery purple spring foliage, large single pink flowers, followed by small edible fruit."

In the United States, "bloodleaf peach" has become a general vernacularism that is applied to any red or purplish-leaved peach. Ornamental peaches in general have suffered a decline in popularity from their status a few decades ago. Oddly enough, I have not knowingly seen even a single purpleleaf peach tree; they are extremely rare in my part of the earth. Nor am I aware of more than one North American nursery (Aldridge, of Von Ormy, Texas) that presently raises purpleleaf peaches. However, at least seven redleaf peach cultivars are reported, although with seven synonyms, the scenario is rather muddy (Table 7).

TABLE 7. Purpleleaf Peach Cultivars.

Name of Cultivar	Origin	Comments
'Bloodleaf'	Mississippi pre-1870	Fair flowers; mediocre fruit.

'Foliis Rubris'
  (= 'Atropurpurea')
  (= 'Foliis Rubis')
  (= 'Purpurea')
  (= 'Rubrifolia')
	Belgium 1873	Fair flowers; mediocre fruit.

'Hiawatha'	New Zealand? 1950?	Ornamental, large, single pink flowers; good, small fruit.

'Kingston Redleaf'
  (= 'Davidson Redleaf')
  (= 'Tennessee Redleaf')
	Tennessee 1946	Rootstock; fruit yellow-fleshed, poor eating quality.

'Rancho Redleaf'	California 1956	Floral excellence with large, double, radiant pink blooms.
'Royal Redleaf' (= 'Ackerman Redleaf')	Michigan 1940	Floral/fruiting clone with large, creamy-white blooms, red-skinned, white-fleshed fruit.
'Rutgers Redleaf'	New Jersey 1947	Rootstock with showy flowers, sweet, white-fleshed fruit.

European Bird Cherries

The European bird cherry, *Prunus Padus*, has given rise to several cultivars with purplish foliage. As usual, confusion surrounds them. They are relatively recent in origin and only one is comparatively common. Regular bird cherry seedlings flush forth cheerfully bright green leaves in early spring. The leaves are large and not as pointed or coarsely toothed as those of most cherries; these unconventional leaves are invested with charm by the accompanying petite, but numerous, pure white flowers in elongated clusters. The name bird cherry is apt because the small, black fruit is too repulsively bitter for humans to eat, yet is relished by birds. Bird cherry is also called mayday tree because of the normal time of bloom—although a "harbinger" strain (var. *commutata*) can begin flowering in late March. The tallest bird cherry measured was 88 feet (27 m), but normal mature specimens grow nowhere near as lofty. It is native not only in Europe, but extends all the way to Japan.

'**Colorata**' (usually spelled 'Coloratus') is the best known of the purplish bird cherry cultivars. It was found, reports Krüssmann (1986, 41), "in 1953 in Smaland Province, Sweden." It is a small tree distinguished by its dark purple twigs, bronzy-colored young leaves, and its flowers that are deep pink in the bud, opening pink. In summer the veins and leaf undersides remain purplish, but overall the tree has a murky green appearance. 'Colorata' received an Award of Merit from the Royal Horticultural Society of England in 1974. It has been offered by some Canadian wholesale nurseries, but is scarce if present at all in the U.S. nursery trade.

'**Purple Queen**' is similar to but darker than 'Colorata'. It is a younger selection, also of European origin, and like 'Colorata', makes a smaller tree. It may be just a nursery trade name for 'Colorata'.

'**Purpurea**' is an obscure name. The best account of it is that of James Searles (1990, 141): "the 'Burgundy-leaf' Mayday, has purplish-green foliage and dark purple flowers." Some Oregon nurseries have listed it. Until additional information is forthcoming, I consider this name, and 'Purple Queen', unvalidated. It may be a nursery name for 'Colorata' or another bird cherry clone.

'**Berg**' is marketed as "Rancho" and is also mentioned by Searles (1990, 141): "A red-leaf variety bred by Dr Skinner and long associated with Clayton Berg's Valley Nursery of Helena, Montana." It is described by Dirr (1990, 659) in a notelike sentence: "Tight globe headed form to 25' [7.62 m] high, new growth green quickly turning to crimson all summer, white flowers in 5 to 8" [126–202 mm] long racemes, Zone 2." It has been in the contemporary North American nursery trade since at least 1971.

'**Wandell**' is the correct cultivar name for what is usually marketed as "Summerglow." Dirr (1990, 659) gives the most complete account: "Excellent red-purple leaf color through summer, strong semi-spreading growth habit has not exhibited suckering that is common to Schubert or Canada Red Chokecherry, well adapted to urban sites, 50' [tall] by 35' [wide], Zone 3 to 7, a Wandell introduction."

In other words, this bird cherry clone is like 'Schubert' (see below) but larger, and does not sucker. It is propagated by the Femrite Nursery Company of Aurora, Oregon.

Chokecherries

Prunus virginiana, the chokecherry, is a North American tree closely related to the Old World bird cherry. Like the bird cherry, it has a vast range, growing over most of the continent. It differs from the bird cherry by being smaller, with smaller flowers, and often it throws up root suckers. Its fruit can be black, but is usually dark reddish purple, or sometimes amber or yellow. The fruit can be acceptable for eating, especially when cooked. A famous purpleleaf selection and several of its offspring exist.

'**Schubert**' is the very well-known purpleleaf chokecherry. In most books it is erroneously spelled "Shubert." Its date of introduction, and often its original nursery, are cited wrongly. The first mention of the tree is in the

60th annual catalog of the Oscar H. Will & Company nursery, of Bismarck, North Dakota (1943, 67): "Purple Leaved Chokecherry. A brand new introduction, selected by our Mr. Schubert from thousands of seedlings. Leaves are green at first then turn dark purple."

The catalog has a picture of Mr. L. Schubert, so, no more should his name be misspelled nor the date of origin given as 1950, nor the Skinner nursery of Dropmore, Manitoba, Canada, given credit for the introduction.

'**Schubert Copper**' "has coppery-purple foliage and red fruit. It was selected by John Wallace of Beaverhead Nursery in Beaverhead, Alberta" (Searles 1990, 142).

'**Mini Schubert**' "is a densely compact small size tree with red foliage. It is an excellent candidate for formal lollipop-shaped trees" (Searles 1990, 142).

'**Canada Red**' began as an improved 'Schubert' selection, but the name has gradually become confused and is usually cited as a synonym of 'Schubert'. The original 'Schubert' might largely have been replaced by this superior selection. Apparently 'Canada Red' has darker color, larger leaves, and possibly paler flowers. It might have been introduced by the Bailey Nurseries of St. Paul, Minnesota. Possibly the "Bailey's Select" and "Red Select" names seen in some nursery catalogs refer to 'Canada Red' in the strict sense. Lawyer nursery of Plains, Montana, reports in its 1991–92 catalog (p. 40) that 'Schubert' chokecherry, when seed-grown, yields "approximately 60–70% true-to-type plants with purple color." This fact explains why the original 'Schubert' clone, like 'Pissardii' plum, has been somewhat lost in the flood of its progeny.

Greenleaf hybrids are known between the bird cherry and chokecherry. Some of the named purpleleaf cultivars may also be hybrids. Since the two species are very similar and nursery growers are not botanists usually, it would not be surprising if an examination revealed some hybridity.

Almonds

The fourth nonplum purpleleaf *Prunus* species is the almond. *Prunus dulcis* (also called *P. Amygdalus*) '**Colbrunni**' is described by Ernest Lord (1970, 86): "Young leaves, stems and double flowers deep reddish purple." The origin of 'Colbruni' is unknown but presumably from Australia or New Zealand. The name does not appear in Northern Hemisphere sources. The almond clone called 'Purpurea' is not purpleleaved, but has single, rosy-purple flowers. Nonetheless, it is sometimes mistakenly described as if it did have purple leaves.

No other purpleleaf *Prunus* is known to me, except in a very imperfect way—the new *Prunus serrulata* 'Royal Burgundy' that is patented #6520 and is, I am led to believe, rather like the celebrated 'Kwanzan' Japanese flowering cherry, except with dark leaf color. The Japanese Apricot (*Prunus Mume*) is one I fully expect to have sported dark offspring.

Endnotes

1. Frank A. Waugh (1901, 211) disputes the assertion that all but two cultivars ('Citation' and 'Purple Pigmy') descended from 'Pissardii'. See "Garnet" in Chapter 12 of this book for Waugh's quote. Of course I am referring to cultivated trees only. One can still find wild purpleleaf plums in southwestern Asia, the homeland of 'Pissardii'.

2. The term "Japanese Plum" applies to two trees: *Prunus salicina*, a regular plum, and *Prunus Mume*, an apricot if there ever was one. The "plum-blossom" of Oriental art is usually the apricot. A widely cultivated, bushy almond-relative from China, known botanically as *Prunus triloba* 'Multiplex', is called a flowering plum by many North American nurseries; its more proper name is flowering almond.

3. The "mystery tree" is a specimen in Seattle that has completely doubled, sweetly fragrant flowers. If other examples of it exist, then it is likely a named clone, albeit an extremely rare and poorly described one. If it is a chance seedling, it may be worth naming and distributing. Its leaves are approximately like those of 'Pissardii' as far as color goes, but have particularly sharp teeth, and are narrower, longer, and more tapered at their bases. The ovary and skin of the plum are hairless but the stone has hairs like the stones of 'Blireiana' and 'Moseri'. Definitely it is a hybrid.

Glossary

Anthers: The pollen-bearing tips of stamens. Plum flowers have usually 10–30 stamens, which are the male floral organs.

Bloom: (1) A thin, powdery or waxy layer on the skin of the plum, easily rubbed off, making the fruit thereby shiny instead of dull. (2) The flower, or the period of flowering.

Budding: A common form of grafting, usually done in the summer. A single bud of one variety is placed carefully onto a rootstock to produce an entire tree of the desired kind.

Clone: A reproduction genetically identical to its source, having been reproduced/propagated vegetatively rather than sexually. A person desirous of a 'Newport' plum tree does not plant a seed to obtain one—it will not work—but instead grows the cloned cultivar 'Newport' via grafting, cuttings, or other asexual reproductive methods.

Cultivar: Cultivated variety; in trees, usually cultivars are clones.

Cutting: One example of clonal (= asexual or vegetative) propagation (see Clone). For example, growers snip off twigs of some plum trees, root them, let them grow, and then sell them as plum trees, not as "rooted cuttings." Trees so grown are sometimes marketed as "own root" stock.

Double flowers: Flowers with extra petals—sometimes just a few, sometimes dozens—that appear fuller, fluffier, and showier than "single" or normal flowers, which, in the case of plum trees, have 5 petals. Double flowers last longer and they usually set less fruit than normal plants, or none. Common roses are doubled, as is the 'Blireiana' plum. "Semi-double" is an intermediate stage between single and fully double. Many purpleleaf plum cultivars bear some semidouble flowers with 7–10 petals.

Glabrous: Devoid of hairs. The opposite of pubescent.

Grafting: A method of propagation by attaching one kind of plant onto another closely related kind. (See Clone.) There are varied motives for grafting and different ways of doing it.

Hybrid: A mule, a cross. When two closely related but separate species of plants interbreed (in nature or in cultivation), the progeny is called a hybrid. Most purpleleaf plum cultivars arose as hybrids. Scientific names of hybrids are often (and properly), but by no means necessarily, marked with a multiplication sign (×) or an x if the math symbol is not available.

Lenticel: A bumpy little dot that serves as a breathing pore on a twig. The relative abundance and shape of lenticels help identify some trees in winter: 'Pissardii' and 'Thundercloud' have no obvious lenticels; 'Newport' has strikingly prominent speckles.

Midrib: The main vein of a leaf, running down the middle. The leafstalk or petiole is a continuation of the midrib.

Ovary: The female floral part that consists of the future fruit and seeds in embryonic form. In plums, it is like a tiny, swollen bulb in the middle of the flower, with a protruding beak (style) that terminates in the stigma. The pollen from the male floral organs (stamens) must come in contact with the stigma for fertilization to take place. In hybrid purpleleaf plum cultivars that have a peach or almond as one parent, the ovaries, as well as fruit, are fuzzy more or less. 'Purple Pony' seems to be sterile because its ovaries are defective.

Pedicel: The flowerstalk, which becomes the plum's stem in fruit. The pedicel can lengthen as the flower transforms itself into a fruit. Only a few purpleleaf plum cultivars have hairs (pubescence) on the pedicels: 'Allred', 'Gerth', 'Purple Pigmy', and one whose name is uncertain.

Petal: The attractive white or pink winglike floral appendages that delight our eyes. Normally plum flowers have five petals, but many plum hybrids have some flowers with extra petals (see Double Flowers).

Petiole: The leafstalk or leafstem.

Pistil: The name given collectively to the female floral organs: ovary, style, and stigma.

Pollen: Yellowish, sporelike dust produced on anthers that sit atop the stamens of the flowers. Pollen serves as the male portion in reproduction. *Pollination* is the process by which pollen is transferred by bees or some other source to the stigma. For *fertilization* to occur, the pollen must make its way down through the style or beak to the ovary's inner recesses.

Pubescent: Hairy, fuzzy, wooly, in any degree, ranging from a few scattered, short, microscopic hairs to thick wooly fuzz as on a peach. The opposite of glabrous.

Rootstock: Plant roots used by propagators for budding or grafting cultivars. For example, a plum tree could be obtained in dwarf, semidwarf, or standard sizes depending on what kind of rootstock is used. 'Citation' is a purpleleaf peach-plum hybrid used as a dwarfing rootstock. Myrobalan, 'Pixie', and 'St. Julian' are other common plum rootstocks.

Sepal: Green or occasionally reddish petal equivalents that are comparatively inconspicuous, hidden beneath the showy petals on the outside of the flower. Instead of being very delicate-textured, colorful, and broad like petals, sepals are usually narrow, small, and plain. Most purpleleaf plum sepals are quite similar, so those that are markedly different help to identify cultivars. The sepals remain, although petals wither and fall away.

Stamens: The male floral organs. Plums bear 15–30 or more, each consisting of a threadlike filament tipped by anthers that bear the pollen.

Stigma: The tip of the ovary, serving as the sticky destination of pollen.

Stipule: Tiny leaflike appendages at the junction of the leafstalk and the twig. Not invariably present. They often fall away very quickly.

Style: The beak of the ovary; the tapering neck between the ovary proper and the stigma.

Sucker: A vertical, fast-growing, strong shoot that pops-up variously from the root, trunk, or branch of a (usually heavily pruned) tree. Suckers commonly have extra-large leaves, and, at least to begin with, do not bear flowers or fruit. As a general rule, they are undesirable eyesores minimized by pruning in the growing season as opposed to dormant-season pruning.

Variegated: Two or more colors in one leaf, such as green and yellow, or green, white and pink. The variegated purpleleaf plum cultivars are 'Hessei', 'Mirage', and 'Purpusii'.

Witches'-Broom: Abnormally congested, twiggy masses growing in tree crowns like cancerous mutations. There are various causes. Some kinds of trees never get them, others frequently do. When plant enthusiasts propagate them, the result is often a dwarfed version of the normal tree, quite suitable in small-scale gardens or rockeries. No purpleleaf plum cultivar is the product of a witches'-broom, but eventually one will come to pass.

Bibliography

Note: nursery catalogs are not included and varietal names are written as they appear in the present volume, not as they appear in the original source; for example where "var. *atropurpurea*" may be in the book, in this bibliography it is 'Pissardii'.

Alderman, W. H. 1926. *New Fruits Produced at the University of Minnesota Fruit Breeding Farm.* University of Minnesota Agricultural Extension Bulletin no. 230 (July).
> p. 47: Minn No. 1, Newport.

Bailey, Liberty Hyde. 1914–1917. *The Standard Cyclopedia of Horticulture.* 6 vols. New York: MacMillan.
> p. 2825: Blireiana, Hessei, Moseri, Nigra, Pissardii, Purpurea, Purpusii, Woodii.

Bailey, Liberty Hyde, and Ethel Zoe Bailey. 1930. *Hortus.* New York: MacMillan.
> p. 501: Blireiana, Cistena, Hessei, Moseri, Pissardii.

———. 1935. *Hortus.* Rev. ed. New York: MacMillan.
> p. 503: Blireiana, Cistena, Hessei, Moseri, Pissardii, Purpurea; p. 736: Woodii.

———. 1941. *Hortus Second.* New York: MacMillan.
> p. 600: Blireiana, Cistena, Hessei, Moseri, Pissardii, Woodii; p. 602: Purpurea.

———. 1976. *Hortus Third.* Rev. by L. H. Hortorium Staff. New York: MacMillan.
> p. 918: Blireiana, Moseri, Newport, Pissardii; p. 919: Cistena; p. 921: Purpurea.

Bean, W. J. 1929. *Trees and Shrubs Hardy in the British Isles.* 5th ed., 2 vols. London: John Murray.
> Vol. 2: pp. 232, 253: Blireiana, Moseri, Pissardii, Purpurea.

———. 1950–1951. *Trees and Shrubs Hardy in the British Isles.* 7th ed., 3 vols. London: John Murray.
> Vol. 2, pp. 542, 544, 570: Blireiana, Hazeldene Variety, Nigra, Pissardii, Purpurea.

———. 1970–1980. *Trees and Shrubs Hardy in the British Isles.* 8th ed., 4 vols. Rev. by D. L. Clarke, chief ed. London: John Murray.
> Vol. 3, pp. 360–361 except as noted: Blireiana, Cistena p. 356; Moseri, Nigra, Pissardii, Purpurea and Rosea p. 410; Trailblazer, Woodii.

———. 1988. *Supplement to Trees and Shrubs Hardy in the British Isles.* London: John Murray.
> pp. 396–397: Hessei, Purpusii.

Bean, W. J., and Blanche Henrey. 1944. *Trees and Shrubs Throughout the Year.* London: Lindsay Drummond.
> p. 21: Blireiana.

Bibliography

Boom, B. K. 1949. *Flora der Cultuurgewassen van Nederland*, Deel I *Nederlandse Dendrologie*. Wageningen: H. Veenman & Zonen.

> pp. 233–234: Blireiana, Hessei, Nigra, Pissardii, Purpurea, Purpusii, Woodii.

———. 1959. *Flora der Cultuurgewassen van Nederland*, Deel I *Nederlandse Dendrologie*.

> pp. 249–251: Blireiana, Cistena, Hessei, Moseri, Nigra, Pissardii, Purpurea, Woodii.

———. 1954–1955. Nederlandse Dendrologische Vereniging, 20ste *Jaarboek*. "Benaming, Geschiedenis en Kenmerken van een aantal Houtachtige Planten."

> p. 83: Hessei.

———. 1956, 1957, 1958. Nederlandse Dendrologische Vereniging, 21ste *Jaarboek*.

> pp. 146–149: Nigra, Pissardii, Purpusii, Woodii.

Brooks, Reid M., and Harold P. Olmo. 1952. *Register of New Fruit and Nut Varieties, 1920–52*. 1st ed. Berkeley: University of California Press.

> p. 127: Hollywood; p. 130: Newport; p. 131: Purple Flame.

———. 1972. *Register of New Fruit and Nut Varieties, 1920–72*. 2nd ed. Berkeley: University of California Press.

> p. 488: Allred; p. 502: Hollywood; p. 508: Minnesota Purple; p. 514: Purple Flame; pp. 522–523: Trailblazer.

Browicz, Kazimierz, and Jerzy Zielinski. *Chorology of Trees and Shrubs in South-West Asia and Adjacent Regions*. 1984. Warsaw: Polish Academy of Sciences Institute of Dendrology.

> Vol. 4, p. 13: *Prunus microcarpa* data.

Burbank, Luther, et al. 1914–1915. *Luther Burbank, His Methods and Discoveries and Their Practical Application*. 12 vols. New York: Luther Burbank Press.

> Vol. 5, p. 222: Othello [cf. plate 70 (p. 196), plate 88 (p. 261), plate 89 (p. 263), plate 92 (p. 269), and p. 300].

Bush, F. A. 1964. *Trees and Shrubs*. New York: Taplinger Publishing.

> pp. 91, 150: Blireiana, Cistena, Nigra, Pissardii, Purpurea.

Caddick, J. W., and Andrew T. Leiser. 1948. *Woody Ornamental Plants Available in Northwest Nurseries*. October 21st. Washington State University Agricultural Experiment Station, Pullman, WA.

> Blireiana, Pissardii, Vesuvius.

Chittenden, Fred J., ed. 1951–1969. *The Royal Horticultural Society Dictionary of Gardening*. 4 vols. and supplement. Oxford: Clarendon Press.

> Vol. 3, p. 1695: Blireiana, Moseri, Nigra, Pissardii, Woodii; p. 1700: Purpurea.

Cochran, George W. 1962. Prunus species in botanical gardens and arboretums. *Fruit Varieties and Horticultural Digest*. 16, no. 4 (July): 63–72.

> Blireiana, Cistena, Gaujardi, Hessei, Hollywood, Moseri, Newport, Nigra, Othello, Pallet, Pissardii, Purpurea, Purpusii, Roebuck Castle, Rosea, Trailblazer, Vesuvius, Woodii.

Creasy, Rosalind. 1986. *The Gardener's Handbook of Edible Plants*. San Francisco: Sierra Club Books.

> pp. 230–231: Allred, Cocheco, Hollywood, Pissardii.

Davis, Brian. 1988. *Trees for Small Gardens*. Emmaus, PA: Rodale Press.

> pp. 59–61: Blireiana, Cistena, Nigra, Pissardii, Purpurea, Rosea, Trailblazer.

Dirr, Michael A. 1983. *Manual of Woody Landscape Plants*. 3rd ed. Champaign, IL: Stipes Publishing.

> pp. 552–553: Blireiana, Cistena, Hollywood, Moseri, Newport, Nigra, Pissardii, Purpusii, Thundercloud, Trailblazer, Vesuvius.

———. 1990. *Manual of Woody Landscape Plants*. 4th ed. Champaign, IL: Stipes Publishing.

> pp. 652–654: Allred, Big Cis, Blireiana, Cistena, Hessei, Hollywood, Krauter's Vesuvius, Moseri, Mt. St. Helens, Newport, Nigra, Pissardii, Purpusii, Thundercloud, Trailblazer, Vesuvius.

Everett, Thomas H. 1980. *The New York Botanical Garden Illustrated Encyclopedia of Horticulture*. 10 vols. New York: Garland Publishing.

> Vol. 8, p. 2825: Cistena; p. 2826: Purpurea; p. 2827: Blireiana, Hollywood, Krauter's Vesuvius, Pissardii, Thundercloud, Trailblazer.

Facciola, Stephen. 1990. *Cornucopia; A Source Book of Edible Plants*. Vista, CA: Kampong Publications.

> p. 178: Allred, Cocheco, Elsie, Gerth, Hollywood, Pissardii, Shalom, Thundercloud; p. 181: Purpurea.

Fogle, H. W., and H. F. Winters. 1981. *North American and European Fruit and Tree Nut Germplasm Resources Inventory*. USDA miscellaneous publication no. 1406. Washington, DC: U.S. Government Printing Office.

> pp. 394–413: Allred, Cistena, Cocheco, Hollywood, Purpusii, Thundercloud, Trailblazer.

Forrest, Mary. 1985. *Trees and Shrubs Cultivated in Ireland*. Kilkenny, Ireland: Boethius Press.

> pp. 70–72: Blireiana, Cistena, Hessei, Nigra, Pissardii, Purpurea, Trailblazer, Woodii

Frederick, William H., Jr. 1975. *100 Great Garden Plants*. Portland, OR: Timber Press; New York: Alfred A. Knopf.

> pp. 70–72: Thundercloud.

Gerard, John. 1633. *Herball or General Historie of Plants*. Rev. and enlarged by Thomas Johnson. London: Adam Islip Joice Norton and Richard Whitakers.

> p. 1498 (in the third book, chapter 126): a cherry plum account.

Grant, John A., and Carol L. Grant. 1943. *Trees and Shrubs for Pacific Northwest Gardens*. Seattle: Dogwood Press.

> pp. 102–103: Blireiana, Moseri, Nigra, Pissardii, Thundercloud, Vesuvius.

———. *Trees and Shrubs for Pacific Northwest Gardens*. 2nd ed. Rev. by Marvin E. Black, Brian O. Mulligan, Jean G. Witt, and Joseph A. Witt. Portland, OR: Timber Press.

> pp. 109–110 (purpleleaf plum section was contributed by A. L. Jacobson): Allred, Big Cis, Blireiana, Hollywood, Krauter's Vesuvius, Moseri, Mt. St. Helens, Newport, Nigra, Pissardii, Purple Pony, Spencer Hollywood, Thundercloud, Trailblazer, Vesuvius.

Hansen, Niels E. 1907–1931. *Bulletins* of the South Dakota Agricultural Experiment Station at Brookings.

    nos. 87, 88, 92, 130, 224, 237, 263: Cistena, Purple C, Stanapa.

———. 1927. Some sterile and fertile plant hybrids. Papers presented at the International Conference on Flower and Fruit Sterility. *Memoirs of the Horticultural Society of New York*, vol. 3 (July): 229–232. New York: Horticultural Society of New York.

    pp. 229: Cistena, Stanapa.

Haralson, Charles. 1915. Minnesota State Fruit-Breeding Farm in 1914. *The Minnesota Horticulturist* (also called Trees, Fruits and Flowers of Minnesota), vol. 43, no. 1, (January).

    pp. 19–20: Minn. No. 1, Minn. No. 2.

Harrison, Richmond E. 1959. *Handbook of Trees and Shrubs for the Southern Hemisphere.* Wellington, New Zealand: A. H. & A. W. Reed.

    p. 267: Purpurea; p. 271: Blireiana, Festeri, Moseri, Nigra, Pissardii, R. W. Hodgins, Thundercloud, Vesuvius, Wrightii.

———. 1963. *Handbook of Trees and Shrubs for the Southern Hemisphere.* 3rd ed. Wellington, New Zealand: A. H. & A. W. Reed.

    p. 272: Purpurea; p. 275: Blireiana, Festeri, Moseri, Nigra, Pissardii, R. W. Hodgins, Thundercloud, Vesuvius, Wrightii.

———. 1967. *Handbook of Trees and Shrubs for the Southern Hemisphere.* 4th ed. Wellington, New Zealand: A. H. & A. W. Reed.

    p. 272: Purpurea; p. 275: Blireiana, Festeri, Moseri, Nigra, Pissardii, R. W. Hodgins, Thundercloud, Vesuvius, Wrightii.

———. 1974. *Handbook of Trees and Shrubs for the Southern Hemisphere.* 5th ed. Wellington, New Zealand: A. H. & A. W. Reed.

    p. 320: Purpurea; pp. 325–326: Blireiana, Festeri, Moseri, Pissardii, Thundercloud, Vesuvius, Wrightii.

Haworth-Booth, Michael. 1951. *Effective Flowering Shrubs.* London: Collins.

    p. 44: Blireiana, Moseri, Nigra, Pissardii, Purpusii, Woodii.

———. 1973. *Effective Flowering Shrubs.* Rev. ed. Newton Abbot: Gardeners Book Club.

    p. 44: Blireiana, Moseri, Nigra, Pissardii, Purpusii, Woodii.

Hazlewood, Walter G. [1960] 1968. *A Handbook of Trees, Shrubs, and Roses.* 2nd ed. Sydney: Angus & Robertson.

    p. 181: Blireiana, Festeri, Moseri, Nigra, Pissardii, Vesuvius.

Hedrick, U. P. 1910. *The Plums of New York.* Albany: J. B. Lyon Co. (New York State Department of Agriculture 18th Annual Report. 1910. Vol. 3, part 2).

    p. 421: Coleus; p. 450: Garnet; p. 516: Pissardii; p. 521: Purpleleaf Kelsey; p. 43: Purpurea; p. 559: Vesuvius.

———. 1917. *The Peaches of New York.* Albany: J. B. Lyon Co. (New York State Department of Agriculture 24th Annual Report. 1916. Vol. 2, part 2).

    p. 188: Bloodleaf Peach.

———. 1950. *A History of Horticulture in America to 1860.* New York: Oxford University Press.

Heiges, Samuel B. 1897. *Report of the Pomologist, 1895.* USDA. Washington, D.C.: Government Printing Office.

   p. 45: Garnet.

Hériteau, Jacqueline. 1990. *The National Arboretum Book of Outstanding Garden Plants.* New York: Simon and Schuster.

   pp. 167, 218–219: Big Cis, Blireiana, Cistena, Diversifolia, Krauter's Vesuvius, Moseri, Mt. St. Helens, Newport, Pissardii, Purpurea, Thundercloud.

Hillier, H. G., R. Gardner, and Roy Lancaster. 1971. *Hillier's Manual of Trees and Shrubs.* Winchester, England: Hillier & Sons. [1972 (2nd ed.), 1973 (3rd ed.), 1974, 1975, 1977 (4th ed.), 1981 (5th ed.) editions have the exact same information on the same pages.]

   pp. 234–235: Blireiana, Cistena, Diversifolia, Hessei, Moseri, Nigra, Pissardii, Rosea, Trailblazer, Vesuvius; p. 243: Purpurea.

Hottes, Alfred Carl. 1928. *The Book of Shrubs.* New York: A. T. De La Mare.

   pp. 275: Othello, Pissardii.

———. 1942a. *The Book of Shrubs.* 4th ed. New York: A. T. De La Mare.

   pp. 328–329: Othello, Pissardii.

———. 1942b. *The Book of Trees.* 2nd. ed. New York: A. T. De La Mare.

   p. 311: Pissardii, Woodii.

Howard, Walter L. 1945. *Luther Burbank's Plant Contributions.* University of California College of Agriculture, Agricultural Experiment Station Bulletin 691 (March).

   p. 26: Othello; p. 27: Purpleleaf Kelsey; p. 90: Thundercloud; p. 29: Vesuvius.

Hunkin, J. W., the Right Reverend Bishop of Truro. 1945. The making of Lanarth. *The Journal of the Royal Horticultural Society,* 70: 63–72, 104–110, 132–135.

   p.105: Paul's Pink.

Hyams, Edward. 1965. *Ornamental Shrubs for Temperate Zone Gardens.* New York and South Brunswick: A. S. Barnes; London: MacDonald.

   Barnes edition: p. 45: Nigra, Pissardii.

   MacDonald edition: p. 79: Nigra, Pissardii.

Isaacson, Richard T. 1989. *Andersen Horticultural Library's Source List of Plants and Seeds.* Chanhassen, Minnesota: Andersen Horticultural Library, University of Minnesota Libraries, Minnesota Landscape Arboretum.

   p. 158: Allred, Blireiana, Cistena, Hollywood, Mt. St. Helens, Newport, Pissardii, Thundercloud, Trailblazer, Vesuvius.

Jacobson, Arthur Lee. 1989a. Purpleleaf plums on the West Coast. *PlantSource* 5, no. 7 (July): 5-7.

   pp. 5–7: Allred, Big Cis, Blireiana, Cistena, Hollywood, Krauter's Vesuvius, Moseri, Mt. St. Helens, Newport, Nigra, Pissardii, Purple Pony, Spencer Hollywood, Thundercloud, Trailblazer, Vesuvius.

———. 1989b. *Trees of Seattle.* Seattle: Sasquatch Books.

   pp. 283–291: Allred, Big Cis, Blireiana, Cistena, Hollywood, Krauter's Vesuvius, Moseri, Mt. St. Helens, Newport, Nigra, Pissardii, Purple Pony, Spencer Hollywood, Thundercloud, Trailblazer, Vesuvius.

———. 1990. Purpleleaf plum trees. International Dendrology Society *Yearbook* (May): pp. 107–112.

> Allred, Atherton, Big Cis, Blireiana, Cistena, Cocheco, Coleus, Festeri, Garnet, Hazeldene Variety, Hessei, Hollywood, Krauter's Vesuvis, Minn. No. 1., Minn. No. 2, Moseri, Mt. St. Helens, Newport, Nigra, Othello, Paul's Pink, Pissardii, Purple C, Purple Flame, Purpleleaf Kelsey, Purple Pigmy, Purple Pony, Purpusii, Rosea, R. W. Hodgins, Spencer Holywood, Stanapa, Thundercloud, Trailblazer, Vesuvius, Woodii, Wrightii.

Johnson, Hugh. 1973. *The International Book of Trees*. London: Mitchell Beazley.

> p. 202: Pissardii, Purpurea.

Kourik, Robert. 1986. *Designing and Maintaining Your Edible Landscape Naturally*. Santa Rosa: Metamorphic Press.

> pp. 171, 175: Citation.

Krüssman, Gerd. 1951. *Die Laubgehölze*. Berlin: Paul Parey.

> pp. 253, 263: Blireiana, Cistena, Hessei, Moseri, Nigra, Pallet, Pissardii, Purpurea, Purpusii, Woodii.

———. 1962. *Handbuch der Laubgehölze*. 3 vols. Hamburg and Berlin: Paul Parey.

> Vol. 2, pp. 249, 250, 252, 274: Blireiana, Cistena, Festeri, Hessei, Moseri, Newport, Nigra, Pissardii, Purpurea, Purpusii, Thundercloud, Woodii.

———. 1978. *Handbuch der Laubgehölze*. 3 vols. Hamburg and Berlin: Paul Parey.

> Vol. 3, pp. 19, 21, 23, 49: Blireiana, Cistena, Festeri, Hessei, Moseri, Newport, Nigra, Pissardii, Purpurea, Purpusii, Rosea, Thundercloud, Trailblazer, Vesuvius, Woodii.

———. 1986. *Manual of Cultivated Broad-Leaved Trees and Shrubs*. Originally published as *Handbuch der Laubgehölze*. Translated by Michael E. Epp. London: B. T. Batsford; Portland, Oregon: Timber Press.

> Vol. 3, pp. 24–27, 51: Blireiana, Cistena, Festeri, Hessei, Moseri, Newport, Nigra, Pissardii, Purpurea, Purpusii, Rosea, Thundercloud, Trailblazer, Vesuvius, Woodii.

Lord, Ernest E. 1970. *Shrubs and Trees for Australian Gardens*. 4th ed. Melbourne and Sydney: Lothian.

> pp. 86–87: Blireiana, Festeri, Moseri, Nigra, Pissardii, Vesuvius; p. 89: Purpurea.

———. 1982. *Shrubs and Trees for Australian Gardens*. 5th ed. Rev. by J. H. Willis.

> pp. 66–68: Blireiana, Festeri, Moseri, Nigra, Pissardii, Purpurea, Vesuvius, Wrightii.

Manning, J. Woodward. 1927. *Manning's Plant Buyers Index*. 2nd ed. Reading, MA. J. Woodward Manning.

> Blireiana, Newport, Othello, Pissardii, Vesuvius.

———. 1928. *Supplement* to *Manning's Plant Buyers Index*. 2nd ed. Reading, MA. J. Woodward Manning.

> Cistena.

———. 1931. *Manning's Plant Buyers Index*. 3rd ed. Reading, MA. J. Woodward Manning.

> Blireiana, Cistena, Newport, Othello, Pissardii, Vesuvius.

———. 1934. *Supplement to Manning's Plant Buyers Index*. 3rd ed. Duxbury, MA. J. Woodward Manning.

> Moseri, Thundercloud.

———. 1939. *Manning's Plant Buyers Index*. 4th ed. Duxbury, MA. J. Woodward Manning.

> Blireiana, Cistena, Diversifolia, Hessei, Moseri, Newport, Nigra, Othello, Pissardii, Purpurea, Thundercloud, Vesuvius, Woodii.

———. 1949. *Plant Buyer's Guide*. 5th ed. Ed. Edwin F. Steffek. Boston, MA: Massachusetts Horticultural Society.

> Blireiana, Cistena, Hollywood, Moseri, Newport, Pissardii, Purple Flame, Thundercloud, Vesuvius.

———. 1958. *Plant Buyer's Guide*. 6th ed. Ed. H. Gleason Mattoon. Boston, MA: Massachusetts Horticultural Society.

> Blireiana, Cistena, Hessei, Hollywood, Minnesota Purple, Moseri, Newport, Nigra, Pissardii, Purpurea, Thundercloud, Vesuvius

McClintock, Elizabeth, and Andrew T. Leiser. 1979. *An Annotated Checklist of Woody Ornamental Plants of California, Oregon, and Washington*. Berkeley: University of California Agricultural Sciences Publications.

> p. 95: Blireiana, Cistena, Hollywood, Krauter's Vesuvius, Newport, Pissardii, Thundercloud, Trailblazer, Vesuvius.

McEachern, George Ray. 1990. *Growing Fruits, Berries & Nuts Southwest—Southeast*. Houston: Gulf Publishing.

> p. 32: Allred.

Mitchell, Alan F. 1982. *The Trees of Britain and Northern Europe*. London: Collins.

> p. 190: Blireiana, Nigra, Pissardii.

———. 1985. *The Complete Guide to Trees of Britain and Northern Europe*. Limpsfield and London: Dragon's World.

> pp. 76–79: Blireiana, Nigra, Pissardii, Purpurea.

———. 1987. *The Trees of North America*. New York: Facts on File.

> pp. 78–79: Blireiana, Nigra, Pissardii.

Neitzel, Jim. 1980. Deciduous fruit varieties. *Yearbook of the California Rare Fruit Growers Association*. pp. 20–40.

> p. 27: Elsie, Gerth, Oaks.

Okie, W. R., and J. M. Thompson. 1989. 'Clark Hill Redleaf' plum. *Fruit Varieties Journal*. 43 (2): 58–59.

Ordnance Survey. 1989. *The Ordnance Survey Gazetteer of Great Britain*. 2nd ed. London: MacMillan; Southampton: Ordnance Survey.

> p. 343: Hazeldene geographic information.

Bibliography

Overcash, J. P. 1963. Heat and chilling requirements for plum blossoming in Mississippi. *Fruit Varieties and Horticultural Digest.* 17, 2 (January): 33–35.
Allred, Hollywood.

Palmer, Stanley J. n.d. (pre-1979). *Palmers Manual of Trees, Shrubs and Climbers.* Glen Eden, New Zealand: A. W. Palmer & Sons.
p. 234: Blireiana, Nigra, Wrightii.

Philip, Chris, ed. 1988. *The Plant Finder.* 2nd ed. Pub. for the Hardy Plant Society. Whitbourne, Worcestershire, England: Headmain Ltd.
pp. 293–294: Blireiana, Cistena, Hessei, Nigra, Pissardii, Purpurea, Rosea, Trailblazer, Woodii.

———. 1990. *The Plant Finder.* 4th ed. Pub. for the Hardy Plant Society. Whitbourne, Worcestershire, England: Headmain Ltd.
pp. 377–381: Blireiana, Cistena, Hessei, Mirage, Nigra, Pissardii, Purpurea, Rosea, Trailblazer.

Prockter, Noël. J. 1960. *Garden Hedges.* London: Collingridge.
pp. 80–81: Blireiana, Cistena, Nigra, Pissardii.

Rehder, Alfred. 1927. *Manual of Cultivated Trees and Shrubs.* New York: MacMillan.
pp. 454–456, 466: Blireiana, Cistena, Moseri, Nigra, Pissardii, Purpleleaf Kelsey, Purpurea, Purpusii, Woodii.

———. 1940. *Manual of Cultivated Trees and Shrubs.* 2nd. ed. New York: MacMillan.
pp. 455–457, 468: Blireiana, Cistena, Moseri, Nigra, Pissardii, Purpleleaf Kelsey, Purpurea, Purpusii, Woodii.

———. 1949. *Bibliography of Cultivated Trees and Shrubs.* Jamaica Plain, Massachusetts: The Arnold Arboretum of Harvard University.
pp. 318, 320–321, 333: Blireiana, Cistena, Moseri, Nigra, Pissardii, Purpleleaf Kelsey, Purpurea, Purpusii, Woodii.

Royal Horticultural Society. 1884. *The Journal of the R.H.S.* 13.
p. 87: 'Pissardii' First Class Certificate.

———. 1912. *The Journal of the R.H.S.* 38.
p. lx: 'Moseri' Award of Merit.

———. 1914. *The Journal of the R.H.S.* 40.
p. lxii: 'Blireiana' Award of Merit.

———. 1923. *The Journal of the R.H.S.* 49.
p. xlv: 'Blireiana' First Class Certificate.

———. 1928. *The Journal of the R.H.S.* 53.
p. 329: 'Blireiana' Award of Garden Merit.

———. 1928. *The Journal of the R.H.S.* 53.
pp. 328–329: 'Pissardii' Award of Garden Merit.

———. 1939. *The Journal of the R.H.S.* 64.
p. 231: 'Nigra' First Class Certificate.

Rosendahl, Carl Otto, and Frederic K. Butters. 1928. *Trees and Shrubs of Minnesota.* Minneapolis: University of Minnesota Press.

    p. 225: Newport.

Rowell, Raymond J. 1980. *Ornamental Flowering Trees in Australia.* Sydney: Reed.

    pp. 172–173: Blireiana, Festeri, Moseri, Nigra, Pissardii, Vesuvius.

Schneider, Camillo Karl. 1904–1912. *Illustriertes Handbuch der Laubholzkunde.* 2 vols. Jena, Germany: Gustav Fischer.

    vol. 1, pp. 628, 632: Blireiana, Pissardii, Purpurea

    vol. 2, p. 991: Hessei, Purpusii.

Seabrook, Peter. 1982. *Shrubs for Your Garden.* 2nd ed. Calverton, England: Floraprint.

    p. 105: Cistena, Pissardii.

Searles, James D. 1990. *The Garden of Joy; A Primer for the Chinook Zone, Plains States, Prairie Provinces,* and *Rocky Mountain Inland Empire.* Great Falls, Montana: Medicine River Publishing.

    pp. 141–142: the best account of purpleleaf *Prunus Padus* and *Prunus virginiana* cultivars.

Sedenko, Jerry. 1991. No time to be tasteful. In *Perennials: Toward Continuous Bloom; New Voices in American Garden Writing.* Ed. Ann Lovejoy. Deer Park, WI: Capability's Books. 44–48.

Silva Tarouca, Ernst Graf, and Camillo Karl Schneider. 1931. *Kulturhandbücher Für Garten Freunde.* 4th ed, 3 vols. Wien and Leipzig.

    vol. 2, p. 276: Blireiana, Moseri, Nigra, Pissardii, Purpurea, Purpusii, Woodii.

Stace, C. A., ed. 1975. *Hybridization and the Flora of the British Isles.* London: Academic Press.

    p. 229: Pissardii.

Standardized Plant Names. 1923. 1st ed. Pub. for the American Joint Committee on Horticultural Nomenclature. Salem, Massachusetts: J. Horace McFarland Company.

    p. 385 Pissardii.

———. 1942. 2nd ed. Pub. for the American Joint Committee on Horticultural Nomenclature. Harrisburg, Pennsylvania: J. Horace McFarland Company.

    p. 261: Purple Flame; pp. 501–503: Blireiana, Cistena, Moseri, Newport, Nigra, Othello, Pissardii, Purpleleaf Kelsey, Purpurea, Purpusii, Vesuvius, Woodii.

Sudell, Richard. 1933. *The New Illustrated Gardening Encyclopædia.* New York: Charles Scribner's Sons.

    p. 742: Blireiana, Diversifolia, Hessei, Moseri, Nigra, Pissardii, Woodii.

Sunset. 1934. *Sunset's All-Western Garden Guide.* 3rd ed. San Francisco: Lane Publishing.

    p. 48: Blireiana, Nigra, Pissardii, Purpusii, Vesuvius.

———. 1940. *Sunset's Complete Garden Book.* Ed. Richard Merrifield. San Francisco: Lane Publishing.

    p. 178: Blireiana, Nigra, Pissardii, Purpusii.

Bibliography

———. 1954. *Sunset Western Garden Book.* Menlo Park, CA: Lane Publishing.

    p. 274: Blireiana, Cistena, Hollywood, Newport, Pissardii, Thundercloud, Vesuvius.

———. 1975. *Sunset Garden Trees.* Ed. Philip Edinger. Menlo Park, CA: Lane Publishing.

    p. 54: Blireiana, Hollywood, Krauter's Vesuvius, Newport, Pissardii, Thundercloud.

———. 1979. *Sunset New Western Garden Book.* 4th ed. Menlo Park, CA: Lane Book Company.

    p. 432: Allred, Blireiana, Cistena, Hollywood, Krauter's Vesuvius, Newport, Pissardii, Thundercloud.

———. 1988. *Sunset Western Garden Book.* 5th ed. Menlo Park, CA: Lane Book Company.

    p. 489: Allred, Big Cis, Blireiana, Cistena, Hollywood, Krauter's Vesuvius, Mt. St. Helens, Newport, Pissardii, Thundercloud.

Ulmer, David. 1989. Southern plum tests. *Pomona* 22, 2 (Spring): 10–12.

    p. 10: Allred.

Van Melle, Peter J. 1943. *Shrubs and Trees for the Small Place.* New York: Charles Scribner's Sons.

    p. 223: Blireiana, Newport, Othello, Pissardii.

Vermont Experiment Station. 1900–1901. 14th *Annual Report.*

    pp. 272–273 describe the 'Omaha' parent of 'Newport'.

Waugh, Frank A. 1901. *Plums and Plum Culture.* New York: Orange Judd.

    pp. 206–207, 211, 361: Coleus, Garnet, Pissardii.

Webster, A. D. 1908. *Hardy Ornamental Flowering Trees and Shrubs.* 3rd. ed. London: Smith, Elder.

    p. 138: Pissardii.

———. 1920. *London Trees.* London: Swarthmore Press.

    pp. 105–106: Pissardii.

Whealy, Kent. 1989. *Fruit, Berry and Nut Inventory: An inventory of nursery catalogs listing all fruit, berry and nut varieties available by mail order in the United States.* Decorah, Iowa: Seed Savers Publications.

    pp. 194, 198: Allred, Citation, Thundercloud.

Wickson, Edward. 1921. *The California Fruits.* 9th ed. San Francisco: Pacific Rural Press.

Witham Fogg, Harry George. 1972. *Coloured Leaved and Berried Plants, Shrubs and Trees.* London: Garden Book Club.

    p. 55: Blireiana, Cistena, Nigra, Pissardii, Rosea.

Wister, John C. 1947. *Woman's Home Companion Garden Book.* New York: Doubleday.

    p. 240: Blireiana, Cistena, Newport, Othello, Pissardii, Thundercloud, Vesuvius.

Wyman, Donald. 1951. *Trees for American Gardens.* New York: MacMillan.

    p. 284: Blireiana, Newport, Nigra, Pissardii, Thundercloud, Woodii; p. 364: Moseri, Othello, Purpusii, Vesuvius.

———. 1964. Prunus boasts some of the best flowering plants. *American Nurseryman* (1 May): 96–97, 105, 107–108.

Blireiana, Cistena, Hessei, Hollywood, Newport, Nigra, Othello, Pissardii, Purpurea, Purpusii, Thundercloud, Vesuvius, Woodii.

———. 1965. *Trees for American Gardens*. Rev. and enlarged ed. New York: MacMillan.

p. 378–380: Blireiana, Hollywood, Moseri, Nigra, Pissardii, Thundercloud, Vesuvius; p. 488: Hessei, Newport, Othello, Purpusii, Woodii.

———. 1971. *Wyman's Garden Encyclopedia*. Expanded second ed. New York: MacMillan.

pp. 885–886, 890: Blireiana, Cistena, Hollywood, Nigra, Pissardii, Purpurea, Thundercloud, Vesuvius.

———. 1990. *Trees for American Gardens*. 3rd ed. New York: MacMillan.

p. 373–375: Blireiana, Hollywood, Moseri, Nigra, Pissardii, Thundercloud, Vesuvius; p. 474: Hessei, Newport, Othello, Purpusii, Woodii.

Yeo, Peter F., and Clive J. King. 1981. *Catalogue of Plants in the Cambridge Botanic Garden*. Cambridge: Cambridge University Press.

p. 94: Crimson Dwarf, Purple Flash.

Zielinski, Quentin B., and W. A. Sistrunk, and T. P. Davidson. October, 1961. *Plum Varieties for Oregon*. Bulletin of the Oregon Agricultural Experiment Station at Corvallis Station, no. 582.

pp. 6, 16: Hollywood, Trailblazer.

People Index

Nursery Index

Subject Index

Species and Varieties Index

Permissions Acknowledgments

Grateful acknowledgment is made to the following for permission to reprint previously published material:

A. S. BARNES: Excerpts from *Ornamental Shrubs for Temperate Zone Gardens* by Edward Hyams. Copyright ©1965.

CAPABILITY'S BOOKS, INC.: Excerpts from "No Time to be Tasteful" by Jerry Sedenko, in *Perennials; Toward Continuous Bloom; New Voices in American Garden Writing* edited by Ann Lovejoy. Copyright ©1991.

COLLINS/ANGUS & ROBERTSON PUBLISHERS: Excerpts from *A Handbook of Trees, Shrubs, and Roses* by Walter G. Hazlewood. Copyright ©1968.

DRAGON'S WORLD: Excerpts from *The Trees of Britain and Northern Europe* by Alan Mitchell. Copyright ©1985).

FACTS ON FILE: Excerpts from *The Trees of North America* by Alan F. Mitchell. Copyright ©1987 by Dragon's World. Reprinted with permission from Facts on File, Inc., New York.

KAMPONG PUBLICATIONS: Excerpts from *Cornucopia; A Source Book of Edible Plants* by Stephen Facciola. Copyright ©1990.

LOTHIAN PUBLISHING COMPANY: Excerpts from *Shrubs and Trees for Australian Gardens* by Ernest E. Lord. Copyright ©1970. Excerpts from *Shrubs and Trees for Australian Gardens* by Ernest E. Lord and J. H. Willis. Copyright ©1982.

MACMILLAN PUBLISHING COMPANY: Excerpts from *Trees for American Gardens* by Donald Wyman. Third edition. Copyright ©1990.

METAMORPHIC PRESS: Excerpts from *Designing and Maintaining Your Edible Landscape Naturally* by Robert Kourik. Copyright ©1986.

MITCHELL BEAZLEY PUBLISHERS: Excerpts from *The International Book of Trees* by Hugh Johnson. Copyright ©1973.

THE NEW SOUTH WALES UNIVERSITY PRESS: Excerpts from *Ornamental Flowering Trees in Australia* by Raymond J. Rowell. Copyright ©1991.

OCTOPUS PUBLISHING GROUP (NZ), LTD.: Excerpts from *Handbook of Trees and Shrubs for the Southern Hemisphere* by Richmond E. Harrison. Copyright ©1959. Reproduced by permission of Reed Books, a division of Octopus Publishing Group (NZ) Ltd, from *Handbook of Trees and Shrubs for the Southern Hemisphere* by Richmond E. Harrison.

RANDOM HOUSE, INC.: Excerpts from *100 Great Garden Plants* by William H. Frederick, Jr. Copyright ©1975.

SEED SAVERS PUBLICATIONS: Excerpts from *Fruit, Berry and Nut Inventory* by Kent Whealy. Copyright ©1989.

UNIVERSITY OF CALIFORNIA PRESS: Excerpts from *Register of New Fruit and Nut Varieties, 1920–72* by Reid M. Brooks and Harold P. Olmo. Copyright ©1972.

WARD LOCK, LTD.: Excerpts from *Trees and Shrubs* by F. A. Bush. Copyright ©1964.